Waiting for the Train

John MacDonald - An Undated Photograph, probably from the late 1920's. (Courtesy of Mary Elizabeth Warner)

Waiting for the Train

A Depression-Era Journal

John MacDonald

Warner House Press

Published by Warner House Press of Albertville, Alabama, USA

Cover copyright © 2022 Ablaze Media

Copyright © 2024 Warner House Press

Waiting for the Train is a lightly edited transcription of a journal by John MacDonald kept during the Great Depression. The circumstances, exchanges, and conclusions drawn are strictly those of the author and may or may not coincide with the recollections of others. It has not been edited to remove material that may be offensive to others and is very much a product of its place and time.

All rights reserved. No part of this book may be used or reproduced in any manner whatsoever without written permission, except in the case of brief quotations in critical articles and reviews. For more information, contact:

Warner House Press
1325 Lane Switch Rd.
Albertville, AL 35951
USA

Published 2024

Printed in the USA

ISBN: 978-1-951890-45-2 (Print)
978-1-951890-58-2 (eBook)

28 27 26 25 24 1 2 3 4 5

Contents

About the Journal   1

Introduction   5

1. New York City   9
2. Newark, New Jersey   21
3. Welcome to the Jungle   29
4. First Freight   39
5. Philadelphia   43
6. Washington DC   53
7. Charlottesville, Virginia   63
8. Lynchburg   75
9. Decatur   85
10. Mobile onto New Orleans   93
11. Heading West   105
12. El Paso   119
13. A Bad Night in Tucson   127
14. On to L.A.   141
15. Daytime Los Angeles   149

16.	Los Angeles at Night	163
17.	Los Angeles - Obstacles, Red Tape, and Danger	169
18.	Oakland and an Old Friend	181
19.	San Francisco	187
20.	A Coastal Trip and An Escape	195
21.	A Very Close Call	203
22.	From Colton to Tucson	211
23.	An Owl Named Peter	229
24.	New Mexico	239
25.	Traveling in Style to El Paso	247
26.	A Reefer to San Antonio	255
27.	San Antonio to Houston	267
28.	Leaving Texas	273
29.	New Orleans, Again	287
30.	Back to Mobile	295
31.	On to Montgomery	309
32.	Birmingham	315
33.	An Eventful Ride to Chattanooga	327
34.	Chattanooga and Knoxville	335
	Obituary for Robert L. MacDonald	341
	Death Notice for Willard MacDonald	343

About the Journal

It is more typical today. A broken home: absent father, daughter and sons yearning to understand, a wife left to manage alone. My mother had a dad-sized hole in her life that never was filled. Her father, the author of this journal, fought in World War I and never returned to his family afterward, at least not emotionally. A Scotsman married to a Swede, there was conflict between the two natures, exacerbated by the absence of his family—and the presence of hers.

The details are hazy, but by the opening of his journal in 1932, it is clear that John MacDonald had given up any ideas of reconciliation with his wife Hannah and was preparing to enter a new phase of his life. And what a phase it was! We are fortunate to have a detailed description of his journey across the United States during the depths of the Great Depression. This journal was most likely kept daily, capturing his experiences in close to real time. Most *likely* kept daily, but not *certainly*, since John (along with his sons Willard and Robert) possessed an almost perfect autobiographical memory, a type of explicit memory focused on events rather than facts. Some would call it a blessing; John's son, Robert, who served as a sniper during the Korean War, felt it a curse.

The publication of this journal is a thread that continues through three generations of our family. It is an uncensored, unalloyed relation of life on the road, full of wonderful insights into the life and thoughts of a relative never met, one infrequently mentioned, and of whom only a single photograph remains. Written in a crabbed, almost indecipherable hand, the notebooks landed in my possession upon the death of my uncle, Robert L. MacDonald. Bob made several attempts to prepare the journal for publication but was unable to complete it. I played a small part in transcribing portions during the 1980s and '90s but did not resume work until three years ago, spurred on by the founding of my son Robert's publishing firm, Warner House Press. Robert Warner completed the transcription and copy editing in 2022. I spent 2023 arranging the text, adding supplementary material (including chapter splits and headings), and doing the final proofreading.

And a Herculean task it has been. Transcription of the work was made difficult, not only by the crabbed writing, but by John's minimal use of punctuation, his highly sophisticated and sometimes idiosyncratic vocabulary (including Hobo slang), and many, many, run-on sentences. The author also frequently slips into the present tense to highlight significant actions or thoughts, a style that has long since gone out of favor. Present tense is used most in passages of declamation—to use a too-infrequent term—which occur throughout the journal. These passages contain the most lyrical writing found in the journal and provide the best insights into the character and soul of John. The editors have retained the declamatory parts in the present tense, along with some action scenes for heightened effect. They are set apart and italicized. Although the writing may seem stilted and inaccessible at first, it soon falls into a recognizable and pleasant rhythm.

My thanks go to my son Robert, who completed the transcription of the work and did the lion's share of the editing, and to my wife,

Vicki, who helped with the transcription during many "Shut Up and Write!" sessions. Uncle Bob kept this journal safe for decades and kept its memory alive in the family. An introduction by him is provided, as well as his obituary at the end of this volume. His sister, my mother, Joanna Warner, did not live to see the journal published. I dedicate this to you, Mom.

— Dave Warner

Introduction

In 1932, when I was four years old, my mother and father separated because he was suffering from the effects of shell-shock and gassing from his experiences on the fields of France during World War I. I saw him on only four occasions in my life, the last being when I tracked him down in New York City to tell him of the death of my older brother Willard in World War II. This was in August 1945.

The only person in our family with whom my father communicated was my older brother. I remember occasionally a postcard arriving in the mail from various cities around the country. Like most men who were drifters during the Depression, my father sought warm climates in the winter because he lacked adequate clothing and shelter. The Southwest and California were suitable places.

The last correspondence from him placed him in Tucson, Arizona, but I had no known address for him. I was seventeen years old in 1945, with no experience in finding missing persons. I took my story to the Missing Persons Bureau of the New York City Police Department. There a friendly, experienced Sergeant told me that if I involved the police in my search, I would probably drive all those who might know my father's whereabouts underground. He told me to go to the Mills Hotel in the Bowery section of New York City and tell my story to the manager. The Sergeant was certain that the manager would set in motion a network to locate my father.

The Mills Hotel was a place where drifters could find room and board for a very low price. Men drifted in from all over the country. These men would provide the network that the Sergeant told me about. I went to the Hotel and told the manager my story. He said that he would begin the network to find my father and that, sooner or later, someone would check into the Hotel who had recently seen or heard of my father's whereabouts.

It did not take very long. Within a few weeks, my father was located in New York City and I made contact with him. I was told to meet him at a Bickford's Cafeteria at Sixth Avenue and 10th Street, at an hour and date which I have since forgotten. But I knew the area well, for I had walked in the area many times when I was a chorister and student at Grace Church School at 10th Street and Broadway. His eyes brimmed with tears when I told him of my brother's—his oldest son's—death.

I have said my mother and father separated because of his war experiences. But there may have been other reasons. One of the last words my father spoke to me that day in August 1945 was to the effect that he and my mother might have made it, "except for those people in New Britain."

Throughout my boyhood my mother had always told me that "Daddy was sick." I clung to this reason for the absence of a father in my life. When other boys asked me where my father was, I was able to account for his absence by saying, proudly, that he had been wounded in WWI and couldn't live at home. But now, in this cold, strange, sheetrock cafeteria, he was hinting at other reasons, and, at age seventeen, I could neither understand nor respond. We said goodbye and walked out onto Sixth Avenue together. He turned to the right, I

WAITING FOR THE TRAIN

to the left. When I had gone a short way, I stopped and looked back at him. He was walking slowly, bent over. It was the last time I saw him.

I ask the questions, but seek no answer from any who may read this.

Any except one who no longer can answer.

Between 1928 and 1932, the volume of men who were riding freight trains jumped from 13,745 to 149,773. A new subculture was created, and it dwelled in the Hobo Jungle. The name Hobo probably was chosen because the point of origin for most freights on the eastern seaboard was Hoboken, New Jersey, although there are other suspected derivations, including "Hoe boys," and "Ho! Boys!"

In addition to the documentation of those who dwelled in the Hobo Jungles and those who rode the freights, my father's journal also gives interesting insights about the lodging places where itinerants could get a meal and bed for the night, usually no more than one night as they were encouraged to move on. Places such as the Salvation Army ("the Sally"), YMCA, Army hospitals, missions, and ten-cent-a-night flop houses. Access to these lodgings was not always easy. Living conditions in some were primitive and, in many cases, sanitary conditions were unhealthy. In many places, men were exploited by staff who got kickbacks from police who staged raids on the dormitories in order to clear the city or town of drifters. In many towns and cities, gangs of men waited at freight stations armed with baseball bats to prevent men from dropping off. My father's journal accuses the relief system of the 1930's of managing its lodgings under a jail management system.

Throughout the journal narrative there are statements about the compassion the homeless showed each other, trying to help each other "see it through" a desperate time in their lives.

—Robert L. MacDonald

Chapter One

New York City

There is a time in the course of every individual's life when they experience what may be called their darkest hour or time of utter despair. It may be occasioned by the loss of some beloved one, or some failure in business, or perhaps being forced to leave those dearest to them or the surroundings held sacred and necessary to their happiness and success in life. And so, like any other mortal, I had mine when that period of Depression had fully set in back in the year of 1932[1].

Up and until that year, I had enjoyed to the fullest almost everything a working man could expect according to his salary and station in life: A car, good clothes, a good time when I cared to have it, and never being without money, shelter, or a meal.

I was always carefree, with no worries for the future. In fact, I can never remember when I really ever had cause to worry about having to give thought to any impending trouble ahead; in other words, I enjoyed to the fullest a sense of security to the effect that in my old

---

1. The author intentionally leaves the date blank here. Based on internal references the journal probably starts in late 1932.

age I would be independent and self-sufficient and not beholden to anyone.

If any of my friends even hinted at the possibility that at some time I would be classed among the needy or on the verge of hunger or without a roof over my head, forced to walk the streets looking for a few hours' work for a meal and the price of a night's lodging, I would have undoubtedly judged them as being somewhat light in the head or else losing control of their imaginations.

No one realizes until they go through the experience what havoc it causes to anyone's mental or moral equilibrium, or the change in their views or opinions towards their fellowman and things in general. Especially when things go topsy-turvy through no fault of your own.

That Depression was one of those depressions that hit everybody, so that made it still more difficult to get at least enough work to eke out a mere existence.

There was only one consolation in regards to the whole situation, and that was that you yourself were not the only one up against it. In my own case, I was perhaps not so bad off, for I had no immediate responsibilities like a great many had. But when you are hungry and without shelter, you feel these things personally and start to turn against the fates, and against those whom you feel could have found some way to avert such conditions.

Any sudden or drastic change is bound to have its reactions. For some, it was a tragedy and they thought suicide the only way out, while in the case of others, they clung on to life and worried it out, and trudged along in their suffering and mental anguish, sometimes to the point of insanity. For the latter class, those that clung on hoping and worrying, I have the greatest sympathy, for not even on the battlefields of France did I worry or go through so much mental anguish as I did in the early part of the upheaval caused by the Depression.

It was not until I took a little time off from thinking how bad things were, that I realized how foolish it was to worry and fret over something no one seemed to have any control over. After summing up my own situation as compared to others, I began to think in a more hopeful train of thought, and thereby came to the conclusion that about the only way out was to sort of float along with the tide and pray for an early return to normalcy.

I don't know how it affected some people, but I started to miss some of the good things of life. I started to hark back to all the years of good living and some of the fun I used to get out of life, and some of the things I wanted to do but never got around to, either because I never had the time or didn't have the guts or couldn't or wouldn't give up a life of comfort and ease.

Now there was many a time when although things were going at their best with me, I had often wished for a complete respite from the humdrum existence one has to go through while living in a city as large as New York. Every day I went to work, I used to give thought to how great it would be to get away from the great canyons of buildings that made me feel I was walking between great walls of stone that had no color. Always the same drabness whichever way you looked. And, too, how great it would be to get away from the monotony of having to get up at the same time every morning and take the same old route to work, and finally, when you arrived at the shop, to have to punch a clock and then have to hear the same old voices and look upon the same old faces day in and day out[2]. And worst of all, to have to listen to a bellyaching Boss and his demand for just a little more production caused (as he claimed) by the keen competition of other firms. All this

---

2. John MacDonald's death certificate listed his occupation as cook. However, his description here suggests a manufacturing job.

and a lot of other irritating occurrences that go to spoil the even tenor of a day's existence while working for your bread and butter.

Yes, I often was on the point of chucking up the whole damn business and taking up some other type of business or packing my things and going to the places I had read about in travel books of far off places, and seeing the things that some of my friends had told me about.

So here it was as though out of a clear sky: An opportunity had presented itself to fulfill all those past desires to get away from it all, if only I took advantage of it.

Now for some reason, it is hard to break away from your own hometown and your friends of many years standing. But here was a situation in which your own hometown or your friends couldn't help much in the way of getting anyone a job, for they too were perhaps walking the streets. So summing up and going over every angle of my troubles, I decided I would take a chance and go to it and leave the rest to "Lady Luck," for I had nothing to lose one way or another. I couldn't be any worse off in one place or another and, too, my room rent was due and from all indications when the day came to pay it, I wouldn't have it, and that meant eviction for sure.

So thus it was that after exhausting every effort in trying to find work or some way to hang on a little longer in New York, I called on a few friends and said goodbye and started to prepare for what turned out to be the greatest time and experience of my life.

I was really happy in the thought that at least I would be free of a great many of my troubles, for there is nothing in this world like having your mind occupied to help you forget your troubles and those about you.

I gave thought to the fact that I ought to be more thankful that I was really free (or would be soon) of that stuffy existence in a city and, too, that I was free of all those disagreeable things I had longed to be free of these many years; really free to go do what I pleased, and go where I pleased, with no questions to be answered to nobody.

Let it not be said that I didn't still have my own opinions concerning the mess the country was in, for I am still not so sure but that conditions could have been alleviated somewhat if those who had the means to help only had tried a little harder than they did. Or perhaps if those who didn't help had only been a little more liberal and sympathetic in their attitude and treatment of the most unfortunate. At least it would have helped to keep up their courage.

Perhaps I have too much faith in what humanity can do for one another; perhaps I expect too much from my fellow man, and it may be that I have the wrong slant on life in general. But it seems to me that there is considerable lack of civic pride in those who deliberately stand by and see people suffering unnecessarily, for one would naturally think that, by a combined effort on the part of those who were able to help, they would know that to keep up the health and morale of the unfortunate and unemployed would only make them more of an asset instead of a burden on the general public. I cannot help but believe that a great deal of our many taxes have been brought about by this very indifference to the welfare of others.

I have heard many of those who were getting along nicely snarl at others who were walking the streets with not even a place to lay their head or knowing where their next meal was to come from when they appealed to them for even a cup of coffee, saying to them with a sneer on their faces, "No, we can't help how hungry you are, that is nothing to us. Why should we worry? Why don't you go to the Government—they should take care of you people who are in such need."

I often thought when I heard people talk like that to a hungry man or woman who had a couple of kids at home (who were perhaps hungrier) just which of the two parties were in the greatest need, for I would far rather be hungry than have such a mental attitude towards anybody's misfortune. In fact, I would rather be a little bit more inclined to give what I had and go without myself, even if it were the last grain of coffee. And so, by such an attitude on the part of those who would turn down an unfortunate or an unemployed fellow, the Government had to step in and see to it that all did their share through public support or a relief program. So it followed that those who could and wouldn't lift a finger for their fellow man were paying double and forced to do their share.

By way of experience I have found that there are certain reactions to certain attitudes one takes in regards life and their obligations to others, especially in times of distress. For I have found that as a rule the "Law of Averages" finally catches up with you one way or another and retaliation does at times come swift and sure, so you get good for good or, if you are inclined the other way, well, you will by the same token get the same in return.

I feel I can truthfully state that most of our troubles are brought about through the unfairness of others and that a great deal of our sufferings are of our own fault or making. You must play the game on the square or take the consequences. Life is too much in earnest and she casts aside those who try to make a fool of her. She will have none of those who play traitor to her precepts.

Such were the conditions around and about me and, with that knowledge, in respect to hoping for any improvement in conditions in or around New York City, I could see none for some time to come. So, having informed my landlady I could no longer afford paying for a room I was leaving, I left there absolutely destitute. With what I thought I could use, I started out to God knows where.

I didn't even have the price of a subway fare to downtown New York. All I had were the clothes on my back, what little I had in a small bundle, my self-respect and, best of all, my health, and that was something really to be thankful for, under the circumstances.

And now I am (or can consider myself) an indigent and subject to the whims and fancies of all my brothers and the public in general. They can ask questions if they want to, for am I not just one more burden on them? But rest assured, I won't dwell long on that angle of the situation, for if I am to get anywhere or have a place to sleep and something to eat, I will have to get a move on, and at this particular moment I am well in need of my breakfast.

So, I stood on a corner of Broadway and one of the cross streets in Washington Heights, not many blocks from my old room that I had occupied for almost five years, trying to sort of get myself together and take a last fond look at the old scenes. I hadn't the least idea when I would ever see them again, if ever.

Somehow or other, I just couldn't decide in which direction I should go in my first lap on what proved to be a wandering life of six years[3].

Whether it was by force of habit or some guiding hand, I don't know which (and at the time I had other and more important things on my mind), I suddenly woke up to the fact that I was walking slowly down Broadway towards downtown New York. After finding I had really walked almost ten blocks, it suddenly dawned on me that from now on, if I didn't want to wear myself out, I should begin to save

---

3. The journal documents a span of ten years. John did not spend all that time traveling.

steps and mileage as best I could. So, instead of taking Broadway any further, I turned to the right and walked as far as Riverside Drive and then went down as far as 72nd Street and thus so returned on down Broadway. When I got as far as 59th Street, I began to feel somewhat hungry and that of course called for action of some sort if I cared to appease it.

The first place I stopped in was one of those "Hamburger Joints" as some call them. "Hamburger Joint" or not, that made no difference to me, so I boldly walked in and offered my services for something to eat or a meal.

The man behind the counter looked me over from head to foot and then finally shook his head signifying there was nothing doing. So I backed out feeling somewhat disappointed in having no success on my first bid for a meal.

That first refusal did discourage me a little, but the more I thought of it the more determined I became that somewhere along the line I would finally find some place that would be glad to let me work out a good meal. So I sauntered on down 7th Avenue until I finally reached 73rd Street, and there I decided this would be as far as I would venture downtown.

As I stood on the corner, I took a survey of all the restaurants and stores, giving them a close observation as to the likelihood of a possibility of obtaining an hour or two of work. None of them appealed to me as being any too prosperous looking, so I walked back a block or two to where I thought (when passing it) was a pretty busy restaurant. So, instead of hesitating, I walked right in and sat down close to the cash register as though I were able to buy the best meal on their menu.

The man looked up from what he was doing and politely asked me what I would have, so I put the question to him point blank and told him I was willing to work out a meal if he would be so kind as to let me. That was one of those times I got sat on as never before.

Said he: "You get the hell out of here you lousy bum and go to work! You only think you want to work for a meal. Why, you big bum, you wouldn't work and besides, you haven't the nerve to ask right out for it. Every one of you bums is too lazy to work very long, so get the hell out of here—and be damn quick about it!"

Having finished his tirade against me and those who would dare enter his place for any form of aid, he started for the end of the counter, no doubt to see to it I did get out as he ordered. I really believed he would have done me bodily harm if I had tarried much longer, so bitter did he seem.

It would be hard to describe the extent of my feelings and the thoughts that went coursing through my mind as I once more found myself out on the street. I only know I felt like a whipped cur, or like some innocent school boy who had just been chastised for something he hadn't been guilty of while in full view of his classmates.

Rest assured it was a few days before I could muster up enough nerve and courage to offer my services for anything in a restaurant.

After I left that restaurant I continued on down 21st Street more or less unmindful of what direction I was going. My one thought seemed to be to get as far away from the vicinity of that restaurant as I could.

I must have had somewhat of a defeated look about me as I shuffled on down the sidewalk trying to keep more or less in the shadows of the buildings, for I still felt the sting of that bawling out.

I was awakened out of my aimless steps by someone bumping into me and near knocking me off my feet, all the while growling at me something to the effect of: "Did I know where I was going and what the hell was the matter with me?"

I gave no notice and took no offense, but it did wake me out of my thoughts and none too soon, for I was in the middle of a crossing and against the traffic lights.

After just escaping being run down by a truck and being bawled out by the traffic officer, I finally reached the opposite sidewalk to find I was pretty well over on the western extremity of 73rd Street.

It was only a few months back that I had been working not so far from the very spot I now found I had arrived at, so, naturally, familiar scenes and places conjured up more pleasant times, which as a rule, bring with them former friends and acquaintances. Among those acquaintances was a restaurant worker, but for some unknown reason I couldn't for the life of me remember his name. However, I did know where he was last working, so, recalling a remark he had made on our last meeting, I finally decided to take him up on it.

Said he on that last meeting: "Now, if ever you get up against it, be sure to come around and see me."

I had only a few blocks to go, but for every step I took on my way to that restaurant, my fears grew that he either had left his job there or was finished for the day and had gone home.

I finally reached the restaurant and, being somewhat agitated from the past hour's experience and somewhat worried, I fairly lunged into the place. As I did, his name came to me. So I asked the young lady behind the counter if such a person still worked there and if he did, could I please speak to him. Instead of answering my question, she called out his name, and when I heard him answer I felt as though a ton had been lifted from my shoulders, for by that time, I was hungry and ready to do most anything for a cup of coffee.

Much to my relief, my friend seemed more than pleased to see me. After a few words of salutation I explained to him some of my past difficulties in making things meet and then he asked me if had I eaten anything that day. And believe me those words were the sweetest words that I had heard in days.

After a long talk about things in general, a good meal, and the loan of a one-dollar bill, I left feeling like a new man and a human being once again.

Let me pause for just a few moments from the events and happenings of my first day of real destitution to jot down a few hints on how it feels to be really good and hungry. For I don't know of anything that will get a man down in spirits more than hunger; yet it spurs a person on and on to find food to appease it.

I thought of more schemes and ways I might be able to get a meal and don't think for one moment that I didn't go to some extremes in my thoughts, even on to stiffing someone or stepping into some eating place and demanding it. At one moment I gave thought to stepping into another place I saw hundreds eating at to put up a fight for it. The only thing that stopped me was that I was afraid of being clapped in jail, or suffering some other dire consequence.

Yes sir, hunger does really set you thinking along queer channels of thought, and will likely as not cause anyone to commit acts that one would never think of doing under normal conditions.

After this first day's experience, I made a resolution that I would never turn down another hungry being asking for a bite to eat, even if it was to take the last nickel I had in my pocket and I had to walk twenty miles to my home from work.

Well now that I had a substantial meal under my belt and a one-dollar bill in my pocket, my worries as regards eating and shelter were over, at least for the next twenty four hours. Now I had only one other worry, and that was: *Will it pay to stay on in New York City, or shall I follow out my original intention of leaving it for other fields and pastures?*

I was now within a stone's throw of a ferry which takes you over to New Jersey and for some reason or other I just couldn't resist the temptation to get on it and get going.

While watching one or two ferry boats come and go, I was reminded of the last time I used them on a trip I took a few years ago, but that was in better circumstances and then there was no need for hesitation and no need to give any thought as to whether I should take it or not.

Something kept telling me to go and then some other thought would raise a doubt as to the gain of continuing. Again would come that little voice egging me on until finally I succumbed and, first thing I knew, I was on the ferry boat and soon on my way to New Jersey.

Well, I am off. Where to I couldn't say, but I am on my way, and, funny thing about it, I feel a thrill and I am not afraid and, in fact, I feel very much relieved and pleased to be moving, and all these things bring me to one conclusion: That it would make no difference one way or another whether to stay in one place, or wander here and there until I find something to do.

Chapter Two

Newark, New Jersey

The ferry boat finally slips into its dock and so I prepare to get off and let come what might.

It was rather late when I arrived on the Jersey side, and traffic seemed to be exceptionally light. Consequently, there were very few people or vehicles about.

I knew from the ferry landing I could branch out in a good many directions, but I had no first-hand knowledge as to which of the many streets close by to take in order to get to Newark, New Jersey. That city, I thought, would be just about as far as I could make before it was time to be looking for some kind of shelter for the balance of the night.

After looking about and seeking some information from the few I met coming and going (some seemed to know but weren't sure, others didn't know at all, and others just smiled a knowing smile and shook their heads, no), one fellow suggested I take the bus. To that bit of advice I only smiled and said, "Thanks, but not tonight," and then thinking it no use to bother asking any more, I started up the highway trusting to luck I was going correctly.

I continued on for quite some distance and then all of a sudden I realized:

Instead of being on the highway, I am in a railroad yard and all tangled up in a maze of freight cars, old engines, piles of old tracks, switches, fences, and buildings of the Jersey Railroad[1].

I cursed my luck and myself for not watching where I was going and my foolhardiness for even starting out without some knowledge as to where I was really going.

Funny how a person can get all turned around and lose their general direction entirely. So being in that state more or less, I figured any direction was as good as another. I selected a line of tracks and followed it blindly and soon I came out on a road, then I took another chance and turned left and continued on until I noticed I was slowly going uphill and, as I came to the top of it, I saw a bridge which crossed the road at right angles. Now (thought I) I am getting somewhere, but when I arrived at the bridge, I found I was just as much at sea as ever.

There was a slight embankment on each side of the bridge, so I decided if I could only get up on higher ground, perhaps I could get my bearings.

So up I climb to the bridge and from it I can see two lights off in the distance which I figure are beacons of some sort in Newark, but I am not sure.

Now, how to get to where those lights were, if they really were in Newark, was my next problem. So, I looked over the bridge and found

---

1. The New Jersey and New York Railroad (NJ&NY) was a railroad company that operated north from Rutherford, New Jersey, to Haverstraw, New York beginning in the mid-to-late 19th century.

I was right in the midst of what looked like a marshland or a swamp of some kind and, winding across it, was a road which must have been the one I had just left.

Looking in the other direction, I made out a dimly lit highway and down I went, feeling my way as best I could, hoping it would finally get me near Newark.

Walking along a highway that is lighted so poorly as this one wasn't a very pleasant evening's stroll. However, I was going someplace and wherever that was would sometime or other present itself if I walked long enough.

I finally came to a crossroad and here I turned left and not fifty feet from there I banged smack up against a wooden building.

I must have created an awful racket, for before I recovered from the impact, I heard someone shout out: "Who is that?! What do you want?! What do you want around here—get the hell out of here!"

I made no answer but instead I got the hell out of there as he told me, turned about, and got clear of the place as fast as I could.

As I continued on in the opposite direction, I happened to glance back and see the rays of a big flashlight stabbing the inky darkness, no doubt looking for me. But by that time I was out of the focus of his light, and thought I was safe and gave attention as best I could to the road in the darkness. Thinking everything was OK, I started to search my pockets for my cigarettes and, just as I struck a match, I heard the crack of a revolver shot, and not a split second later, heard a bullet whip over my head, and that galvanized me into instant action.

Hearing bullets whizzing through the air was not new to me,[2] so past training came to the fore and I dropped flat on the road and rolled over and over on down into a nice muddy ditch. How I got under

---

2. The author saw action as an infantryman in World War I.

the extremely low railing of the fence bordering the road is still one of those rare accomplishments of getting through small spaces that do happen once in a while. That railing couldn't have been more than eight inches from the ground.

I crouched down in the weeds as flat as I could, waiting and listening, hoping that would satisfy whoever it was that got so worked up over someone just bumping up against a building in the dark but, no, two more bullets went whipping overhead and these were too low for comfort.

"Cripes, that guy means business and things certainly are getting too hot in this neck of the woods. Well, I asked for it and so I'll have to take my medicine if he takes it into his head to hunt me up." Thus I reflected as I lay in that muddy ditch, getting wetter and wetter every second.

After another minute or so, I crawled up the ditch and took a look back towards the direction of the shooting and I saw no flashlight. Things apparently were OK, so I got back onto the road and hot footed it as fast as I could, seeking some way out of that vicinity, for any minute I would hear the siren of some highway patrol car.

Much to my relief I notice as I glance to one side of the road some cultivated land and, after a patch or two, I come abreast of an old barn. A little further on I am walking amidst a clump of dwellings.

This encouraged me somewhat and, at the first crossroad or street, I turned onto it and beat up it as fast as I could get my legs going. After dodging around corners and taking side streets (and once I went down a small back alley and came back on the same street that I entered it), finally I emerged onto a business street.

Much to my relief I am in Newark at last, but madder than hell over the events of the night and my wet condition.

It was just breaking day when I came to a park and there I sat down cursing myself for a damn fool for ever thinking of leaving New York City.

I glance down at my clothes and I find that I am covered with mud and thistles and streaks of whitewash from the fence I went under. One of my trouser legs is torn. To say the least of my appearance I certainly look a mess. Besides all this I am cold from the dampness of my clothes, I am hungry and tired and, if anyone was to dare make a false move or remark it would be woe onto them.

I felt so mean and miserable I hated myself.

I cleaned up as best I could and then got up and walked through the park. I was not the only wayfarer there, for here and there I saw forms all huddled up on the benches, trying no doubt to get a few winks of sleep. It being in the month of December accounted for so few transients sitting throughout the night. Those that I observed were shivering from the cold air of the early morning, and some were shifting from one side to the other vainly, no doubt to rest one side and then the other.

Such things as men and even women sleeping in the park was nothing new to me, so I didn't pay much attention to them. I finally reached the opposite side of the park and as I passed the last seat, occupied by a middle aged man, he called out to me for a match. As I gave it to him, he offered me a cigarette, so I took it and sat down beside him, and that was all he needed, for said he: "You haven't a spare nickel about you you could spare?"

"Yes, I got a spare nickel to spare, but if you care to and are able to walk, and can show me a reasonable priced restaurant for such as we, I'll be willing to spend more than a nickel," I answered.

For a minute or two I thought the man had a spell or something, for I never saw a man get into action as much as he did; he fairly leaped out of that seat and said, "I'll say I can. Come on buddy, I know where we can get hot cakes and coffee for a dime. Come on, let's go."

As we walked out of the park, we met another man who stopped and spoke to my companion and asked him where he was going.

My friend told him and to my surprise, he said to him, "Come on along and have a cup of coffee!"

I looked my friend over and then gave the other fellow a questioning look, for here was something that looked rather queer. So I said to both of them, "Just who is taking who for that cup of coffee?" Believe it or not, he said, "Why, you are."

That answer made me boil over, so I told him and his friend that, as far as I was concerned, I was going on my way alone. So I did, and left the both of them standing there.

I returned to the park in a roundabout way and sat down again. As I did, another fellow spoke to me as he was passing, so I nodded and, first thing I knew, I had another guy on my hands who asked for the price of a cup of coffee. I told him yes, but as for handing it out, he would have to show me he was alone.

While waiting for his answer, I looked the man over for signs of dissipation from drink but I couldn't see nothing but that vacant stare that so many men had when they are more or less down in spirits. So I told him I guessed he was alright and then arose and told him to come along.

We left the park and finally we came across one of those cheap restaurants. As one, we turned into it and sat down and, as I did, I looked the place over and gave the customers a glance. And who do I see sitting not three seats from me, but the other two fellows who tried to take me over for whatever they could get out of me, and now that I had a second look at them, I felt I was right by getting away from

WAITING FOR THE TRAIN

them. For in front of them was a pretty substantial breakfast which only proved they had money.

While waiting for our orders, I gave the restaurant a second close scrutiny and all I could see was filth and dirt and dust. The proprietor was as dirty and as grimy as the surroundings, and blended well with the whole place and his customers, the majority of which looked like a lot of professional bums or panhandlers. None of them would have been presentable in any other environment than just where I found them.

We ate our hotcakes and coffee more or less in silence, for this man I could see was really hungry, so I left him to himself until both of us had finished. Then, I asked him for some information in regards to the direction I would have to take to get onto the highway to Philadelphia, Pennsylvania.

I ordered another cup of coffee and, while we sat there, he told me first how to get there and what to do and where to go when I got there. I bid him goodbye and hot footed it to the spot he said anyone could get a hitch hike to Phila.

I finally find the place, but if I judged the case with which he claimed I would get a lift to the number of hours I stood there thumbing for that ride and the number of refusals when I asked orally for a ride, I'd say I either was experiencing some real hard luck, or else he certainly didn't know what he was talking about.

I stood there from about ten o'clock to about five in the evening. So I gave it up, and was just about ready to chuck the whole business up and return to New York City and stay there, when I happened to notice a freight train pulling out from some railroad yard that ran parallel with the highway, and that chased away all thoughts of abandoning this trip.

I gave the highway a few more minutes of attention but with no different luck, so I crossed over on the other side and walked along the highway to find some opening or way to that railroad yard.

Chapter Three

Welcome to the Jungle

Now, for some reason or other I had always had a slight fear of railroads. Why, I could not fathom, unless it could be some fright I had gone through as a child. I am still leery of crossing a number of tracks to this day, but this was a time when I had to do something regardless of fear or anything else if I was to get out of Newark, so I gave full attention to the possibilities of using that railroad as a means of at least getting to Philadelphia that evening.

My feet were bothering me terribly from the walking and standing I had done since the day before, and if I didn't get someplace to get my shoes off to give them a rest, it wouldn't be long before I would be laid up in some hospital with them. Every step I took it felt as though my soles were seared and raw. Never before did they ache and burn and throb so badly.

It was getting close onto darkness and, like every other time when one is trying to accomplish something and has so little time to do it in, everything seemed to be going against me.

I must have walked almost a mile before I came to any kind of an opening that I could use to get to that railroad yard. Finally, when I did, I had to climb up an embankment and then cross over a field of weeds and stubble, only to come to a barbed wire fence about six feet high—and that was a fence, for the wires were so close together I could hardly get the toe of my shoes in-between in order to climb over. But over I got in spite of this and, as I was just topping it, I lost my balance and rolled over the top and fell to the ground, minus damn near one sleeve of my coat.

As I got to my feet cursing a blue streak and damning those who had invented such blasted damn kind of fences, I came face to face with a sign that informed me I was on private property and also that I was now facing a fine of fifty dollars or thirty days in jail for daring to do so.

Well here I am, thought I, and here I stay and the hell with signs and warnings and such things as private property and fines and any number of days in jail I might be facing. I didn't give a damn. I'll take the chance and investigate anyway, I decided. So with a firm determination, I proceeded to get up on the track and look the yard over.

I was expecting any minute to have some watchman or guard hail me and tell me to get out of it, or hear a shot fired like that crazy guy last night did, but none came, and that sort of encouraged me to proceed further on.

As I look up and down the track I see about a block away a string of box cars standing on another track and to those I make a beeline, if only to use them to keep out of sight just in case someone is about.

Now that I was actually in the yard good and proper, I decided to walk to the end of the cars and, as I stepped past the last car, my eye caught sight of a head disappearing in a clump of weeds not far from the tracks. This made me make a hasty retreat back to the offside of the cars for cover, for I had no way of knowing whether that head belonged to a railroad man or not.

After a minute or two, I cautiously looked around the end and, instead of one head, I saw two, and this time whoever it was stood up and beckoned me over. From their frantic motions I deduced that they were warning me to get over there quickly.

I dodged back to the cover of the car I was standing by to sort of think things out, and to try and decide whether or not to heed their invitation or warnings, and once more I decided to take a chance.

So I boldly walk right out in the open and descend the short embankment and on to that clump of weeds, and as I just get down to get out of sight, I see out of the corner of my eye someone appear at the far end of that string of cars.

I was sure I saw some kind of badge on his coat so after all, thought I, there was somebody about and it was just luck that I didn't run into him. My heart skipped a beat or two as I heard footsteps approaching and I expected that any minute whoever it was would come crashing in on us. If they did, and they happened to be someone of authority, that would be all it would take to make a very miserable ending to a still more miserable day. But, much to my relief, no one stopped and the footsteps went out of earshot.

My fellow wayfarers didn't seem to be worried in the least and seemingly paid no attention to what I thought an imminent danger to our freedom.

After I got more or less settled, I began to take stock of my companions, and I found that I was one of seven men whose ages ranged from twenty-four to sixty-five years of age. After having fixed their ages in my mind, I took stock of their appearance and general character and, summarizing that part of my observations, I found I was in the midst of the most decrepit and unkempt lot of men I have yet looked upon.

There wasn't one of them that I would care to walk on the street with, and not one of them I can safely state had even washed their faces for days—and perhaps for weeks. I shuddered inwardly at their uncleanliness. Their clothes were filthy with dirt and grease, not one of them had a decent pair of shoes and one or two of them had on two different kinds.

I wouldn't have been surprised to see cooties crawling about them, so I kept as far away from any close contact with them as I could without causing any offense, for I have been good and lousy myself but under different circumstances.

It must have been fully fifteen minutes before any one of them spoke, and when one of them did he asked me, "So where was I bound for?" and "Had I been on the bum long?"

Such a straightforward question as that sort of took me by surprise and I thought I detected a hint of sarcasm in it, so I evaded answering the last part of the question and only told them I expected to go to Philadelphia and would like to get there that night.

The oldest of them sort of smiled knowingly and tendered his opinion or thought by remarking, "I thought so, but let him alone—he'll learn," and, "I guess he is OK." Then, looking me straight in the eye he asked, "You're not a cop or a railroad dick, are you?"

The last question sort of made me hot under the collar, so I asked him if he was trying to be funny and then told him that I was not, in as emphatic a tone as I could put on.

He ventured no more questions and after a few minutes of silence everybody seemed to be more at ease.

So, with that as my first inspection or examination, I might say I was duly accredited as being OK'd by the first lot of hobos. I might add too that this was my first real contact and introduction into the "Realm of the Jungle of the Hobos."

I felt more at ease now that I had apparently passed their scrutiny, so I took a closer look at my companions and the immediate surroundings.

We were sitting in a circle, all facing each other, which struck me as being from force of habit, or perhaps it was a matter of convenience, or that they got more benefit of the heat from the fire that had apparently gone out just before I arrived. I could see a few coals were still hot.

Once in awhile, I detected in their conversation and actions a want of confidence and freedom that is felt among friends. They talked to each other as though they were perfect strangers, yet at times they seemed to have met before. All had that haunted look in their eyes, and one of them acted as though he might be a hunted and wanted man.

Every time any one of them started to speak, all the rest were alert to every word that was said, as though weighing every syllable. I took special notice that there wasn't a subject that was brought up but that it wasn't contradicted, and therefore I listened to some of the silliest arguments that didn't have an ounce of sense in them. From that I judged that none of them had more than a fourth-grade education to their credit, and that, I thought, answered the riddle of why they didn't have any pride in themselves as regards their appearance and uncleanliness. I couldn't make myself believe that the conditions which then prevailed would be any excuse for not keeping clean and somewhere near tidiness.

They all appeared suspicious of each other and from their general want, I'd judge them as being rightly so in that respect. I must admit that I wouldn't care to leave anything of value around loose and have any one of them know about it or, for that matter, bring to light or show anything that I would care to keep.

I was somewhat disappointed in the fact that I couldn't see any resemblance in them to what I had always pictured in my mind of these so-called Hoboes or "Gentry of the Road." The one thing that disappointed me the most was the total absence of that romantic atmosphere that is supposed to go with living a life in the "Jungles."

After looking my companions over once more for some signs or evidence of having some breeding or background and seeing none, I gave thought that perhaps this lot of men were not what one could call real Hoboes. However, they were in the environment and, from their conversation, they had been living as such for some time, so I had to give them the benefit of the doubt. So, until I had more experience living this mode of life, I didn't waste any more time thinking about it.

As silence fell over us and as nightfall was coming on pretty fast, I began to get a little bit worried about having to stay up all night again. So I shifted into a prone position as best as I could to try and get a wink or two of sleep, but, somehow or other, I couldn't get into a comfortable position and, too, thirst was bothering me somewhat. So I got back into a sitting position and ventured to ask the man who sat to my right if he knew where I could get a drink. He informed me that he didn't know of any, but if I cared to, I could have a drink of what coffee was left.

I looked around, but I couldn't see no coffee about and naturally I began to think he was kidding me or waiting perhaps for me to refuse it. Why I should think that he wanted to hear a refusal rather than an acceptance I don't know, but it did seem to me his actions expressed that intent, so, just to see whether he was fooling around or not, I told him I didn't see no coffee around.

Instead of making any remark in answer to that, he reached to the rear of him in the weeds and brought to light an old rusty tin can and handed it to me.

I thanked him and began to sort of sample what he called "coffee."

After taking a sip or two I had to sit the can down and, not meaning to, I made a sort of wry face. One of the men, noticing the expression, took exception to it and asked me in a sarcastic tone, "What's the matter with it? Isn't it good enough for you?"

Under different circumstances, I no doubt would have told him in plain words that it was not, and I might have added too that it was pretty rotten, but here was a time and a place I had to use precaution and a certain kind of diplomacy if I was to still remain in their good graces.

So I told him that it was alright but it certainly would taste better if it had a little sugar in it, and by way of a suggestion I further added it would do more good if it was hot.

Everyone was giving me their full attention, so when I had finished my suggestions, one of them started to laugh and said in a derisive manner and tone, "Sugar? Sugar! Did you hear him? Sugar—can you beat that—he wants sugar in his coffee! Ha ha ha, that's a good one! Sugar!"

"Sugar!" piped another one and then almost fell prone, he laughed so heartily.

"Sugar!" said still another one. "Just imagine that! Say buddy, let me tell you something, just so you will know. If it's fancy things to eat and comforts you're looking for in the Jungles, you are certainly going to be sadly disappointed before you go places."

To all this derision and criticism and advice and information, I gave no answer. I just let them have their way and let it go at that, but it did give me a pretty good idea of the kind of men I was dealing with.

Now, when I am thirsty and there is anything around that is wet or that might possibly appease my thirst, even if it isn't the most pleasant drink, I can hardly pass it up. So, to show these men I could drink that coffee, I finished it down to where I was getting mostly coffee grains, and that seemed to satisfy them. Why? Don't ask me—I certainly wouldn't know, and to this day, I can't figure out why there should have been so much ado over anyone's dislikes or how anyone likes their coffee: sweet, bitter, hot, cold, black, or otherwise.

When I had finished drinking what coffee there was left in that old rusty can, I sat it down on the ground and, no more than my hand had left it, one of the other men grabbed it up. To my amazement, he picked up an old piece of newspaper and proceeded to dump the used coffee grains onto it and then wrapped them up and stuck the parcel in his coat pocket, saying to all in general, "That will come in handy sometime, somewhere down the road."

I didn't dare make any comment on such an economical act, and none came from any one of the men, but I did do a deal of thinking. For I couldn't help but think it must be a hell of a condition when men get down to such need and want that they have to use coffee grains over and over.

Well, I am learning and it only goes to show there is always something new to learn and see and also there are more ways than one to eke out an existence.

Thus it was that I got my first introduction to that famous "Jungle Coffee" I had so often read and heard about.

Nothing more happened or was said that was of much interest, except that perhaps it was now almost dark and all of us were more or less restless. This was due to the fact that, since we were sitting there, none of us had noticed any activity that would have given us any encouragement on being able to get a freight out that night.

I didn't know how the rest of the men there felt but, as for myself, I was getting cold. So in order to get my blood into better circulation, I got to my feet and, as I turned around, I noticed a heavy engine standing some distance down the track, and to that spectacle I called my companions' attention.

They all got to their feet, and one of them exclaimed in a pleased tone, "That's her! Let's get ready. Come on!"

Chapter Four

First Freight

So up the embankment as one we climb and proceed down the tracks towards the engine, yet at the same time trying to keep out of the focus of the engine headlight.

This being my first experience of riding on freight trains, I naturally was somewhat excited and a little nervous; worried, too, that I wouldn't be able to get on if it happened to be going at even a five-mile speed.

One of the men noticed my excitement and nervousness, so he told me not to worry, he would show me how it was done.

We had arrived just abreast of the engine when the engineer gave two blasts of the whistle. Coming so unexpectedly, those two blasts almost scared me to death, so much so that I started to dive down the embankment to our right. One of the men got ahold of my sleeve and held me back and said, "I guess you need someone to take care of you, so keep right in back of me and don't worry—we won't let you down."

I liked that and began to think that I had judged them unfairly and that perhaps in spite of their apparent slothfulness and want of breeding, they were not bad fellows after all.

Just a second after the echo of those two shrieking, ear-splitting blasts had passed away, the engine started and slowly it took up the slack and was rolling by us.

It was then that I got panicky and, if two of the men hadn't grabbed me under the armpits and lifted me up bodily between them until I got my feet on one of the steps, I certainly would have been left behind.

To say the least, I never felt so thankful towards anyone as I did to these two men. That, I thought, was what anyone could call helping one another. That was seeing you through.

After we got settled, one of the men sort of called the roll. No doubt he was a little worried as to whether all of us got on, and that little bit of thoughtfulness started me to thinking along channels that brought me all the way back to the beginning of my independence.

It seemed a queer thing. In these men who were not even very well educated, most likely the product of a very poor environment, and who seemed to have been in dire want a long time, I had found one of those rare qualities that go to ease the burdens and vicissitudes of life: A helping hand and seeing you through. In comparing it with past experiences during all this Depression so far, I thought it put to shame some of the people whom I knew and their attitude, the hard things they had said, and their absolute disinterest in regards to having any sympathy or even giving a helping hand. When I compared it further, especially in respect to the conditions those same people were living under and the many comforts and conveniences they had at their command, these men certainly struck me as being like a ray of sunshine in a darkened sky.

These men were hard; they were dirty and close to being filthy. They perhaps wouldn't let a chance go by to take something that didn't belong to them, and they were seemingly always ready for a fight at the drop of a hat. But damn it all, they were considerate when you were stuck or in trouble. They encouraged you by word and backed it up by action. Yes, they even went fifty-fifty with you, whether you were friend or foe or stranger, if you were hungry or not. Glory be, could it be possible that I had found the kind of men I like, and must it be amidst such as these? Does one have to live amidst squalor and want and ignorance to enjoy real brotherhood?

What the hell, where does this talk about education being the medium by which mankind is supposed to race to a higher plane and have a better understanding of each other come in? Here was a glaring example that certainly refuted such reasoning.

Such were the thoughts that ran through my mind as we rode on through the night towards Philadelphia.

This being my first experience of riding on a freight train, I naturally was more or less nervous and a little frightened. Every jerk and squeak and rattle of the car we were riding made me jump, but after covering about twenty-five miles, I began to feel a little more confident that nothing was going to happen. It wasn't until we had covered about half the distance that I became fully composed and aware of what my companions were doing.

Being old hands at riding freights, my companions naturally were acting in a matter-of-fact way and all had by this time found a place to sit. But I, being a novice, was still standing up, getting the full blast of the cold air as we rode on. Not only that, but I was getting the full benefit of the smoke and hot cinders every time the fireman started throwing more coal on his fire. After getting one of those cinders in my eye, I got wise to myself and found a place and sat down, and from then on felt more comfortable.

It is only a short run by rail to Philadelphia from Newark, so I figured it would only take three or four hours to get there.

Every once in a while, one of my companions would get up on his feet and look around and, just as soon as he got his bearings, he would announce about where we were. Gradually we came nearer and nearer to our goal and then, all of a sudden, the train slackened speed and, as one of the men expressed it, we would soon be "sliding into the Penn. Yard." When the train came to a full stop, we started to file off as one and drop to the ground and, no more than we had touched the roadbed, three or four men with nice shiny badges on their coats surrounded us.

That, I thought, would be all for tonight, for all I could see ahead of me was a nice sojourn in jail.

Now, I had never been arrested or in jail before, and if there was any way to prevent it from then on, yours truly was going to take it, but I had my few moments of worry for nothing.

The officers certainly gave me a big surprise when all they did was to tell us to "get the hell out of those yards and, if they ever saw us around there again it was going to finish bad, so get going," and then directed us to cross the tracks towards the left of us.

We finally came to a gate and, as we were going through it, there were five other officers standing outside. As we passed through, they sprang into action and as many as could reach us gave us a damn good boot in the pants. Rest assured, I had to be the one they didn't miss. The guy that connected with me must have had muscles in his leg like a mule. That boot in the pants actually lifted me off my feet.

Thus ended my first trip on a freight train, my first contact with hobos, and my first experience of straying away from my hometown.

Well, so far, so good and, as they say, "I made it." Now for Philadelphia and what it may have to offer, and for further experiences on down the Road.

Chapter Five

Philadelphia

After we really got clear of the Railroad yards, my companions went one way and I another, as though by mutual consent. I didn't venture to ask them for directions to downtown Philadelphia, or rather to that section where I might get a place to sleep according to my means. By now, I was almost flat broke again and didn't feel I should even spend carfare. Naturally, not knowing the way, I walked about three times the distance that was necessary.

I will never forget those brick sidewalks of Philadelphia. In comparison, I'd say that walking on cobblestones would be preferable. I certainly was pleased when I finally found the section I was looking for.

Previously, I had heard a great deal about what a great city Philadelphia was, and perhaps it is to some people who don't know any better or who never saw a first rate city.

It was this much-talked-about city that gave me my third surprise after I saw some of it that night.

Now, I am pretty well acquainted with the slums of my own home town, and I am willing to admit that they are nothing to be proud of. But after wandering around those of Philadelphia, I will have to own up to some pride now for those of New York City. At least they are cleaner and safer, and, too, those who live in our own slums seem to be sharper and more alive. Those of Philadelphia seemed to walk along with a hang-dog appearance. They all seemed to be afraid of something.

It was the early hours of the morning when I arrived to where I felt I could start to look for shelter. The first place I stepped into almost knocked me over from the stench that greeted me when I got up one flight to the office. This was one of those "thirty cent" lodging houses commonly known as "flop houses." Yes, we have them in New York City, but I bet you couldn't find one like this there. Gee, did that place stink.

I was really pleased when the man whose breath reeked of cheap booze told me he had no more beds, but he recommended another place further down the street. I thanked him and hastened on down the stairs to the street, for that place really made me sick to my stomach.

I looked up the place he had sent me to, but that house was filled up too. There was plenty of evidence to the fact, for I could make out forms lying on the floor in the hallway leading from the landing of the stairs. The man in this office not only stunk of bad booze, he was drunk. So drunk that he could hardly stand up. He must have felt mean, for when I asked for a bed, he started to curse and complain about the g— damn bums and the time of the morning and so forth.

It was now getting around to about four in the morning, so I gave up looking for a bed and started out to look for someplace where I could sit down and rest my weary feet.

In wandering about, I finally came to what they call a mission and, noticing a group of men loitering outside of it, I stopped and looked the place over.

After about five minutes of observation I learned that it was possible to go inside if you cared to and sit the night out. This mission no doubt was run by some religious denomination for those who perhaps didn't have the wherewithal to buy or pay for a bed.

So I decide to take advantage of the accommodations and step inside, and what a sight I see.

I couldn't believe my eyes. I couldn't believe that the poverty I saw in that room full of men was real. It was almost unbelievable.

After weaving between those poor unfortunates, I finally found a vacant chair and almost fell into it. When I got the weight off my feet, I thought they would never stop tingling as if they had been asleep. Did I give a sigh of relief when I took my shoes off! My God, how good it felt, for it must be remembered that I had been on them for almost three days without having my shoes off.

After my feet began to feel a little bit rested, I got myself in as comfortable a position as I could and proceeded to take advantage of every minute of rest I could get. I overheard one of the men say, "Well, we have two hours more to sit here." So, from that remark, I deduced that the place would be cleared of all at about six.

I couldn't begin to describe the scene in that room. I don't believe anyone could, it was so terrible and sad: Terrible in the absolute destitution and conditions of those men, and sad in their apparent helplessness to help themselves.

I don't believe I shall ever see such utter hopelessness written on the faces of men as I saw that night. I couldn't see a smiling face, try as hard as I might. Some had murder in their eyes.

Gee, what I wouldn't give if I only knew or could read the thoughts of any six of the one hundred to one hundred and fifty men that sat there. What a story could be written; what a shame that such material was wasted and lost.

I fell asleep and was awakened by someone shaking me and informing me that the time was up. So I got into my shoes and stepped outside into the street and into some nasty weather. Rain—and if I judged by the way the temperature was falling—I wouldn't be surprised if I were to see snow before long.

I turned left and started on down the street, looking for one of those restaurants that are frequented by such men as I who didn't have the price for a "deluxe" breakfast. I didn't have to go very far, for after walking about one block, I found about six of them all in a row. So I picked out the cleanest of them and stepped in, and, as I got inside, I was accosted by a big burly Swede who wanted to know if I had the "price."

"The price? What do you mean by the price?" I asked him.

"Have you the price for what you want to eat?" he replied.

"Why, of course I have," and then I inquired of him what was the big idea of asking me that.

"Oh," said he, "We can't be bothered in here with guys asking us for something to eat if they haven't the price."

"Well then," I said, "I haven't got much, but I am willing always to pay for what I get when I have it. But now that you've mentioned it, how about working a couple of hours for a damn good breakfast?"

He looked at me as though he didn't know what to make of me and scratched his head. Then, in an abrupt manner he said, "Say, come to think of it, I could use a man for a couple of hours on the dishes. The fellow I had didn't show up—just wait here a minute. I'll see."

In about five minutes he returned and said, "OK for two hours, and, if you are good, I'll give you your dinner if you are around here near noon time."

He led me towards the back and into the kitchen and if ever I worked for two meals, it was that day.

This was one of those restaurants they call "hash houses," but "hash house" was no name for it. Calling it a "garbage dump" would come nearer being a correct name for it.

But "hash house" or "garbage dump," I was glad to get those two hours of work and that breakfast. It did taste good in spite of what I saw in the kitchen.

When I had finished eating, I got up and started towards the door. As I passed the cash register, the cashier handed me a fifty cent piece and said, "Good luck."

Well, there you are. I went into a restaurant to buy my breakfast and I was challenged at the door. There is a doubt about not having the price to pay for what you eat; no beggars are allowed, no handouts. And yet I wheedled two hours of work out of them, got a good breakfast, and fifty cents to boot. Now, if I *didn't* bum a meal, I'd like to know, for I know that the most I would ever get per hour wouldn't be more than twenty-five cents.

Well, that was more than I could do on the day I started out from New York City. Perhaps, I thought, I had found the way to do it without knowing I had gone at it in the right way, i.e. professionally. It was still raining and at the same time it was gradually getting colder, so I dodged under one shelter to another, trying vainly to keep from getting wet through. I kept asking pretty near every man who looked like he might know the shortest way back to the railroad yard or one where I could catch a freight to Washington DC. This was the route I had been advised to take, to go in a southerly direction to get into warmer weather. I finally met the right man at last and, after getting all the information I could, I started out immediately. For, as he said: "If you can catch one about noontime you'll be in Washington DC that night."

On my way there, I observed any number of men panhandling. What amazed me was how openly they were doing it. Even on some of the main thoroughfares they stopped pretty near every man who looked a little bit prosperous without any interference from the authorities.

Some were standing in the middle of the sidewalk, some were walking against the traffic holding their hands out, and if the handouts didn't come fast enough to suit them, they started to curse and berate the pedestrians. I watched some of them with a certain degree of awe for the technique they used in their approach to an intended victim.

It was these men that might have been called professional panhandlers, for I noticed pretty near every one of them made some kind of contact. At least they seemed to get more handouts than those who were of the beggarly type of panhandler, and, too, they were far better dressed and more intelligent looking.

To get a better idea of the many ways there are at your command to eke out an existence while knocking about, one must really live as they do.

Begging and panhandling seemed to be the most prevalent method of getting by, and it takes considerable nerve and a certain lack of shame and pride to be able to do it. In other words, it is only a certain type of man that does it.

There was many a time I thought of trying it, especially when I couldn't "make the grade," as they call it. But just at the moment I got to a man, I always lost my nerve; my pride wouldn't let me. I felt ashamed, and instead of asking them for a handout, I would ask them for the right time to cover myself up.

Some of these men do make a fair day's pay and, naturally, they live very comfortably on the proceeds. It is to them that the ordinary tramp and bum takes his hat off. Real hobos detest all three. One cannot help but admire them in a way, if you take into consideration the many types of men they must stop and ask for a handout and the many refusals, as well as the added risk of perhaps being put in jail for thirty or sixty, and at times, ninety days.

Such audacity and persistence and perseverance. If put to better use, no doubt it would net them as good a living as every man would want.

To my way of thinking, some businessmen would do well to look for some first-class salesmen among them. They never let up until they have made enough to tide them over. You never see them down in the slums, and never have I seen them in a breadline or a mission.

These men really lived by their wits.

After a few more minutes of observing these men, I continued on my way. About halfway there, I caught up with a fellow whom I had seen in the mission I had eaten in that night, and as I passed him he recognized me. Of course, I couldn't very well pass him up.

As it so happened he was on his way to some railroad yard to get out of Philadelphia too.

From what I could make out, he didn't like the city any more than I had, so when I told him I was trying to get to Washington DC, he asked to go along. Being pleased to have company I said, "Sure thing, come along."

We finally reached the spot that I had been informed would be the best place to catch a freight.

Apparently my companion was as new on the Road as I was, and naturally was as unacquainted with the time or track the freight left on or took. So, between the two of us we agreed to take any one that came along.

It was almost five hours before a freight finally came into view. It went by too fast for both of us to get on, so we returned to our place of hiding to wait for another one.

While we were waiting for the next one to pull out, someone crashed in on us. From his appearance I judged him to be one of those "old-timers" that could boast of years of knocking about.

The first question he asked us was, "Say, how did you find this spot?"

From that, I figured he had spotted us instantly as being new on the Road. While he was right, if that's what he thought, I wasn't going to let him think for one moment that he had two easy marks. So I asked him how he found this spot himself and what difference it made one way or another.

Instead of getting a comeback, he asked another question in regards as to where we were headed for, so we told him. To that, he volunteered to show us the way.

I looked at my companion to see how he took the offer but he only shrugged his shoulders as though signifying it didn't make any difference to him. I was of a different opinion.

In the first place, this old-timer acted too damn smart and sure of himself and I don't like men who act in that manner, so I thanked him and said, "No, we don't need to be shown. Washington DC isn't so far away that we can't find it somehow."

"Yeah?" said he, "Well, you have a long wait ahead of you. There will be no freight out of these yards for Washington DC now until tomorrow afternoon." With that remark he rose to his feet and made some kind of smart remark about "punks."[1]

---

1. The force of this insult was much greater during the time of this journey than it is now.

Not having caught the first part of his remark, I asked him what did he mean by "punks" and was he talking to me or both of us?

Instead of answering me, he just stood there staring at me with a sort of mocking smile and sneer on his lips, as much to say, "You heard me—what are you going to do about it?"

Sensing trouble, I got to my feet and shifted to a place where, if he was looking for trouble, I would have a good foothold. My companion also got on his feet and as he did, he said, "Come on, let's get out of here."

I told him that I was staying, and that if anyone around here didn't like it, well, they could go to Hell.

By this man's actions, he resented our presence and apparently he was trying to get rid of us by putting on one of those "bully" acts. Finding that we didn't jump or get scared at his actions and words, he was picking a fight.

I don't know just how to describe how it was that both of us went flying through the air at each other, with both trying to get a hold on the other.

The impact of our heads coming together almost put me out, and for a few seconds I thought for sure I was out of action. Somehow I managed to keep my grip on him until my head cleared up.

We were about the same weight, and he a trifle stronger and perhaps more experienced at rough-and-tumble fighting than I was, so he forced me to that style.

After a few more moments of weaving and jostling around, I finally got a good grip on one of his wrists and started to force his arm up behind him. Every move he made showed me that he was trying to get me by the throat.

I finally managed to get that arm to a position where I could put on some pressure and, when I did, he dropped to his knees to try and break my hold. But I had such a hold on that arm that any amount of effort on his part couldn't break.

Somehow or another, he managed to get into a position that enabled him to get a hold of one of my legs and, by raising it off the ground, I lost my balance. To break his hold, I fell as heavily as I could on top of him, but I still had that hold on his arm.

The moment I landed on him, he started to roll. Being on a hill, and slightly heavier in weight, he carried me with him on down that hill. We rolled over and under each other, he vainly trying to break my hold on his arm and I trying to keep it and to stay on top.

We finally reached the bottom of the hill and, just then, our attention was distracted from ourselves when we heard two blasts of a whistle.

"What's that?" he asked.

"That's a whistle," I answered.

"Yeah," said he, "and it's a freight. Come on, get up, if you want to catch it."

"That's OK with me. But remember this: no tricks, and when we meet again, don't forget I don't like you and you don't like me, so let's go."

We got to our feet and made for a spot where we could get on safely.

In that whole line of cars there was only one empty box car, so all three of us piled in. My adversary was the first to get on, my companion the second one, and I the last. The one thing I'll never forget was how my adversary gave a hand to helping my companion and myself onto that freight.

Chapter Six

Washington DC

I will never forget that ride for as long as I live.

It was just turning dark when we finally did get underway and the weather was turning colder every minute. Once in a while, a flake of snow could be seen flying about and, by the time we had covered about two miles, it started to snow in earnest.

This was one of those locals that makes all the stops, but this one did more than that. It not only stopped at the stations, but it also stopped at damn near every telegraph pole along the route.

It seemed that every mile we went it got colder and colder and finally, in order to keep from freezing all together, my fellow travelers and I had to pace up and down inside of that box car.

I had thought in the past that I had known what it was to suffer from the cold, but comparing how I felt on that night with past experiences, I had to admit to myself I really didn't know what it was to be really cold.

I don't know exactly how many miles it is from Philadelphia to Washington DC, but on that night it could have been only fifty miles as far as getting there was concerned. From stops and speed that freight train made, we wouldn't have gotten there any sooner than we did, and I do believe that if I had started out to walk it I could have made better time. I might as well have, for if I had any way of computing the number of steps I made up and down that car trying to keep warm, I am pretty positive I had at least done as much walking as I perhaps would have done covering at least half the distance there.

My friend and the other fellow were suffering terribly from the cold as well. Neither of them had an overcoat, and from what they told me one didn't have any underwear and the other one was still wearing his BVDs.[1]

My old adversary was the one who had no underwear, so from the time we left Philadelphia he shivered so at times I thought he would lose his teeth, and did he curse his luck and the weather and everything else! My friend seemed to be taking things in a more sensible manner, for I didn't hear him make one complaint.

It was just breaking day when we arrived at the outskirts of Washington DC, so all three of us got ourselves prepared to leave the freight the minute she stopped.

When it finally stops, we discover that we are in between two highwire fences with about four barbed wires strung along the top.

My old adversary started to run things again, so I told him to get along or get going and take care of himself.

He didn't like being told to get, so he got mad and started to cursing and swearing again and then came that word "punk" again. This time I didn't bother asking any questions; I just pulled my arm back and put every ounce of my one-hundred-and-sixty pounds behind my fist

---

1. A brand of men's underwear. In the early twentieth century, the term was commonly used to refer to all men's underwear in the same style regardless of manufacturer.

and let it go right smack in his mouth. Like all "bullies," he howled like a pig on its way to be slaughtered.

"What did you hit me for?! That wasn't fair! Now look at me, that's a hell of a way to treat a pal," said he, half-crying.

"Pal?! Why, all you have done on this trip is to curse and swear and complain, and then you started that 'punk' talk again. Didn't I warn you back in Philadelphia that I didn't like you? While we are at it, if you care or think you ought to get a chance to crack me one in return, right here is as good a place as I know of to try it." But apparently he had had enough, so he turned his back on us and went his way.

When I hit him, I thought my arm had cracked in half, so cold and stiff was every muscle and bone in my body from that night's ride. My feet were practically numb, and every time I took a step it felt as though I was walking not on my feet but on stumps.

We were lucky in the fact that we had made a stop about five miles from the railroad yards that saved us much walking. So, when we finally managed to get over that fence, we discovered much to our elation that we were right near Capitol Hill.

Before I left that freight train entirely out of sight, I took one last look at it and discovered we had been riding in a steel car, which accounted for why we had suffered so badly from the intense cold. Being a steel car made it practically a refrigerator.

After walking a short distance, my blood started to get back to its normal circulation and while this was going on, my feet started paining me so badly I had to stop. For a few moments, it felt as if a thousand red-hot needles were being hammered through them, or that someone was pulling all the nerves out of them one by one.

Nobody will ever convince me from that time on that feet can't talk and, suffice it to say, mine were telling me plenty on that morning. There was about three inches of snow on the ground and the weather indications were such as to make us think of finding some place to stay and rest up.

While I was back in Philadelphia, I overheard two men talking about a place they had heard about in Washington, DC. From the gist of their conversation, I learned that there was a place run by the government where men, and women as well, could stay. I related to my companion that information and we started to look for it.

As we were just about to start on our hunt, an old colored man came down the street, so we stopped him and asked if he knew where it was. He seemed surprised we didn't know, for said he pointing to the left of us, "See that one-story building over there?"

"Yes we can see it. What about it?" my companion answered.

"Well, that is where they eat."

"Where they eat? Thanks, Mister. Come on," said my companion. Then he smiled for the first time since we had joined company back in Philadelphia.

We finally reached the entrance of the building and entered almost abreast of each other. The only thing that forced me to get into a single file was that the door wasn't wide enough for both of us to get through it arm in arm. No more than we got inside someone hollered out, "Come on you guys, step on it if you want to eat! You just have time—one minute more and you would have been out of luck."

There was no need to dwell on the fact that for just one moment I forgot the soreness of my feet going to that counter that we saw filled with steaming kettles of food and coffee. Oh boy, did that coffee smell good. The odor of roses would have been compared as being like the scent of stink weeds to the aroma of that coffee that cold morning.

Each of us got our plates and cups and, after finding a table, we sat down, but for some reason or other I was afraid to start eating.

My companion must have been terribly hungry or else he was blessed with a wonderful appetite. I thought for a few moments he would founder himself.

I didn't eat very much, so as soon as we were through, the man in charge instructed us to report to the Social Service Department, which was in another building about two blocks away. The building was an old church, and I mean *old*. There were still some of the church furnishings in use as seats, etc.

Just as we entered, we were stopped by a man who said in a gruff voice, "Where are you going and what do you want?" We showed him the slips of paper which had written on them the information from where we had eaten. From that time or till about closing time for the day force, we did nothing but answer questions and go from one clerk to another.

Some of the clerks might ask us just one question and then type the answer, put their signatures on the paper and pass it on to the next clerk. While we were at each clerk's station, a cart like an applecart followed the paper around.

If ever I did a "ring around the rosie," it was on that day. I don't believe I will ever live to see so much red tape and unnecessary help doing actually nothing.

We finally got "checked in proper" as they call it and, rest assured, they had in their files pretty near our life's history.

After being checked in, we were issued a meal card for twenty-one meals and another card for seven nights lodging. And don't forget the work ticket that, so all the boys said, "They never failed or missed on."

We were assigned to a building about three blocks distant from headquarters. This building had once been an apartment house but remodeled to suit the requirements for using it as a "Lodging House."

We slept in double bunks, one over the other, and I will say this for that "Lodging House": It was really clean.

About every state in the Union was represented in the hundreds of men staying in that lodging house. They were from every part of the compass.

They called these places "Transient Bureaus,"[2] and in order to gain admittance you had to be a transient. No resident of whatever city had a transient bureau could use them. These places naturally were a haven for wayfarers and, as time went on, they became what might be termed a paradise for all manner of men and women and sometimes young boys. Tramps, bums, and hobos used them as well.

Such a conglomeration of men only made it that much more difficult to manage them. I noticed that there was a considerable lot of agitators among them who were continually berating the government and those in charge.

Having to do any kind of work seemed to cause considerable dissatisfaction and it was surprising the extent to which some would go to dodge or get away from doing what work was assigned to them.

It has always been a mystery to me. Where is the gain in shirking one's responsibilities or one's share of work?

The amount of work that was assigned to men who were able to work couldn't be considered laborious or unreasonable. From what I could see, no one put in more than three or four hours a day and, on some days, we had practically nothing to do. It was amusing how some men kept up ducking the Boss Detail Man, or stalling around and absenting themselves from the premises only to go walking around the neighborhood wearing their feet out.

---

2. The Federal Transient Bureau was a program that was part of the Federal Emergency Recovery Act (Roosevelt Administration).

I couldn't see much difference in the amount of energy it took to do a couple of hours walking compared to working a couple of hours around our sleeping quarters on one of these details.

We had an old hard-boiled Army Sergeant for a Boss Man and when he caught up with these fellows who didn't and wouldn't work or try to help…well, it wouldn't be many hours after you would see them packing up and on their way.

Among the great many forms of relief the government was trying to use as a medium for alleviating the misery and suffering caused by the Depression, none were more unappreciated or taken advantage of than this one. There were the same petty jealousies, the same petty thievery, the same conniving, and the same favoritisms that cause so much unpleasantness and trouble among a large body of men or women.

If I was judging rightly the actions of some of the men and women who were taking advantage of the benefits of this particular Transient Bureau, they certainly were living under better conditions than they had been living under previously. To some no doubt it was just the other way around, and there were the men and women who never made any complaint.

The tramps and bums and the shady characters that managed to get admitted found this form of relief fertile ground for getting by, while the hobo who will work found here an opportunity to get some sort of menial job which satisfied his pride in not asking for anything. But he never stayed in one of these places for any length of time, for the hobo loves too well to be footloose and on the go and away from the "stinking mess," as he sometimes so truthfully calls some places and conditions in general.

In the intervals between our work, my companions and I took in Washington DC from stem to stern, as my companion called the thoroughness of our tours about the many interesting buildings, institutions, libraries, and best of all the Smithsonian Institute.

It was after a two week rest in this Bureau that I decided to leave it and continue on down south. I spoke to my companion about moving on, but he decided to stay on in Washington, DC for a while longer, so on the following morning I checked out.

In the two weeks I was in the Transient Bureau, I had gathered considerable information in regards to the best railroads and routes and "stop overs" to use on a hobo trip going south.

The missions, the Salvation Army, the Volunteers of America, and jails of different cities and other forms of shelters, including the many transient bureaus that were distributed all over the country, were termed as "stop overs" by indigent travelers. More about these places as I go along.

I had accumulated about eight dollars from wages and other sources of revenue while resting up, so I was starting out on this phase of my wanderings rich in comparison to the day I left New York City. It was approximately seven miles to the place I had been told would be the best to get a freight train to all points south, so I started out by walking the entire distance on foot. What a walk and how foolish it was, for I could have ridden that distance for the small sum of fifteen cents and saved myself from some worrisome moments all along that seven mile stretch.

The highway wasn't one of the best, so I had to keep a sharp ear and a watchful eye on the trucks and pleasure cars for fear of being run down.

I finally reach there at about noon time and when I find the specific spot I am looking for, I discover about one hundred other men, all waiting for the "next freight out" going south. From the general appearance of the majority of them, they look as though they've been there all night.

My deductions were also substantiated by the fact that all over the area under that bridge, there were drum fires, half-filled rusty old cans of coffee grains, newspapers, and debris of all kinds strewn about the place. Off to one side of the bridge there was a small area that showed plenty of evidence of it being used as a public toilet, and the flies hovering about it were as thick as bees around a hive, and this was in December.

It was three o'clock before a freight came along and, if ever I saw a general scramble for some object, it was then as the freight had finally come abreast of us. Every one of those one-hundred-odd men seemingly was trying to get on at once, and I in the middle of them as well.

By the time the end of the freight had passed the bridge, I looked back towards the bridge to see if there would be any left behind, but the place was deserted.

We were on a Southern Railroad freight train which, according to most of the men in the box car I managed to be lucky enough to squeeze in, was one of those "through trains" that only made a few stops along the route and sometimes only for coal or oil or water.

We had only covered about ten miles when the freight came to a sudden stop and naturally this caused considerable comment, for as one of the men said, "That's funny, I never knew of a freight stopping here." Just as he finished his comment, someone called out, "Here comes the 'Dicks'!" If ever one-hundred-odd men left a train like some burning building, it was after that warning had reached the end of the train.

It seemed that every one of us reached the ground as one, and in order to get out of sight all of us made a grand dive into the weeds along the track.

After lying there a few moments, heads started to pop up here and there and finally a few stood up. Finding it was only a couple of train men coming down the side of the train, they gave the signal that all was well and once more we filed on.

The scenery along this particular stretch of the Southern Railroad didn't interest me much. I was more interested in my companions who were in that box car, for this was my first experience of being among so many men who were on the "bum."

I counted no less than forty men and, after looking them over closely, I couldn't find in any one of them one that I would care to travel any great distance with. That is, if I cared to keep out of trouble enroute. Not in one of them could I see that substantial quality that is necessary to a pleasant companionship and dependency. Every one of them I knew in an instant would run on you in a pinch, or perhaps rob you in the end.

It struck me as a queer instance that I should have met a lot of men all of whom should strike me as being of the same character and stamp, and before we reached Charlottesville, Virginia, my suspicions were fully rewarded with whisperings about one another and some of them accusing others of swiping food and clothing. We had no less than four fist fights and the dirty tactics I saw used while fighting reminded me of so many cats or wild animals.

Chapter Seven

Charlottesville, Virginia

It was late in the evening when we reached Charlottesville, Virginia, and due to the darkness I couldn't make out what kind of a place it was I finally sat down in. Here I spent the night sitting it out around a fire with ten other men.

I didn't dare stretch out for a few winks of sleep for I felt pretty sure I would have been set upon and cleaned of everything I had. So I was sitting and shifting and once in a while getting up to hunt around in the dark for any kind of fuel I could find to keep that fire going for the night, and hoping and wishing for daylight to come. Finally, when daybreak did come and things started to take shape and form, I had to pinch myself to find out whether or not I was in a dream, for the sight I saw before me seemed so unreal and of another world.

After gazing for a while at the unbelievable sight before my eyes, I stood up and straightened my clothes out the best I could, then went and looked around for more material to replenish the fire. It wouldn't do for me to leave that fire without doing some little thing for the general good of those who used it. You might call it a matter of principle or a code of the Road or one of the "Jungles."

So now that I had done my little bit, I told the rest of the men that I was going uptown to see what I could do and that I would be back if I got anything.

I did go uptown, but only to buy my breakfast and after a reasonable time I came back not to the fire but to get a close look at that "Jungle" of men.

This was a Jungle, and I mean a *Jungle*. Back in Philadelphia, I thought I had seen some bad cases of men who had given up, but in this Jungle I was looking not only at men who had given up but men who had gone completely to "Hell."

What a conglomeration of humanity there was in that Jungle; it ran into every conceivable station in life.

Everyone was there: Down and out lawyers and doctors who had lost their lease on life through booze and dope; hobos, bums, panhandlers, habitual drunkards, dope fiends, young uncaring ables, and off to one side of the Jungle, I was surprised to see a whole family huddled up against a fire. There were three children in this little group, all of which didn't even have on sufficient clothes to keep them warm.

Taking this mass of humanity as a whole, I didn't see one of them that looked any too well, and some of them should have been in a hospital instead of where they were. In fact, one of the men, while I was talking to him, started to cough up blood. He no doubt was in the throes of Tuberculosis.[1]

I estimated the number of humans in this Jungle at about two hundred and fifty men, and every one of them showed in their faces

---

1. Tuberculosis would eventually lead to the author's death in 1953.

and actions the marks of the strain from privation. All went about as though they were walking dead men.

There was one man who seemed to keep to himself and who appeared to be suspicious of everyone that came near him. It was this that got me interested, so I went straight to him and asked him right out, "What's the matter—are you sick?" He didn't even let on that he had heard me, so I repeated my question and this time I got only a stony stare for my pains. He had a large blanket spread over his legs and somehow or other one corner of it was lifted by the wind. It was then that I caught sight of one of his legs which had a running sore that covered the whole length of it.

From its appearance, anyone could see that it hadn't been treated for some time. The stench from it almost stifled me. I couldn't help after seeing that leg but offer to help him, but to my offers he only gave me that stony stare again. It struck me then that perhaps he didn't dare go near a hospital, for after taking a closer look at him I detected that hardness and wickedness that is to be found in criminals' eyes. This man had no doubt taken cover among the tramps and bums and the Jungles. Undoubtedly, the condition of his leg came from extracting a bullet from himself and not having the necessary facilities to treat it, so infection had set in. I tried once more to let me get him some place to have it treated, but he only shook his head no.

It was in this Jungle that I saw some terrible cases of dissipation, for just to one side of the Jungle I ran across about six men, all of them sprawled out apparently unconscious and their faces half buried in the mud of a small stream. A little further on up this stream, in the shadows of the brush, I observed a man using a hypodermic needle taking a shot of dope.

After mingling among them for a while, I attempted to try and get some of them into a conversation. The one or two who did respond shut up like a clam when I asked them the simple question as to what part of the country they hailed from.

After trying a few more times to get some one of them to tell me a little about themselves and getting no results, I left them—but not before I paid that little family group a visit, for I was curious as to how they should have chosen such a place to stay rather than appealing to the relief authorities for aid.

I greeted the man first as I approached them, asking in as pleasant a manner as I could as to how he was getting along. He gave me a look first before he answered. It was an inquiring sort of look; one that seemed to say, "What do you care?" After feeling that I had no ulterior motive in my interest in them he said, "Oh, we can't complain, it could be worse." After a moment or two of silence he continued on by saying, "All that is worrying me now is where I could get some milk for my children, especially the youngest one."

I asked him then, "Why don't you appeal to the Relief Station or the Salvation Army or some other such organization to help you out?" They certainly would help him, especially where a family is concerned, I told him.

"Not me, Mister. I wouldn't ask them for nothing. They wanted to know too much about your business for me. Nope, not me," was the answer I got.

That sort of answer made me wonder what all his worry about his children not having no milk was about. Here, I thought, was a case of a man's family suffering just because he didn't care to answer a few questions that might be asked of him.

I was just about to leave them when I happened to catch his wife looking at me as though she was terribly sorry and disappointed at the outcome of my visit. She looked so downcast that I ventured to ask her if she thought the children were so badly in need of milk as her husband claimed.

"Yes they are," she answered, and it was then that I noticed she had another child coming, and that settled my opinion of her husband. I couldn't help feeling like giving him a darn good thrashing.

With the husband's permission, I took this woman into the business district to a grocery store and after purchasing some groceries and milk she asked me just how to go about getting on the relief rolls. There being no Transient Bureau, I took her to the Salvation Army and they sent one of their workers with us, and a police officer. Inside of two hours her husband was in jail and she and her children were put up in a fair-price hotel in Charlottesville.

It seemed a queer thing that this man should worry so much about his family's welfare, yet when the officer asked him to take his family Uptown, he refused.

"Well then, my man, there is only one way to deal with men like you." So he puts his hand on the man's shoulder and says, "You are under arrest for cruelty to your children so get ready and come with me."

It was getting late and as I left the Jungle to get my supper, it began to drizzle. Such weather called for better shelter than one could get in one of these Jungles. As I went about Charlottesville looking for a reasonably priced lodging house, I gave thought to those little children. Gee, I said to myself, what terrible suffering those kids might have gone through as a result of spending a night like this in such a place as I found them.

The drizzle had turned to rain and, finding no place that suited my purse, I decided to have a fling at sleeping at the expense of the Salvation Army for once. I figured as bad as some have told me it was, it certainly couldn't be as bad as sitting the night out in the rain in a Jungle. I had heard all along the routes about these shelters and if I were to believe all that I heard about them, I was going to have a terrible experience on this night.

When I arrived at the Salvation Army's headquarters, I found that I was to be the fourth man in line. As time went on, that line kept on increasing until there must have been 150 men lined up for a "bed."

According to the first man in line, there were only twenty-five or thirty beds in this "Sally" and then, as though talking to himself while looking down at the line, "The poor suckers, and it's raining too."

I deduced he had reference to the fact that all but twenty-five or thirty men wouldn't get a bed.

That word "Sally" interested me, so I asked him what he meant by it. I'll never forget how he looked at me. I thought he was going to laugh out loud, but he seemed to think better of it and said, quote, "That is what the boys call the Salvation Army."

The door into the shelter finally opened, and the first five men were told to step inside. But instead of five men, about twenty squeezed in. This made the Man In Charge mad, so he turned on us and said in a loud voice, "I said the first five men, so fifteen of you back out of here or the doors will be closed again," but not a man moved. So he backed up his command by putting us all out in the rain again.

There was only one man among that twenty who took serious offense, and of all the cursing and berating and damning the Sally ever got, it sure got its full share on that night.

I never knew a man could say as much against anything in so few minutes, for said he, "These places are rotten, their officers are rotten, the place is lousy, G— damn the sons of b—s, damn their dirty hides! If I had my say I'd have them all burned down or closed up, the dirty damn robbers! All they do is go around begging, the bastards! The hell with them, I'd sooner sleep in a box car!" With that tirade off his chest, he disappeared around the corner in the rain. The first man in line looked at me and smiled and shook his head and said, "He's nuts."

I smiled in return and said, "Not only nuts but crazy, and that still isn't the half of it." I couldn't figure out any good reason why he should get himself worked up about the whole affair. If, as he claimed, the whole place was wrong, what the hell was he doing here if all he said was true, I asked myself.

In about ten minutes, the door opened again and as before the first five men were told to step inside. This time only four men stepped inside.

When the man in charge saw only four, he hollered out, "I said five! Where is the other one? I want five in here."

What the hell, thought I. What kind of a man is this? He must have exactly five men in or he doesn't start admitting them, and it's raining outside and men are getting wet. What the hell is the idea of just five men? I gave up on figuring it out, so I said to him "Would it be all right if I called in one more to make it just five men?"

"Sure, sure, go ahead. I don't know what is the matter with these men. They don't seem to understand," and then sat down on his chair in such a manner that I thought he was going to pass out.

I opened the door and simply called out, "One more man wanted in here!" Once there were five men standing there, he proceeded to check us in, saying to us, "That's better. I want five men in here each time, and I mean five men, not one or two or three or four. I want five!" and with that ultimatum he banged the table with his fist.

After taking our names, where we slept the night before, where we came from, where we were born, our age and religion, where we were going, and then finishing up by taking down our marital status if we had any, he handed each one of us a slip of paper and told us to go and take a bath. Then he told us to make it snappy for, said he, it's raining outside and those men out there will get wet.

As I was taking my bath, I gave thought to what kind of a man this was. He didn't seem to worry much about men getting wet all through his queer idea of wanting just five men at a time, and now he was hustling everybody else around as though they were to blame for all this unnecessary hold up. My wonder increased as I took in the size of that shower room. It could have accommodated ten men easily.

I was awakened from my thoughts by another man opening the door leading to the showers and calling out, "Come on you fellows, let's go, that's good enough. We ain't got all night, come on."

We wiped ourselves on what looked like pieces of cloth from those worn out bed sheets which didn't have much absorption qualities, so we emerged from the hot steaming shower room into the cold air of another room almost dripping wet.

When I got outside, I started to look for my clothes and the man who stood there asked me in a hard-boiled manner, "What are you looking for now? Come on, get into this and get to bed. You can't have your clothes now, they are being deloused. Ask for them in the morning."

The garment he told us to get into was a short cotton nightgown, and with it he also handed us two brass tokens. These, he told us, had the number of our bed and the other was the number for our clothes in the morning. All five of us said nothing and proceeded to look for our beds and was I glad to get into it, for by this time I was almost frozen. I didn't even inspect the bed nor bother looking the room over, for my attention was called to an argument that was going on in the office between one of the men and that "Five-at-a-Time" nut. The argument seemed to be over the man being accused of being too lousy for admittance.

"So I am lousy?! And what makes you think I'm lousy?" were the first words I overheard. "Yes you're lousy, and you can't sleep here!" said the man in charge.

"But how do you know that without an examination?" parried the man.

"I just know it. I don't need an examination. You're lousy and that's all there is to it, so get out!"

"Okay," said the man, "I'll get out, but for your own sake save just one bed, for I'll be back inside of ten minutes," and then he disappeared through the shut door.

About fifteen minutes passed before he came back, and when he did, he had a police officer and one of the officers of the Sally with him.

"Now," said the officer, "Just what is the matter here? What is this about this man being lousy? How do you know he is lousy? Have you a doctor around here who said so? Was he examined?"

"No, we haven't the doctor around here but I know he's lousy. I don't need any examination to know that. I know my business, and for any further information ask my superior there," meaning no doubt the Sally officer.

"Well," said the Sally officer, "I don't know what to say. As far as I can see, the only thing I know to settle this argument would be to have this man examined," and then he asked the man in question if that would satisfy him.

"It certainly will. In fact, I demand an examination," said the man.

"Very well then. Strip off your clothes and the officer here and I will examine you and your clothes," said the Sally officer.

About twenty minutes passed before anything more was said, and finally when the examination was over, I heard the verdict announced by the police officer. Apparently he was peeved at being bothered, for I could detect somewhat of a bored tone to his words as he said, "You say this man is lousy, but damned if I can find any. How about you, Mister?" he said, addressing the Sally officer.

The Sally officer only said in answer, "I can't either, so I guess he can stay here."

That seemed to settle the argument, and soon after someone put the lights out, and all I could hear were the grunts and groans and snores and heavy breathing of tired and sick men; tired physically, and sick in mind from worry and uncertainty and living the life of a dog, and from dissipation.

We were awakened out of our slumbers in the morning at six o'clock and given only twenty minutes to get dressed and be fed and on our way.

Well, after thinking over my first experience with the Salvation Army or Sally, and comparing it with all the hearsay, I came to the conclusion that the only way to find out about places and other things is to go there and see for yourself.

To my way of thinking, I couldn't see where anybody had any kick coming in regards to this particular shelter. It must be remembered that in spite of all other features of this particular organization, whether good or bad or otherwise, one couldn't, to be fair, be too critical or expect too much when asking for something you can't pay for. In other words, to be more explicit, I might use that old saying that "beggars cannot be choosers."

On this particular night, I felt thankful for that shelter, for it rained all through the night, and if I didn't get anything else but that bath and bed, I felt I was doing pretty good for an inexperienced itinerant traveler.

Charlottesville will always remain in my memory as the real starting point of my hobo life, for here it was that I saw my first real Jungle and my real first insight into the sort of life I had ahead of me if I chose to follow it. Also, it was here that I had my first contact with "Sallys."

Before returning to the Jungle, I stopped in and bought a good pair of gloves, for it seemed that the further south I went it grew colder and colder. I arrived at the Jungle just as another lot of riders were piling off and another lot were piling on, so taking advantage of so fortuitous a coincidence, I piled on too and got settled in a box car full of the dirtiest men I ever saw. To add to their general ragged condition, most of them were wet through from the rain of the night before.

In a way, I thought, they should be admired for their indifference to their wet condition, for riding on a freight while wet through is not a very pleasant experience to go through, especially in the month of December. Such unmindfulness to suffering and discomfort certainly spelled plenty of nerve and guts. I, for one, wouldn't care to do it and would only in an emergency.

The only thing about most of them I could not stand was their filthiness. Some of them were black with grime from head to foot. There is no excuse even for men living as they did for being in such a condition, for all along the routes there are plenty of streams to take a bath in, missions and Transient Bureaus to check into and clean up in. But for some unknown reason, they seemed to like to actually be unclean. As unclean and unkempt as this lot of men were, I had not as yet met up with still dirtier men than these. This lot of men could be considered fairly clean compared to what I saw later on.

Well, we are off to the next real stop which, according to all the men, will be Lynchburg, Virginia.

Chapter Eight

Lynchburg

The trip between Charlottesville, Virginia to the Monroe railroad yards, about 7 miles south of Lynchburg, was uneventful.

Riding in a boxcar, especially one that is sealed on one side, you get only a one-sided view of the countryside. You do get a pretty fair idea of the terrain in general, but it is not a complete picture.

What little that did attract my attention was just duplication of previous scenic views. Perhaps the only real thing of interest was that the ground was covered with about two inches of snow, which caused considerable comment from most of the men.

"Can you beat that? We go south to get away from winter, and so far the further south we go, the colder it gets. Rain in Charlottesville and snow 100 miles further south," was the thoughtful comment of one of the men.

We finally arrived in the Monroe yards and this, said one of the men, is where the riding gets "hot." No more easy traveling from here on, and you had better watch your step too, for the Dick in this yard gets real mean sometimes.

We all piled off and made for the weeds and bushes or whatever cover was handy, but I couldn't see any need for worry for there wasn't anybody around who cared to bother us.

After finding our way to the highway, we all started for Lynchburg proper which, if ever you walked it, you will remember it for the steep hill that descends to the river.

I didn't attempt to walk it. Instead, I hung back and caught a bus and arrived there before dark.

It was about six pm when I finally arrived in Lynchburg, and my first impressions of it were not so good. There was something about it that I instinctively didn't like, and I wasn't long in learning what it was.

Anyone traveling about as I was of course didn't look any too prosperous and naturally in a small place a new face is noticed by the police. So I had not walked up one of its many streets more than two or three blocks when one of its guardians of the law stopped me and wanted to know if I belonged to Lynchburg.

"Say there, young fellow. Are you from Lynchburg?" was his first question.

"No sir, I am not. Why do you ask?" I answered.

"Now look here, you young fellow. I'll ask the questions, all you do is answer," said he, putting on his best air of authority.

"Okay, ask all you care to. I'll answer," I told him.

"Now that's better. Where did you say you come from?"

"I didn't say, and you didn't ask me that, but for your information—if you must have it—I am from New York City."

"Oh, you're one of those New York guys, eh? Well, be on your toes in this town, fellow. We don't monkey around much with strangers," and with that warning and piece of advice he passed on down the street.

Every minute I was in Lynchburg, I was more or less worried that I was going to be picked up by some policemen just on general principles, but I wasn't bothered again. That incident only increased my dislike for Lynchburg. That place, I thought, is no place for an itinerant traveler.

For a while that incident sort of riled me, but on second thought, I couldn't blame the authorities for being on their toes, for there were plenty of men and boys wandering about who no doubt would stop at nothing short of murder to obtain a living. So I let it go and gave attention to a place to hole up in until the following morning, but in Lynchburg the places were few and the prices were too high for such as I. In such emergencies, there are only two things or perhaps three to do. One: go to some free shelter. Two: leave town or sit it out, or Three: walk around until the next morning.

In my wanderings about I had passed the Salvation Army shelter so, not being able to secure a room or a lodging house, I decided to give one of these shelters another fling. They surely couldn't be all the same. Surely in different towns and cities there would be better ones, I thought as I took all the side streets I could to get back to it.

In this shelter you have to go to the head office where an officer takes down the preliminary paperwork for your history. After that and a little bit of fatherly advice, you are given a slip of paper and then told to go to the rear of the building and wait.

When I got back to the rear of this building I found the place already open and supper being served. From the comments of the men, it wasn't so good.

I finally got in and sat down and if ever I had never before run into a bunch of men who all had that "boarding house reach," I could claim these to be them. Why, it was everybody for himself, and just to such a degree that you weren't sure of the very food on your plate or the coffee in your cup.

I finally managed to eat my supper, such as it was, and got out without being covered or messed up with food. These men actually ate like a lot of hogs.

I went through about the same procedure as I did back in Charlottesville, and I swore thereafter that if weather and climate permitted I would take to the open air for sleeping.

The place itself wasn't so bad, but the stench from the old clothes, especially the shoes and socks, was almost unbearable. This place didn't delouse your clothes, nor did they force everyone to take a bath. Consequently, some of those who were passed up really needed a bath, and body odor can pollute the air of a room full of men quicker than anything I know of.

For some reason or other I couldn't get to sleep. The things that seemed to bother me in this place were the stench and heat and closeness of the room. As I lay there vainly trying to doze off, I gave thought to the hell of a mess an economic upheaval can cause, and the number of lives that are blasted—and the suffering humanity must go through as a result.

Surely all these men that I have been mingling and living with are not wandering around in rags and half sick because they like it. Surely they would gladly turn back and go to work and live a decent clean life if they could only do it.

Gee, what a tragedy and disappointment it is going to be for some of them when things get back to normalcy, only for them to find that they will be of no use or out-of-date. Some are no doubt doomed to a life of "pillar to post" and, until they die, will be a burden on the public. None the less of them so will I be, I fear. What a dull life that will be. What readjustments will have to be made, and will they be able to survive the change?

These and a thousand other things ran through my mind as I finally managed to fall off into a fitful sleep. My dreams were of trains and Jungles full of poor unfortunate souls from far-off places, until I was awakened from my troubled sleep by someone shaking me and at the same time telling me, "Rise and shine. It's six. Get up and out of here; this is no home, come on."

Everybody was up and some had been up for some time, or perhaps they had slept in their clothes and now were on their way out to wait for breakfast.

I don't know why it was, but somehow or other I felt rotten and sick. My head was bursting from a severe headache, so I was somewhat slow in getting to the breakfast table. As I sat down the Man In Charge hollered, "Where the hell have you been?!" But before I could answer him, he hollered out, "No breakfast for you! Outside if you can't get up in time. Don't come in here to eat."

I felt too sick and disgusted to say anything one way or another, so I got up and started for the door but found the exit locked. Not wanting an argument, I stood there and waited until all had finished and left with them.

After walking a few blocks in the open air my headache abated somewhat and, after having a good cup of coffee in a restaurant, I began to feel somewhat better. Then I made up my mind to get the hell out of Lynchburg as quick as I could for, apparently, this town was my nemesis, or I was a marked man, or something else was the matter.

So I get my bearings and hotfoot it for the place I got off the bus when I first arrived here the day before.

I had a half hour to wait for the next bus to Monroe, so in my anxiety to get clear of Lynchburg before something else unpleasant happened, I started out to walk that five to seven miles, and what a walk that was.

I had to cross a short bridge which ended at the very foot of a steep hill and, like all hills, it doesn't start to tire you until you are halfway to its top and then, when you finally decide you will take the bus from some point on it, you discover they don't stop on account of its steep grade. It is then you begin to realize you just about bit off more than you can chew and start to damn yourself for trying it, but you keep on climbing and climbing until you finally reach its end. Then, after you've climbed and walked the greatest share of the way, someone stops and asks if you want a lift. You laugh to yourself and say, "I guess I am a damn fool at that," and have no one to blame but yourself for your tired legs and sore feet and once more you swear you will not climb no more hills like that if you never get anywhere.

I finally arrived at Monroe and gradually eased my way towards the Southern Railroad yards, keeping in mind the warnings of the day before in regards to the railroad being "hot" here and from here on.

You shall never want for company along the railroads when it comes to riding freights down in this section of the country, especially in the winter months. I'm not mentioning what kind of company it is, but it *is* company and at times very welcome for a novice who hasn't been on the road for very long. So I was not surprised to find about twenty-five men waiting when I finally found the right place to catch a freight out of the Monroe Yards.

It is at this division that the rails of the Southern Railroad from Washington DC end and the rails of the Norfolk and Western Railroads begin to points further south. I wanted to get down deeper into the South if for no other reason than to get into warmer weather, and I didn't know just exactly what freight to take. From information I had overheard while in the Sally, there were two which went in a different way so, right after sizing up the men now waiting, I ventured to ask one of them which would be the right one to take if I cared to go by way of Greensboro, North Carolina. The answer was the next one.

We hung around trying to keep out of sight as much as we could, but there was just one smart guy who wouldn't heed our warnings—if only for the other fellows' sake—to keep back. Through his damnable bullheadedness, our presence was called to the attention of one of the railroad officers further on down the yards.

Naturally, he has to do his duty, and first thing we know he steps off a string of cars that were being switched and comes over and orders us off the premises and at the same time he draws his revolver and points it in a threatening manner to emphasize his orders.

We scurried in all directions to obey his orders, but the same fellow who had given us away just stood there as though in defiance of the officer's orders. When we had cleared the railroad property we stopped and turned to see how things were going on with the officer and that smart guy who didn't seem to give a darn.

"Well, what's the matter? Didn't you hear what I said? Come on, let's get going," said the officer as he advanced towards the man.

"Yes I heard you, so what?" as he still stood there with his legs spread apart.

"A tough guy, eh? Well now, isn't that great. Say, now that I get a good look at you, it seems to me that I have seen you before somewhere. Your face sure is familiar," said the officer as he slowly advanced again, for he had paused for a minute or two apparently to study and measure this man who dared to stand up to an armed officer on his own ground.

"You sure have, pardner, and not so long ago either. What's the matter? Is your memory failing you or are you getting old?" said the man, who by this time had shifted himself into a more advantageous position, for the officer was slowly and cautiously getting nearer to him.

"No, I am not losing my memory and I am not getting too old either. At least, not too old to handle you, young fellow. I've met tougher men than you, and now that I am a little closer I know who you are, so get ready to come along with me and this time you won't get away."

"Yeah," said the man, "Come and get me if you're so good," and then he turned like a flash and started to run for cover, but the officer had the advantage. There was no time needed to draw his gun, so all he did was to pull the trigger and in a split second I saw the man stumble, grab his leg, and hold up his other hand in surrender.

After this little drama of wits between himself and the wanted man, the officer looked in our direction and called out, "Alright boys, go on and get on that freight standing three tracks over, and get the hell out of here."

None of us needed a second invitation and, while we were all going by, we thanked him. About five minutes after we got on, we heard two blasts of the whistle, and soon we were on our way.

I was lucky to get in a boxcar, for the air was getting pretty keen and, if by chance we had to do any night riding, a box car was going to be a Pullman in comparison to riding on a car that had no protection from the wind.

While a good many of the men who were in that boxcar were standing in the doorway looking back to see if they could see the finish of that battle of wits (which was lost by a darn fool, who if he had only used his head, could have been with us), I was rustling up enough of the paper that was strewn on the floor to lay on and cover me up. Paper, I had found, if there is enough of it, can keep you fairly warm, so after getting myself nicely fixed up in a corner I proceeded to lie down and get what sleep I could.

Chapter Nine

Decatur

Sleep is one feature of traveling on a freight that I had not yet found the way to do, so I lay there getting all the rest I could. One could not predict what might happen knocking about, so I lay there listening to the rhythm of the train and the click of the rails as we rode on into the fast closing day.

The freight was not one of the locals that stop at every telegraph pole, so after getting speed up, we just ate up the miles. I estimated the speed at about fifty or sixty miles an hour and figured it wouldn't be long before we would be in Greensboro, North Carolina.

This lot of men I was riding with on this freight were the easiest going bunch I had yet met, for aside from an occasional remark or begging for a smoke and a light, nothing much was said by anyone.

There was one Old Timer among us who was more or less cranky and, from the tone of his voice, I figured he was just naturally that way and harmless. Nobody paid much attention to him, so he too finally stopped his complaining after he saw that it didn't do him any good.

I really enjoyed that trip as far as Greensboro, but my hopes for an entirely perfect night of it were blasted when we did finally arrive there.

One of the men who had taken it upon himself to be lookout finally announced that we were near enough to see the yard light and that was the signal for everyone to get on their feet and to get off before we actually reached the yard limits, if the speed of the train permitted. But this was one of those times that didn't permit us to risk our lives by dropping off in the darkness of a railroad yard, so we all got back into the shadows of the car and waited until she came to a sudden stop, and then it was too late. When no more than one of the men had stuck his face beyond the casing of the doorway, a ray of light flashed by his face and then back again only to rest there. Then Wham! ping! zip!, two bullets crashed into the side of the car.

I couldn't begin to describe the pandemonium those two bullets and that ray of light caused as it kept constantly stabbing through the darkness and the open doorway.

I hadn't gotten up as yet and as I lay there about all I could make out in the darkness were shadow-like forms bobbing about. It reminded me of a flock of bats flitting about in the air, bumping into each other; or of ghost-like images doing a death dance. The rays of the light shifting about and stabbing through the darkness only added to the grotesqueness.

As suddenly as pandemonium had broken out among those fifteen or twenty men, so was the suddenness to which it had abated to a calm, for I heard someone say, "Come you fellows, be your age. What the hell is the matter with you? Come on, follow me."

That remonstration sort of snapped them out of their panic and all was once more back to normalcy, but only for a moment, for the same voice cried, "Well, here goes!" He no sooner said that than I saw him preparing to leave the car, and like a lot of sheep following a leader all the rest prepared to follow suit. As of one accord, they all crowded in the doorway and jumped off into the darkness, and it was then that the real fireworks started.

Crack, crack, crack! Crack ping ping ping ping! Boy I would have given anything to witness those fellows running for fear of their lives across the tracks and vainly trying to get under cover from those revolver shots.

I'll bet it was funny in some respects.

It was on this night I gave thanks to my experience of having served overseas in Uncle Sam's Army. I am pretty sure I would have reacted to the occasion as those men did when they became so panicky at the sound of revolver shots and on hearing them go crashing into the walls of that car if I hadn't had similar experiences. So instead of following the mob, so to speak, I kept my head down and stuck to my corner and let come what might. I was right in my strategy, for after all those men had finally cleared the car, the officers' interest in it seemed to have ceased and I was left alone in apparent security.

The freight stood there for about thirty minutes before it started to move and, finally, as it went on down the track it picked up speed. Soon it was on its way again and clear of Greensboro and on down towards Winston-Salem.

It is in this vicinity that the Southern Railroad starts to run along the Catawba River and as we entered the valley I noticed a change in the atmosphere. It seemed to dampen and the cold seemed to penetrate more.

We entered this valley at a pretty good speed and, not wanting to get up from my bed of papers and its comfort, I could only get a blurred or hazy view through the darkness and the door of the car.

It was early in the morning and still dark when we finally stopped in Winston-Salem, but only for a little while. Winston-Salem is not a very large place, so I didn't get off. Now that I had ridden most of the night and in comparative comfort I decided to continue on while the going was still good.

The only interference I experienced in this place was the "shack"[1] who was going over the car as a matter of course. As he passed the car I was in, he stuck his head in and inquired if I was OK and, getting my answer in the affirmative, he went on his way.

I couldn't figure out how it was he knew I was even on the train, let alone the box car I was occupying, but I guess these old "shacks" are pretty "wise old birds" and know the ways of "Mr. Hobo" as well as they do themselves—and maybe better.

We left Winston-Salem with a jerk and bang and a rattle and a terrible shriek of the wheels. I thought for a moment that we had backslid into some busy boiler shop, the din was so great and noisy. But after we got underway everything seemed to relax and none the less did I, for I thought for a moment or two that we had left the rails.

I was somewhat disappointed in not being able to get a good look at the countryside and the river, for now I was really down South and I wanted to compare by eyesight with what I had often read about it while in school.

The only thing I really could make out very well was the river, but that had to have the moonlight shining across it to actually prove it was a river I was looking at.

No one got on in Winston-Salem. At least, if anyone did they didn't bother with the car I was in, so here I thought would be a good time to get a few winks of sleep. So I returned to my trundle bed in the corner and covered myself up and proceeded to do so. For the first time I managed to go fast asleep and didn't wake up until the train stopped.

---

1. Slang for brakeman.

It must have stopped suddenly, for it was my head banging up against the car walls that really woke me from my slumbers.

It is broad daylight so I get up quickly and go to the door and, on looking out, I find I am on a side track and off to one side of a railroad yard. Here I pile off to look up a place to eat and most of all to find out where I am at.

I judged the time to be near high noon, for the sun was up high and not giving off much heat at that. The wind that was blowing against me was damp and bitter cold and off to my right there was a heavy mist like one that is seen hanging over a body of water, which led me to think I might be near a lake or the sea.

I had not gone very far after clearing the railroad yards before I came to a crossroad on the corner of which was a sign showing me the way to the business section. It didn't mention what town or city that business section was in, so I followed the road and came upon a combination grocery and restaurant and ordered a meal and asked what town or city I was now in.

The man behind the counter looked at me in surprise, and then he said, "What town or city are you in? Why? Don't you know?"

"No, I don't and if I did, Mister, I certainly wouldn't bother asking," I answered back, feeling somewhat peeved at his apparent joking at my expense.

"Well my boy, this is Decatur, Alabama, and that river you see out there is the Tennessee River," and after imparting that much information, he retired to the back of the restaurant and returned with my order of "Hot Cakes and Coffee" and real maple syrup.

There is no need of me dwelling on how good those hot cakes and coffee and maple syrup tasted. Suffice it to say they were the best I ever ate.

After leaving the restaurant, I decided to return to the railroad yard to ascertain when the next freight would leave before I wandered about very much. On the way there, I caught up with a very old colored man and asked him if he knew. For being an information bureau about the time all trains arrived and left that yard, he was a wonder. He even knew the numbers of the Engines.

It was from him I learned I had only fifteen minutes to make the next freight out if, as he said, "You all can get on with that Bull always hanging around there day and night."

I thanked the old fellow and hurried on down the road hoping I would be on time to catch that freight and with no interference from that Bull.

I got there on time alright, but in my haste I didn't notice or give any heed to the overcast and darkening sky overhead. Just as I was about to get into a position where I thought by crawling over two or three lines of cars I might be able to make that freight with nobody seeing me, it started to rain and then all of a sudden, as though the heavens had opened up, it came down not only in sheets but like a waterfall.

When the first drops started falling, I looked round for shelter but in those two lines of cars I couldn't see one that was open. Then, thinking I could get back to the road, I started back over the cars again. Then I thought of getting under the cars but I had no way of knowing that they didn't have an engine on one end that might start them going. So there I was and by that time it was no use, so I sat. Talk about feeling like a drowned rat. To tell the truth about it, I felt and looked like a dirty old mop that had been soaking in muddy water for a week.

If ever I was mad and in a jam this was the time. Here I was, down in the open, wet clear to the skin, and with only six bits in my pocket. As though Mother Nature was in one of her mocking moods, the sun came out as though there had been no weather disturbance for a month back. I had been in a cloud burst as near as I could make out, for it lasted but ten minutes.

Well, now what to do?

It would take two days for my clothing to dry if I walked around in them, and to do that I would run a good chance of landing in the hospital. To light a fire in the open would only attract attention and, perhaps for my own good, I'd be thrown into jail. So I left everything to fate and started on down the tracks looking for some warm place to get into and get at least my overcoat off.

As I emerged from between those two strings of cars, a colored man came out of a small building to my right and I hailed him while on the run.

He stopped to wait for me and, without even a word of inquiry on our parts, he said, "Follow me."

He led me a short distance along the tracks and then took a shortcut towards the river through a field until we came to a shack. The door was not even locked, and as he opened the door he said, "Get in there, boy, and get those clothes off before you catch your death of a cold."

I entered and started to strip off my clothes while he piled more wood on the fire that was burning slowly and then he reached for a coffee pot and soon we were conversing as though we had been friends for years.

Now let anyone tell me any more tales about the Negroes down South the like that I had been listening to since I left Washington DC, or just let me hear someone recommend that signs should be put up telling them to not let the "sun go down on them."

I had heard of some tall tales of rape and robbery and even murder and every other kind of criminality, all these being committed by Negroes only.

"Never go into a place with a Negro," said one man, "For if you do, you will not come out alive," and a lot of other such nonsense.

This Negro and many other Negroes I have met certainly belie such tales, and this one in particular couldn't have done—nor worried more—over the outcome of the drenching I had received. Nor did he ever give me any questioning or examination or even did he ask where I was from. Not he, he just took me at face value and showed that he was a Christian and brother and it made no difference to him who I was, and that was more than I had ever received from a White man. Such faith and kindness is rare indeed.

I certainly felt thankful to this Negro, for I am sure that if it wasn't for his wonderful kindness, I perhaps would have fallen sick by the wayside. Lord knows what then may have happened.

My clothes were dry in about three hours with the exception of my overcoat. That, it seemed, never would get dry, so this old Negro said, "Well, you can't go on without it, boy, so make yourself comfortable as you can until tomorrow."

We had a very nice supper together and whatever may have been this Negro's breeding or training, he ate his meal with more elegance than I ever knew existed. I spent fifty cents of the seventy five I had on hand, that is in loose change, and it was well spent.

We sat around for a while then we retired, he on his own bed and I on the floor with my back within safe distance of the fire. In spite of my hard bed, I slept throughout the night and my dreams were of the miles and miles I hoped to cover the following day.

All in all, this stop over was the most interesting and most pleasant of any since I had left New York City.

We arose early on the following morning. My overcoat was dry, I had my three cups of coffee, and by nine o'clock I was on my way further South with Mobile, Alabama as my next objective.

Chapter Ten

Mobile onto New Orleans

Nobody needs to tell me now that it does get cold in the south, for it seemed the further I went the colder it got. It seemed when I got cold from riding I just couldn't get warm unless I got up against a fire.

There were four or five other men waiting for a freight when I got in the yards and, naturally, there being only one open box car, all five of us climbed into it. And being only five in number you cannot help but fraternalize somewhat. So, as we rolled on down towards Mobile, we got pretty well acquainted and exchanged stories and yarns about our experiences on the Road.

From what I could make out of these four men they were only knocking about the same as I, but their intentions and views were so different than mine I didn't get much of a kick out of any of them. Most of their talk was about how many houses they had dinged (or begged, to be more explicit) and what they got and what they asked for and didn't get. Some liked to brag considerable about the "set downs" (asked to come and eat at a table) they received and the two bits or so they were handed as they left. Much of this sort of talk I knew to be just so much bulls—, for they spread it on too thick and they didn't look like they had the nerve they were accrediting themselves as having.

It takes a well seasoned tramp or bum to get a handout at every house they hit (as they call it), and these fellows by their actions had not been on the Road much longer than I had. They were too well dressed and well fed, and the one thing that gives all novices away to an old timer was their continual worry about the "Bulls" or railroad officers. They call this fear the "Bull Horrors."

The countryside along this stretch of railroad was quite interesting. It was the first time I had ever seen sugar cane growing in its natural state, and the cypress swamps and sorghum were all new to me too.

The cypress swamps interested me more than anything else. For, when I tried to see further into their dark interior, it recalled to my mind terrifying ghost stories of dismal swamps and crocodiles and other creeping creatures I had often read about when a young boy.

I took special note of some real old colonial homes that, according to their style and architecture, must have been built long before the Civil War. They were quite picturesque in their whiteness and contrast to their surroundings. They seemed to shout out stories of better days back in the days of the Old South when hospitality was its byword. In spite of the changes and the passing away of those folks of yore who doted on good living, they still held their stateliness and grandeur and from a distance they looked as though—like good wine—they had mellowed with age.

It was these old colonial buildings that convinced me to forsake the comfort and protection of the box car I was riding in. I wanted to see more of this country and, it being a sunny day, I left the car at the next stop and got on top. From there I had an excellent view of most of that section of the country, but I paid well for it, for in spite of the sun, the wind was damp and cold and by the time darkness started to set in I was stiff.

I was surprised at the scarcity of the cotton plantations. There seemed to be more sugar cane grown in this section than anything else.

We made another stop, so while the train crew took out a few cars and side tracked them, I climbed down from my roost on top and returned to the cover of that box car. For the balance of the trip I was occupied with trying to get warmed up and listening to more bragging from two of the men. And they were really good at it.

The sun was dropping below the horizon and for every degree it dropped so did the temperature, until the damp cold was almost unbearable. I was pleased when we finally pulled into the Mobile yards.

Now I had only twenty-five cents in my pocket when I arrived there, and twenty-five cents don't get you much more than a cup of coffee and a sandwich, or perhaps a plate lunch. So yours truly had to do some tall rustling before he could think of staying very long in Mobile.

This was really the first time I was up against it badly since I left New York City. And it would be the first test of the many ways I had been hearing about as to getting along or "making it," as most of the itinerant travelers call it.

The business center of Mobile is not very far from the railroad yards, so even before I started looking for opportunities of obtaining a night's lodging and meals, I had arrived at that section. Not wanting to attract too much notice, I retraced my footsteps and about halfway I came abreast a large warehouse about which showed considerable activity both inside and on the outside.

They were unloading five or six big trucks on one side and reloading about ten trucks on the other. It looked for all the world as if they were taking merchandise from one set of trucks through one set of doors, only to take the same merchandise through another set of doors and reload it on the trucks on the opposite side of the building.

As I stopped to watch these men working like a lot of bees it struck me: I might by chance get a few hours work. So I sized up the place for a few more minutes and finally decided to try it. I figured they could do no more than refuse me and in the end no harm would come of it. So over I went and no more than I got up on the platform someone says to me, "Looking for a couple of hours' work, Bud?"

"Sure thing," I said and, to show him I meant business, I grabbed the handles of an idle truck and asked him where to.

"Over there, Old Timer," he said, pointing to one of the trucks they were unloading.

I had no idea of how much per hour I was to get, but I was happy to be once more working. I had visions of steak and onions and french fried potatoes and a nice cozy room for a change from what I had been existing on since I first started out on this business of hoboing it, or going with the tide.

Just as fast as one set of trucks were unloaded, another set backed up and it wasn't until I had put in five hours were we done. So the foreman called me over and sent me into an office and, as he left me, he told the man at the small windows I was pretty good and OK. If ever I fell over when I counted the amount I received for those five happy hours, it was on that first day in Mobile.

I counted the bills three times over before I could actually believe my good fortune. There were five one dollar bills in that envelope! I came near leaping for joy and shouting out in my happiness.

"Five dollars! Five dollars!" I kept repeating to myself as I wended my way back towards the business section of Mobile.

Steak and onions and french fried potatoes, oh boy!

So at the first restaurant I came to I went in and gave the order. The man looked at me sort of doubtful, but he called it out and, if ever I enjoyed a meal, it was in that Greek restaurant. And the best part of it was when I read the check, I found that combination only cost (including coffee) fifty cents.

Before I left the restaurant I asked the cashier to direct me to a reasonably-priced place to stay for the night. She gave me an address at which she said lived a friend of hers who would be glad to let a room out for any length of time.

I had a little difficulty in finding it and finally, when I did, I came to a little house or cottage practically covered with vines. Here it was I obtained as nice a room for fifty cents as anyone would care to live in. That night I slept among the feathers of perhaps a thousand ducks and chickens.

I must have dropped off to sleep immediately after retiring. All I could remember when I awoke in the morning was that when I got into that feathered bed I could just look over the edges of the covers—as if I had laid into a soft fluffy bank of pure white snow.

I was loathe to get out of that bed that morning, it felt so soft and restful. In fact it was too restful, for when I did finally arise, I felt somewhat stiff in the knees, and it was quite a while before I got them limbered up.

After leaving this wonderful stop over, I stopped in the same restaurant and had breakfast. After eating I started back towards the railroad yards but don't think for a moment I was not tempted to return back to that house and hire that room for a couple of nights more. But now that I had a little money in my pocket, I felt it would be better to keep on moving and, too, I felt I could enjoy knocking about knowing I had the wherewithal to maintain myself if I got stuck along the route.

Mobile shall always remain in my memory as one of the most pleasant stops I ever made. There was something about it that made you feel at ease and welcome. The city itself impressed me from the first, like I was returning home, when in fact I had never been there before. I can't express it in as many words but I did really feel at home while there.

Not once in the day and night did anyone as much as ask me my name or where I came from or anything pertaining to my personal business. The only time there was any doubt explaining myself was when the counter man looked at me sort of doubtful when I ordered steak and onions. For that I couldn't blame him; to tell the truth I didn't look so prosperous or quite as I should coming as I did just off a freight train ride.

If there ever would be any choice presented to me in regards to what city I would like to live in down south, just give me good old Mobile, Alabama.

When I arrived at the yards, who did I see but my companions of the day before, and for three forlorn-looking men, they sure looked the part.

I couldn't help feeling sorry for them, but on second thought my sympathy ceased when I recalled all the bragging about how they could make it so easy. In spite of all they deserved I couldn't see them hungry, so I gave them two bits to go to the nearest store to get enough bread and some cheese or sandwich meat for the four of us while riding. True to their breed, I waited until the freight was ready to pull out and I was still waiting for them to show up. That little run out cured me from then on; that was a lesson learned and cheaply so, it might just as well have been a dollar lost.

From Mobile on, this railroad (L&N[1]) took me through a country which abounded in sugar plantations, cypress swamps, and bayous and cedar trees. Here and there I noticed small patches of cotton, but they were few and far between.

I took particular note of the scarcity of insect life one would expect to find in such a terrain. No doubt it being in the Winter months accounted for that. I did expect to find some stray mosquitoes and flies, but there was none to speak of.

A good share of this section of the country seemed to be under water. I certainly wouldn't care to spend a summer in this particular locality, for I can well imagine to what extent anyone would be bothered with mosquitoes and other annoying pests.

I was riding on top (as they call riding on top of a box car), so I got a very good view and an idea of every mile we rode on to New Orleans.

I don't know how many miles it is from Mobile to New Orleans (and generally an itinerant traveler doesn't bother about mileage between points or divisions), but mile-for-mile I would say it certainly has variety in scenery. One minute you are barreling over water, then all of a sudden you hit dry land, then first thing you know, you are surrounded by swamps, and finally you suddenly emerge from a grove of cedars into a clump of houses or a village.

About halfway to New Orleans, we ran into a fog so thick I couldn't make out my hand in front of me, and from then on the cold seemed to stab right through our clothes. The chill that grips you down here makes you shiver until your knees knock together.

We made a stop shortly after the sun started dropping, so I got down and under cover of the car I was riding. But it didn't give much protection in regards that damp fog or the cold, so I spent considerable

---

1. Louisville and Nashville Railroad

time pacing up and down trying vainly to keep the shivers from getting control of my muscles. In spite of the exercise and the heavy overcoat I had on I did shiver some.

I don't know exactly at what hour we finally pulled into the Chantilly Yards, which are about eleven miles outside of New Orleans. Here we found a reception committee waiting for us in the guise of three railroad officers, of whom I can honestly say, they "knew their business."

This being the first time I had ever been in this yard, I would hardly know in which direction to go to get out, even in broad daylight. So it being dark, the difficulties were only tripled in that respect when I saw those three flashlights, one coming from the front end on top. I just stood where I had dropped from the car and tried to figure or decide which way would be the best to go. After I got started and a little off to one side, I sure was hurting, for right behind me was one of the Officers seeing to it I found it or else.

It being pitch dark I didn't know any more where to look for an opening, so I start to run along parallel with the tracks and finally I notice what looks like a foot bridge over a small ditch. So I turn to it and step out, but what I thought was a bridge I discover after falling full length into a muddy ditch, to be only the branch of a tree that had accidentally fallen across the ditch.

About the time I got straightened out, that officer was getting close, so I struck out blindly through a lot of brush when suddenly I was brought to a stop by banging into a wire fence. Over this I vaulted, just as the officer was reaching out to grab me. If it wasn't for the darkness, I guess yours truly would have spent a little vacation down in Louisiana.

I heard him cursing out loud to himself; something about the g— d— bums and tramps and what he wouldn't have done if he only had his hands on me.

Now that I had cleared all railroad property, my next problem was which way to go to get into New Orleans. Once more I struck out blindly and as I went along I realized I was walking on what appeared to be a pretty rough roadway, and then suddenly I heard footsteps. As dismal as it seemed in the dark, those footsteps almost made my heart stop, so eerie did they sound coming on and then stopping and then starting again, until I couldn't stand it any longer. I cried out "Who's that?!" And to make it more mysterious, I got no answer but a hollow echo in return.

I couldn't think of anything else to do, so I continued on and as I did the footsteps started too and then I bumped into them (so I imagined) so sudden and unexpected that I was almost knocked off my feet. Then almost simultaneously we called out, "Where in hell are we?"

I managed to get my wits together somewhat and stammered back "That's what I'd like to know!" After getting those words out, I felt pretty much relieved and then suggested both of us take the same direction until we found some sort of opening.

We stumbled along that rough muddy road until we emerged abreast a small grocery store, so I suggested we go in, and we find we are going in the right direction for downtown New Orleans.

We finally come to where this road is illuminated and here I take a look at my clothes and to my amazement I find I am not covered with mud but I am pretty wet—but not clean through. So we trudge along until we come to a trolley line which was running at right angles to the road we came down on. So I say to my companion, "Well, this is far as I walk, for here is where we wait for a car."

I asked my companion, who I discovered was a colored man, if he cared to come along, but for some reason or other he said he would wait until morning. Just then I heard the wires overhead humming and in about thirty minutes I alighted right abreast the Post Office, which I am informed by the street signs is on Monument Street, New Orleans.

As I was turning the first corner I came to, to get off the "main stem," for I didn't look so hot with half the length of my trouser legs soaking wet, I was accosted by a middle-aged man who had "Detective" written all over him.

"Whoa! Steady there, fellow. Where are you going coming around a corner like that?" and while making those inquiries he got ahold of my arm.

"Why, no place in particular, Mister," I said, and then continued on by explaining I got a pretty bad soaking and I was on my way to a hotel to get my wet clothes off.

"OK, I thought something was up. So go ahead, but don't let me catch you panhandling in this town." Then he stepped back and examined me and then said, "Cripes, I guess you did get a soaking."

I thought sure I was a goner that time and I didn't get over it for quite some time. For every man I met who was dressed somewhat similar, I looked upon them with suspicion.

This business of being chased and bothered and stopped by the authorities was beginning to get under my skin, and sort of making me irritable, to the point of getting somewhat disgusted with the police. Several times when I was stopped, I was on the point of asking them what the hell they were wasting their time on poor Mr. Hobo or the Tramps and Bums, while all around them was all sorts of criminals and crimes and conditions that might be more worthy of their attention.

But it doesn't pay an itinerant traveler to be too pugnacious with the police, so I had to swallow everything they did and said. And particularly must you be very polite and diplomatic when you haven't the means of subsistence in your pocket. And sometimes it doesn't pay to let them know that either way, for on the knowledge that you have money in your pocket, you perhaps will be arrested just to get that money from you through fines; for it is a very easy matter to "vag" you (which is what they call it when they arrest you for vagrancy), or take you in as a suspicious character. Such cases are not at all rare.

I walked about several of those streets that seemed to shoot off Monument Street. until, on one of them, I noticed a restaurant that appeared to be more or less moderate in price.

It was in this restaurant that I learned what good coffee was, and that the best way to drink it is black. The food too was good as any that is served in some of the highest priced restaurants in New York City. And this meal cost me only thirty-three cents, and I was waited upon by the first "Creole" I had ever seen.

After having satisfied my hunger and having another cup of that coffee, I started out to look for a hotel that would have the facilities of a good bath and a private room, for I had some wet clothes to get dried.

I learn after walking a few blocks I am on Royal Street and on this street there are any number of reasonable priced places.

In fact at that time this street seemed to be lined with hotels of every description and price.

The hotel I selected was by far the best I ever was in for the price, so after a good bath I returned and fell immediately to sleep. I didn't wake up until late that evening and by that time my clothes were dry and I was once more set to continue on.

On that same evening after strolling around a little bit I finally find I am standing in front of Monument Street facing a ferry boat which I am told will take you across the Mississippi River and from there on I can make connections going west.

Out West! Oh dream of my dreams! And didn't I long to fulfill those dreams of my boyhood!

Everything that I ever had visioned of the West, and the wide open spaces, and what I had read about it seemed to be on parade before my eyes as I stood looking at that ferry boat which seemed to beckon to me as though saying, "Get a move on, if you are going. You won't get anywhere standing there. Come."

Chapter Eleven

Heading West

I would have felt amply repaid by an extended stopover in New Orleans, but when you have only three dollars in your pockets and the possibilities of obtaining any kind of work to earn more are as slim and uncertain as they were then, it would be the act of a dolt to not try to conserve what you have on hand. Especially when you are knocking about and at the mercy of the Law and the elements, and a hundred other contingencies that beset an itinerant traveler.

I own it didn't take much persuasion on my own part to decide on what I should do. At the end of a summation of my doubts and fears, and my ability to make the grade, I came to the conclusion that if ever I was to see the West now would be as good a time as any.

The going couldn't be any harder than what I had already gone through traveling the fifteen-hundred-odd miles so far and, as an added bit of encouragement, had not I come through OK? And with more money in my pocket than when I had started out? Why, certainly! So what is the matter with you, why do you hesitate? Such were my thoughts as I stood watching that ferryboat and the manner in which they collected fares.

At first the manner of collecting fares only interested me as a matter of curiosity, and in comparison to the manner they collected fares on ferryboats in New York City. There was only one difference and that was, instead of passing by a window each way, you only passed one man who stood in between at a turnstile in two lanes—one coming and one going. It was this sort of system that engendered in my mind as to how easy it would be to get by him without paying any fare. It would be a cinch, I thought, and no sooner had the idea struck my mind than I was on my way up the gangplank to test it out.

It was so easy I couldn't help laughing to myself and I gave thought to a possibility that that ferryboat must be losing thousands of dollars each year. It was so simple to figure out the fact that nobody can look in two directions at the same time.

Well, that was ten cents saved.

"Ten cents," say you. "What good would the saving of ten cents in that manner do anyone?"

Ordinarily it wouldn't, but it is perhaps news to some people that it can be the means of saving a life by more ways than one. For instance, ten cents has been the means of saving many a man from freezing to death, for there are many places all over this country where you can get a bed for a dime.

My conservation was motivated by the stories of what a tough part of the country I was heading into. For an itinerate traveler, ten cents saved was worth the trouble if such stories were true, and I had proved to my own satisfaction that there was always a grain of truth in such stories, especially if it was a Hobo who had been good enough to tell you so.

Well I am across the Mississippi and in a town by the name of Algiers, and here it is I see roses in bloom for the first time in December. There really is no wonder to that down this far South, but it is a sort of novelty to me.

I had only to walk to the outskirts of Algiers to catch a freight going West. So, more from force of habit, I got out of the city limits to avoid the authorities to where I was told would be the proper place to keep under cover and out of sight.

It was about six pm when I started out from New Orleans and, from information, I had to wait until eleven o'clock that night for a freight. So, not wanting to get too hungry, I bought on my way there some food and a pound of coffee.

This was my first experience at "jungling up." So, like everything else, I went at it backwards. But I finally did get my coffee boiling and my eggs fried and all in all I had a good time so to speak.

From then on I took every opportunity to cook my own meals and I felt much better for it.

I stayed out of sight until about ten o'clock. For, not far from where I had to find a freight, there was a nice big County Jail.

My attention was called to a man and woman who were pacing up and down along the tracks. Once when he passed me, he inquired about what time there would be a freight pulling out. The woman was carrying an infant in her arms and for some reason or other I just couldn't connect them with a freight. But being curious about why a man and his wife should be out with an infant at that time of the night, let alone their interest in freights, I took a chance and inquired if he was really going to ride out that night. To my surprise he told me yes and he was sort of worried as to whether he could get his wife and baby on safely.

I offered to help him all I could and I told him I couldn't understand why he had to do that, especially when there were better ways of getting about, especially in regards to his wife and child.

"Well, I got to get to a town about fifty miles up the track," says he, "For there is a job waiting for me if I can get there by morning."

Just then an officer came into view and on seeing a woman and a child he expressed considerable surprise. Naturally he wanted to know how come.

The husband explained matters to him, and the officer told him to go along and get the job and he would see to it that his wife followed him, but not on a freight. The Travelers Aid Society would do that, "on my recommendation tomorrow afternoon."

And so it was that man and I were the only two that boarded that freight out of Algiers, on my first lap to the land of my boyhood dreams.

I never saw a man who worried so much as this man. From the minute he got settled on the floor of the car, he did nothing but complain about everything from the speed of the train to the present conditions.

I was more or less pleased and relieved when we made our first stop, for at this stop we took on about thirty or forty more men, and there being only one open box car, they all piled in.

Talk about a bunch of jabbering monkeys in a cage. This bunch had anything beat I ever saw, and for panhandling tobacco and matches, well, if there was a tobacco store on board, I am afraid that wouldn't have been enough. It looked for all the world as though they were starved out. Some I noticed bummed just for the sake of bumming.

Among this polyglot lot of men there were about a dozen or so very young boys, and of these they were the toughest youngsters I had yet seen on the Road.

After the train got underway, they started to fan off and those of the same language naturally picked each other out.

I counted eight different languages going at one time. It put me in mind of the Biblical account of the Tower of Babel.

The boys interested me more than anything else, for I could hear their high pitched voices above the rest of the jabbering. From their talk and conversations, I gleaned they were as worldly-wise a bunch of youngsters any city could boast of.

There wasn't one section of the country mentioned, but some one of them had been all over it, and to prove it they questioned each other minutely about certain streets and Missions and other hangouts.

It being still dark, I couldn't make out their general make up, so I had to wait until morning to get a good look at them.

We rolled along at a first rate clip between stops. I judged we were on just an ordinary freight train so they dropped off cars as we went along, but the crew didn't bother us. In fact, some of them stopped and inquired if everything was OK.

I stood up all that night. I wouldn't dare stretch out on the floor of that car on that night for a hundred different reasons.

What are the reasons, you ask? Well, for one: Attempted theft or filching of your pockets if you fell asleep, getting lousy another, and still another the sexual perverts who might attempt a sodomy. And then there is a possible chance you might be choked to death to satisfy a lust to kill. So, in as large a crowd of men as this, it's best to stay on your feet just to play safe.

Riding at night has its advantages in one way only as far as I could see, and that was you were more or less under cover from the Railroad Officers and could, if you were forced to, get away from them more readily than in broad daylight.

To me, night riding was an ordeal and terribly monotonous, for about all you can do is to just sit or stand until you reach your destination. You couldn't see those around you or see what they were doing or might be up to by way of devilment, and some are so damn mean and petty, they wouldn't stop even to cut the buttons off your overcoat.

It was useless to try and make out what sort of country we were riding through, for most of this trip we were bothered with fog and a heavy mist.

I was pleased when finally I saw a streak of daylight off in the horizon. Just as soon as it got light enough everyone was up on his feet, and what a sight presented itself.

"My God," I said to myself. "Are these really human beings?" For before me I saw the dirtiest and most unkempt body of men I hoped I would never see again. Those youngsters, were they lousy, the cooties crawling from under their coat sleeves.

There was just one little fellow among that filthy lot that I could honestly have any sympathy for. I didn't have to take a second look at him to judge he certainly was far away or out of his proper environment, and half scared to death.

After observing this boy for a while I am sure he isn't with anybody and too I notice he is in pain, for every once in a while he would wince when his back touched the wall he was setting up against. I thought it would be interesting to know how a little boy found his way on a freight, so I ease my way towards him and finally he catches my eye and sort of smiles at me in a half-hearted manner. Then he gets on his feet and asks me if I knew where we were.

I told him I didn't know any more than he did, and then I asked him what he was doing riding around on freight trains at his age, which I judged to be around thirteen years of age.

He explained his presence there by telling me about the beatings he always got when his father was drunk so he couldn't stand it no longer, so now he was going to Houston to live with an aunt who had sent for him. If I wanted any proof of those beatings he could show me his back if I cared to see it and didn't believe him.

I couldn't help believing this boy, for sincerity was contained in every word he uttered. So I asked him if he felt hungry and, like all young growing boys, his eyes sparkled in expectation as I started to offer the small package I had that contained what food I had left.

We ate our food under the gaze of the hungry eyes of those who were close by us. I felt sorry for them on that score, for I know what that feeling was like and I couldn't blame them. Too, I was sorry I didn't have more to share with all of them.

After talking with a few of the other boys, I find that a bad environment in their homes has driven them to seek a happier place to live. I listen to three or four stories of drunken fathers, and mothers too, and one or two left home because there wasn't enough to eat for the whole family. Now, as one explained, he is eating three square meals a day in the Transient Bureaus or if not there, he would get it in the Missions.

The rest in the boxcar being men who were made up of tramps and bums, and just the riff-raff that played the Transient Bureau and Missions. These men are called "Mission Stiffs," and for whom not even the tramps and bums have much use for. These men are too lazy to work and spend most of the time looking for handouts and free drinks and will steal for it.

So far on this stretch of the Southern Pacific Railroad, I didn't see any real Hobos, and I am sure they wouldn't care to be seen in such a boxcar full of men as I was riding with.

Now that it was daylight, I took a chance on getting a few winks of sleep, so I dozed off with one eye open and one shut, for one has to be on the alert even in the daytime. No matter what one might do to you in your sleep, you would have a hell of a time finding out who it was from any of them.

There is one code that you can depend on from any man, whether he be old or young or a tramp or bum or even a Mission Stiff: None of them will betray one another. They all put thumbs down on a "snitch." There is another way to take care of thieves and those who would roll a fellow traveler. It is done by what is called the "Grapevine." It takes care of snitches and thieves and men who are caught too many times in earnest conversation with Railroad Officers; but for me to explain its workings in detail would be a breach of faith, so suffice to say I am for any form of retribution that might be used to keep such scum off the Road or any other place.

I did get a little sleep but the constant jabbering and pacing up and down of the men, and the click of the rails and roar of the train in general didn't let me sleep long. So, between sitting up and trying to go back to sleep and listening to some of the things those youngsters did to this guy or that guy, I wiled the hours away until some one announced our approach to Houston, Texas.

Talk about a cage of excited monkeys. I thought for a minute or two some of them would be sprawling on the floor in a fit. The youngsters I thought were acting natural, but the men all seemed to have gone back to being youngsters again. This sort animation upon our reaching Houston, Texas led me to think it must be a very friendly city to itinerant travelers and that the pickings there must be good and easily obtained. So, I myself felt a little tingle of excitement.

For I had in my mind to look for work immediately after I got rested up, for now I had only two dollars and fifteen cents in my pockets. On such evident pleasure as I had just witnessed, I built up some high hopes for a very pleasant visit in Houston.

I didn't wait to get into the Southern Railroad yards. About three miles from the yards, the freight came to a very slow speed, so I got ready to drop off at some advantageous spot within a reasonable walking distance of the city limits. As I sat down the youngster I had shared my lunch with sat down beside me ready to drop off also. When I said to him, "Let's go," we both dropped off and hit the ground as one.

We got to our feet and I'll never forget as long as I live how that youngster took a hold of my hand just as though he felt by doing so he was showing his appreciation for my attention to him on the train.

We trudged along the tracks until we came to a crossroad and here we turned down it looking more like father and son than one itinerant traveler and a recently made friend. As we came nearer and nearer to Houston, so did the grip of that little hand become more friendly and protecting in its feel and warmth.

It was on this day that the same feeling came over me as it did when I stopped in Mobile, Alabama, so I hoped that Houston wouldn't disappoint me.

We were not long in getting into the heart of things. When we came abreast of the YMCA, I stopped and told my little friend that was as far as I was going so if there was anything that I could do for him before we parted I would be pleased to do it.

The little fellow looked me square in the eye and said, "Do you really mean that?"

"I sure do," I answered.

"Well, then, Mister, my aunt lives about three miles from here, so if you could loan me a dime I wouldn't have to walk it and if you did, I'll return it tomorrow if you give me your address."

I saw him on a street car and that was the last I saw of him.

I put up in the YMCA that night and, after a good bath and a substantial supper, I started out looking for work. In about two hours I obtained a short-time job in a moderately priced restaurant as a dishwasher.

I went to bed that night blessing Houston and giving up thanks and feeling happy as a lark and like a human being once more.

This job was only good for one week's duration, and when the regular man returned, the proprietor held me on for two more days just to make sure "that the man was able to work and I can at least hand you a ten dollar bill when you leave."

This proprietor was one of those rare men who had begun at the bottom of the business and appreciated a working man. Houston is a hostile city in some respects, but if you tend strictly to your own business the authorities will respect you and even help you.

So after a ten day stop over in this friendly town I decide to move on further West. On one rainy morning I am in the Southern Railroad yards looking for a box car and whether I found one or not that wouldn't have stopped me. For now that I had twelve dollars in my pockets I felt I could make it to the Coast.

I had just arrived in time, for standing all made up and set to go was a "Manifest."[1] As I just got abreast of the engine, the Engineer saluted me and asked me if I was going West and why did I leave my job in the restaurant.

After explaining my presence and why I left my job, he leaned over and waved his hand and told me to hurry up and get on, so I continued on. About halfway the length of the train I met one of the trainmen who stopped me and said "Wait a minute." Then he broke one of the seals and opened the door and said, "Jump in there and keep quiet."

In about five minutes I heard two blasts of the whistle and immediately after the train was on its way.

The Engineer who had signaled I was OK used to eat where I was working and he did like his coffee. So I used to slip him an extra cup

---

1. A fast train.

and never charged him for it and that pleased him. So, as a reward, I am paid back sooner than I had expected.

Well, thought I, it only goes to show that it pays to figure there are other people in this world besides yourself and, if you want the rest of the world to treat you right, you must be the first to show your worth.

This train, being a Manifest, didn't do any stalling after it once got going. Some of these Manifests do better time than some passenger trains, and this one was no exception.

This was the best and fastest ride I had yet had on a freight. We flew through small places like a shot out of a cannon and after leaving it, all you could see was a cloud of dust. When we did stop, we didn't stop long enough for me to get even more than a glance at the one or two stops we made.

It is a pleasure in a way to have a box car all to yourself, so I laid out in the middle and took it easy. I took in what scenery I could but we were going along at such a fast clip everything whizzed by in a sort of blur. I fell asleep after a while and woke up with the sun shining full in my face.

Suddenly I realize we are rolling along at a very slow speed, so I get up and look out and discover we are pulling into some railroad yard. This galvanizes me into instant action, for I didn't want to get this crew into trouble; for I had heard someplace that it isn't well for those who dare to ride on one of these fast freights. So I prepare myself to drop off before we are really in the yard, and it was well I did, for after leaving it I watched after it stopped for some evidence as to how hostile the railroad officers were out this way.

This was San Antonio, I discovered after I got a piece up the track, and as I was approaching the yard limits, I saw no less than five officers going over the freight. When they came to the car I was riding in, all five examined it from one end to the other.

I made no attempt to walk through those yards and after several turns up some back streets, I finally arrived at a railroad station. Right abreast of it was a park, and here I sat down to get my bearings.

While I was sitting there, the engineer who had brought that freight in passed by me and on recognizing me, asked me how I liked that ride.

I had to admit to him it sure was OK and then I thanked him. After a few words of advice on what to do to catch one going further on, he left me.

Now while I was working in Houston, an old Army Sergeant who had retired gave me the name of another sergeant who he said would take care of me if I went to the Army Post in San Antonio and just mentioned his name.

There was another place I was also put wise to by an old Hobo who had wandered in the restaurant in Houston, and who had asked the proprietor for a few hours work for a meal which he got. Taking advantage of this fact, he had traveled around all his life, or so he said, and I asked him for a little information about how things were further on West. So he gave me the address of another place.

Of these two places the Army Post interested me the most and, after getting directions as to how to get to it, I started out to take advantage of its hospitality.

I found the sergeant I was told to look up quite easily and, after I mentioned my informant's name, I was practically taken under his wing and treated like a brother.

I had a message for the sergeant and when he read it, he took me with him to the captain in the company orderly room. In five minutes after reading that message, the captain had written out orders for me to stay overnight and, if I thought it was necessary, I could have still another night. But I did not take advantage of his kindness entirely.

I only ate two meals there and told them to save the shelter for some other time.

I was too anxious to see San Antonio to stick around the Army Post any longer than to eat, so as soon as I was through dinner I sauntered on down towards the business district of San Antonio, Texas.

While I didn't stay in this pleasant city very long, I took in most of its attractions and saw the alligators in a park named after the Battle of the Alamo.

I saw some buildings that smacked of the old days of the West and there was one in particular that interested me more than all else: an "Old Trading Post." Whether this was the original building I couldn't say, but it sure looked like it.

I returned to the Army Post and had my supper, and then returned to the business district to look for a place to stop over in. Unknown to myself, I had passed the other place that I was told about by my friend Mr. Hobo in Houston.

This place was on St. Mary's Street, and one of the best Transient Bureaus I have ever stopped in. It was more like a hotel.

From the looks of the place it couldn't have been more than a week since it had been opened up, so everything was bright and shining.

I was offered a job in this Transient Bureau, but I had in my mind to see the Pacific Coast now that I had come this far. So on the following day, I paid the Army Post another visit and I was given enough food that should last me at least as far as El Paso, which was the next important stop. So that evening found me with about fifty other men waiting for the next freight out of San Antonio, of which city I was just as sorry to leave as I was of Mobile and good old Houston.

The freight is coming.

Chapter Twelve

El Paso

When I arrived at the yards I couldn't see a soul around, but after finding a place that kept me out of sight and after looking around for a few minutes, I saw heads popping up and peeking from every conceivable kind of hiding place along the tracks.

It is well to keep under cover, for what the railroad officers don't see won't bother them. But once in a blue moon you run across an officer who is a little more conscientious in his work and who does take a stroll around the yard and this one was one of them. So, just before the freight pulled out we saw from our hiding places someone coming up the track and of course it couldn't be anybody else but our "friend," or one of them.

Now the country in this section of the U.S is more or less open, so none of us dared show even our nose for if we did, well, all of us would have to wait for the next one out.

In such a case it is better to wait until a freight has pulled out and underway, for then you have a chance of getting it between you and an officer. Then the rest is easy if the freight isn't going too fast.

I had been watching them make up that freight for about twenty minutes and it struck me that from the number of men who were trying to make it things might be popping. I for one didn't want to be around when one of the Western railroad officers got hot under the collar and started shooting; and they do shoot, so I was given to understand.

I wanted to make that freight in the worst way, so when the officer had his back turned, I stepped from my hiding place and started on down the outside track as though I was going into San Antonio rather than leaving it. I figured from the way things looked in the yard that freight was just about ready to pull out and if I could get down to about abreast of its middle I could catch it by making a run for it. By the time it got to where the rest of the men and the Officer were then I would be under cover and out of danger of any shots.

I had figured pretty close so when the engineer gave two pulls on the cord, I did a right face and hopped and run over the tracks like one possessed. But I made it and believe me I got under cover, for those damn fools came from their hiding places like so many ants out of an ant hill—and a little too soon.

I got back as far into the boxcar as I could, for no sooner had that gang of men showed their faces the officer started shooting, and the last I saw of those on the side of the officer, they were running for dear life up a hill and between the structures of a big ice conveyer.

I didn't know how the other men made out, but I knew whoever did make it had to be those who could catch a freight at a pretty fast clip, for I never felt a freight pick up speed like this one could. By the time we cleared the yards she was almost at top speed.

The freight stopped about twenty-five miles outside of San Antonio and here it seemed about every man that had got on piled into the boxcar I was in.

There must have been about twenty men in all, but no one could blame them, for we had headed into a nasty cold drizzle about ten miles from the yards and by the time the freight stopped it was raining in earnest.

Among the men who piled on at this stop was a frail little fellow who was shivering from the cold and dampness. He was shivering so badly his teeth were actually chattering. I stood it as long as I could, so I let him use my overcoat and covered his feet with a lot of newspapers and after a while he seemed to warm up but not completely.

I was running a great risk in so doing, for it was a toss up as to whether my coat would be lousy, but I just couldn't stand seeing that kid suffer so from the cold.

Some of the men I noticed didn't have even any underwear or even a jacket on. How they could stand such chilly and damp weather was more than I could understand, but most of them didn't seem to mind it. As for myself, I felt it keenly even when I had my overcoat on, but when one is Hoboing it you can't very well complain, for if you do out loud you are sure to get the life kidded out of you from those who haven't half the clothes on that you have. So it's best to keep quiet and think to yourself.

I was told I was foolish to let that kid take my overcoat, but I didn't give them any argument so they dropped the subject from then on.

The diplomacy one must use to keep out of trouble is much the same as in any other stage of life, with only one little exception: You can't talk with any nicey-nice talk. You've got to put on your gruffest manner or else it won't be taken seriously; but the best way is to keep silent.

This was one time I could really see the country I was riding through, for in spite of the rain I could see quite clearly for miles distant.

The country along the railroad between San Antonio and El Paso is not very thickly populated. Here and there you see a ranch house in the distance across the sand.

We passed through several small hamlets which seemed to be inhabited mostly by Mexican railway workers who do most of the track work. They say they stand up better under the hot sun. I am not so inclined to believe that is the chief reason for using this kind of labor, for if the truth be known I think they work more cheaply.

There are some large ranches in this vicinity but as for cattle there were very few. From the nature of the soil and the amount of and the nature of the range, I fail to see how cattle really exist or thrive very well on it. Still I am told they do and grow fat on it.

I noticed cattle eating off of what appeared to be spots that were practically barren of vegetation, but I learned after that cattle food is distributed all over the range. Even cattle as well as human beings are fed now from a bag or can.

We moved along through the rain with here and there a stop to change engines or to cut out some cars.

I wasn't enjoying this trip so very well on account of the dampness and cold. The rest of the men were restless and some started to complain about the cold, so one of them started a fire in one corner of the car amid the protestations of the majority of the men. But he wouldn't listen, so at the next stop the boy and I changed cars and it was well we did. When the "shack" was passing, he noticed the smoke and chased everyone out and held them until the caboose just cleared them. He left them stranded there, but they perhaps wouldn't be stranded for long, for freights travel quite frequently along this route.

Starting any kind of fire in a freight car, whether open or closed—it makes no difference—is one of those offenses that a railroad will not tolerate. That, and theft and breaking seals are unforgivable offenses, and in some cases the offender is put behind bars.

The boy who followed me when I left to change cars certainly was pleased he did, for said he, "Gee, that was a close one! I thought for sure that bunch was going to jail. Gee, I wouldn't want that. I wouldn't be able to stand that."

We ate our lunch but I couldn't help but notice this boy certainly was next to being famished, so I asked him when he had eaten last. With quivering lips he told me three days ago and then he began to cry and sob like a baby.

We got off at the next stop and made some coffee and after he got some hot stuff in him he seemed to become more composed and cheerful and expressed a desire to go back home. So I told him we would see what could be done when we reached El Paso.

We had a wait of about two hours before another freight stopped. We piled on and just as darkness was falling on El Paso we pulled into the yards. We het[1] for a street that would lead us away from the railroad and to safety, for out of the corner of my eye I saw one of those police cars easing its way along the road that ran parallel with the railroad yard.

Somehow or other we found our way to a large park which, from what I could make out, was about in the center of El Paso. Here we sat down and we went over as to how my little friend could get back home to New Orleans. It was he himself that suggested I take him to the authorities and let them find out if he was telling the truth. So it was I left him with the officer at the Police Headquarters and bid him goodbye until the following day and—to make this account short—I saw him off two days after on his way home.

---

1. Slang for headed or searched.

"If," says the Chief of Police, "every man that ran across such cases as this boy's would only hand them over like that, we perhaps would have fewer criminals."

I put up at the Army YMCA and ate down on the Skidway, a street where you can have a fling or two at most anything and not be bothered by the Police as much as you might be in better sections of the city. It is on these streets you will find the cheaper grade of hotels, restaurants, and stores; and don't let me forget the sporting houses and gyp joints and honky-tonks.

This section of the city is generally the hangout for itinerant travelers, tramps, bums, habitual drunkards, and the general run of shady characters and down-and-outers.

Speaking again about the restaurants and the price of meals, I certainly wouldn't crow about the quality of the food—and I wouldn't recommend eating in them very long. But I will say that low-priced restaurants certainly have been the means of saving many a man from going hungry. They certainly were well patronized all through the Depression by those who were on the road and the unemployed.

El Paso, Texas is supposed to be the "Gateway to the West," but I fail to see how it can be called that. For to be the real gateway I think it is too far South and too far West.

The city itself is a nice place to stop over in, but for having any scenic beauty within its environs or its surroundings, it falls very short in comparison to, say, San Antonio. In fact all I could see was practically barren country and mountain sides; even the Rio Grande River was almost dry.

It is said that, "About two of every three people living or stopping in El Paso are sick," and I don't know but what that is the truth, if I was to judge from the looks of some of the people who seem to make the parks their hangout. It is almost impossible to get a seat if there is any sun at all, and, too, if I judge by the number of advertisements I noted in the local papers of the numerous sanitorium and hospitals, all of them private. They seem to treat about every known disease, but the majority have made tuberculosis their specialty.[2]

It is also said that, "Half the population of El Paso are pensioners," which perhaps accounts for the great number of aged people I saw on its streets.

The climate I might call mild but on my first full day I was glad I had an overcoat; but when the sun gets high it is quite pleasant.

In the two days I was in El Paso I saw more hobos, tramps, bums, fast-workers, hourlies, panhandlers, and dope fiends than I ever saw before in my lifetime. The police in El Paso are hard on panhandlers, but as for hourlies and fast-workers they seem to have the "Keys to the Town."

On the third day of my stop over I decide to move on, so by early noon I am on my way farther West, with Tucson, Arizona as my next stop and this trip should be the toughest of all if what I am told to expect going through this stretch of country is the truth.

According to some, it was a country of thirst and hunger and the toughest two-gun railroad officers this side of Hell; and for meanness they have no equal.

"Be sure to take a canteen or bottle of water and of no less than one gallon capacity, and be sure to take plenty of food with you for it sure is a hungry country," said everyone I had asked information of concerning the country between El Paso and Tucson.

The more I heard, the stronger did the desire become to see this land of thirst and hunger and real He-men. I had visions of cowboys and

---

2. The author was to die from complications related to advanced tuberculosis in 1953.

all that goes with a Wild and Wooly West. Now thought I, I was going to see something. I had at last got near to that land of my youthful dreams.

It seemed a freight would never pull out of El Paso, so anxious was I to be on my way, and when one did finally come out of the yards, I ran to meet and jump her feeling like a kid full of glee on receiving something he had his heart set on.

It was late in the afternoon, and from the time I left El Paso I was on the lookout every minute and mile as we rolled along into the desert. I expected any minute to see some swaggering two-gun railroad officer come hopping along the top of the cars, telling us (amid the barking of his two pistols) to unload pronto. But after about four hours of riding nothing seemed to be happening, so I gave up and put down all that had been told to me as so much bull s—.

We rolled along over the desert and about every three or four hours we stopped to cut out some cars or to change over to another crew at small divisions, of which I wouldn't ever bother to get off at, so uninteresting did they appear from the car I was riding in.

Chapter Thirteen

A Bad Night in Tucson

This trip was getting terribly monotonous and I had no hankering for food or water and, as for railroad officers, I didn't ever hear of any, let alone see one.

Why there should have been such a glowing account of this part of the country I haven't to this day yet figured out, unless it is their way of having a little fun at the expense of a stranger. But I hardly think so, for nearly every man and woman I talked with seemed to take their West quite seriously. They all seemed to have a tendency to exaggeration without knowing it. It just seemed that was the way these vast open spaces seemed to affect them. In other words, big country made for big talk—big ideas. As, for instance, I was told about a certain mountain I would see at a certain locality along this route: "Boy that's a mountain! Boy that is a mountain! Just wait until you see it, about eleven thousand feet I think it is," said one of my informants. But when I finally saw it, I was amazed to see only what might be called a good sized hill in comparison to what I had already seen before I ever started knocking about in this country.

They have a saying out West which goes in this wise: "We do things out here in a big way." But for the life of me I couldn't find anything done that could be judged as being out of the ordinary, unless they have reference to that much heralded hospitality that you often read about in the past history, or in fiction; and now you only read about in cheap pulp magazines. Even that seems to be in the discard pile, for if ever I had never seen such indifference to one another's sufferings, I certainly was getting an eye-full on this lap of my trip. It seemed to border on brutality in its aspects.

If it would cost them anything, even to a turn of the head, they wouldn't give you the time of day, so miserly are some as you get deeper into the West. And when you asked them how do they get that way, they blame it on the nature of the country out there by this alibi: "It is a hard country."

Yep. They do things in the West in a big way but it is generally done in reverse.

The police are a funny lot too, if you compare them with a well organized police force, for about half their time seems to be spent in worrying about the number of poor unfortunates and floaters and "winos," as they call those who are especially addicted to wine and found under its influence. And while they are chasing these harmless men from pillar to post or out of town, there is all kinds of devilment being pulled off right under their noses.

I arrived at Tucson late the next afternoon, tired and much disappointed in the trip, in the scenery along the route, the monotony, and the absolute lack of that I thought I was going to have in the way of excitement and thrills. To say the least it turned out to be the dullest lap of my travels so far going West.

The first thing I did when I finally got into Tucson was to look up some place to stay overnight. As I was going down one of its many streets, I noticed a sign of a certain organization that takes in itinerant travelers who are destitute of the means to pay for a night's lodging.

Not wanting to spend any more money than was necessary, I stepped in this place and after satisfying the man in charge I had not been there before, he gave me a one night stay over.

Now that my lodging was taken care of, I hied me to a restaurant and ate a good supper and then went back to the shelter. When I got back, I found the place I am to sleep in is on the floor of an old garage, and just in those few moments of absence the place was packed to its full capacity. I couldn't even find a place to stand up in, let alone lie down. Try hard as I might there wasn't as much as an inch of space between those who had arrived during my absence. So, not to be outdone of my share of space, I managed to squeeze my feet in between two of the sleepers and get enough space to sit down.

Unknown to me, if it wasn't for some paper that was on the floor I would have had a nice greasy spot clear across the seat of my pants. This I discovered after trying to lift myself up once in awhile by my hands to stretch my legs from their cramped position. My hand came up covered with what looked like lubricating oil. It can well be imagined without much effort what must have been the condition of some of those sleeper's clothes after a night sleeping on that floor.

Generally this organization had a fairly clean place with at least something to sleep on if only some benches or old mattresses that could be thrown on the floor. But this place didn't even have a covering on the floor and neither was there any effort to clean the place up. When you looked towards the street you could almost make out objects across the street through the cracks in the front wall. And there was no fire, for one of the men had been evicted for attempting to light one, so now nobody dared to try it again. And believe me it was cold on this night; cold enough to freeze over small water puddles in the road.

There must have been about two hundred men in that miserable, cold, ramshackle garage. Talk about packing human beings in like sheep; here they were not only packed—they were wedged in.

The position I was in forced me to get up whenever anyone came in or wanted to go out. Just to give those who might read this an idea of how many times I had to get up: There was no toilet so there was nothing left to do but use the gutter in the road outside the building. I only wished at that time I got just one cent for every time I did get up—I could have left that hellhole "well-heeled."

It was about the one hundred and ninety-ninth time I had been disturbed, and this time it was a late caller who had just come in. He stood in the doorway for about three minutes with the door wide open, no doubt to let in a little light to see where he was going. When he saw that crowd on the floor, he let out an exclamation of surprise saying more or less to himself, "God Almighty have mercy on us. O my God, isn't that terrible, gee whiz." Then he noticed me looking up at him and then he asked me if I knew of another place to stop in around this town.

"Sure, there is a lot of places to stop in if you have the price, buddy," I answered.

"Yes, yes, I know, what I mean is like this," he answered in an irritable tone of voice.

"No, Sir, there isn't. And furthermore there isn't another place like this in the whole U.S.A. Ain't this awful," I returned.

"I'll say it is," and as he finished those last words a light was put on in a little office. Whoever it was hollered, "Quiet out there! Shut up or get out."

"Shut up, did you say? How about keeping your own trap shut and who the hell asked you anything?!" said the man.

"Yes, I said shut up," called back the man in the office, and then he reached over and took a telephone in his hand as though to scare the man into believing he was going to call the police.

"Go ahead and call whoever it is you're going to call, I am not afraid of you or them. Who the hell would, and what attention would they pay to you who is running a place like this hellhole."

The man looked more closely through the wire that stretched across the opening between him and the man and then he put the telephone back into its place and pulled the light out and all was darkness again and quiet resumed once more.

The man stood there in the darkness for a minute or two and then leaning over he whispered to me to come on out of this damn place if I didn't want to catch my death with cold and exposure.

Now it wasn't because the man ordered me to get out of this place that I did. I was more or less curious as to who he was and why he was so friendly to me, a perfect stranger. In fact he had not even seen my face.

I got up and both of us stepped out into the cold air and believe me it really was cold, which certainly made me think I was up around the Canadian border instead of here in Tucson, Arizona, practically in the middle of a desert.

The first words this man said to me when we finally got under a street light were, "You were saying there were plenty of places here to stop in if anyone has the price. That's what you said, isn't it?"

"Yes, that is what I said, so what about it? Is that what you brought me out here in this cold to ask me?" I parried, for I didn't know this man from Adam, so I wasn't letting him believe I was afraid of him nor was I doing what he told me to do without knowing something about him. Yet he seemed a likable fellow but one never can go by what one sees on the surface. Knocking about, you soon learn that funny things do happen in the queerest places and at the most unexpected times, and to me this looked like one of those incidents. In the last two days I had had an interesting time of it and here I thought might be something worthy of following up to sort of make up for that disappointing trip from El Paso to Tucson.

We stood there in the cold looking at each other for a few minutes more, sizing each other up but not in a way to offend each other. After satisfying himself that I perhaps was alright he said in an abrupt manner, "Well, we got to get into someplace. Come on, let's see what we can do further on down the line." Having finished that short piece of logic, he said, "How did you get into such a hell of a place as that?"

I answered him by asking him, "How did you find it? Couldn't I find it in the same manner as you did?"

He made no further answer back while we kept on down the street towards the railroad station. Here we ran into a police officer, who stopped us and wanted to know what we were doing out in the cold at this time of night.

"Looking for a place to sleep or get under cover, if you must know," my companion answered.

"Well, why don't you go on down the street? There is a place there you can stay until morning," said the officer, pointing in the direction we had just come from.

"Yeah, we know where that place is. We just come from there and I wouldn't ask a dog to stay there," my companion answered in a tone of disgust.

"Well, that's the only place I know of here in Tucson, so the only thing I can recommend would be to walk it out for the rest of the night. Take your choice: Walk it or go back where I told you," and with that piece of advice he turned his back on us as if the interview were finished.

Realizing there would be no use in further argument with this officer, we took our leave but suddenly as though on second thought, my companion turned on his heels and returned to the officer. From where I was waiting I caught only the word "buck" and then I saw the officer spring into action by grasping the man by the collar and starting towards me, saying as he came on, "I guess you do want a place to sleep in and I am going to give it to you. We don't stand for panhandling in this town. You sure must be crazy panhandling a cop." As he passed me he gave me a piece of advice by telling me to get moving before he took it into his head to take me along too.

And rest assured I did get moving, for when a cop gets riled up like this one, you can be sure he is going to plaster it on good. You won't have to worry about a place to sleep for no less than ninety days.

"Well, that's that," I said to myself. It only goes to show how easy it is to get into a peck of trouble and for no reason. If I had been taken in it would have been my own fault, for I should have known better than to listen to a perfect stranger. "Well I know better now. I'll have to be more careful from now on."

Unknowingly I had wandered back towards the railroad yards and as I was getting ready to turn back, some one came through the fence and hailed me by saying, "Hello there!"

Coming out of the darkness as suddenly as it did, I gave a start of surprise but not out of fright. So instead of answering immediately I held my silence until whoever it was came up to me.

"Say there, Bo, where in hell can I get under cover around here? I am near froze to death."

I told him where he could go and on second thought I said, "Come on, I'll show you," and then turned back with him following me.

We finally got to the garage and practically had to force our way in, but we got in and got settled down in the best way we could, and that was a night. Or rather the balance of a night that I practically slept standing on my feet.

If ever I blessed the beginning of the dawn, it was on the following morning as I saw that faint streak of light in the sky and its gradual broadening into full daylight, and then the sun. Oh, it certainly looked glorious to me after that terrible cold damp night in that nightmarish place I stood up in. A thousand strained and taut nerves seemed to have relaxed as I stepped out into the open and daylight. A one ton weight seemed to have been lifted from my head.

My thoughts of the night's experience were soon forgotten when I was standing on the curb watching the men coming out of that awful dark place one by one. I certainly couldn't help laughing to myself, even in the face of such abject destitution and misery, as they stepped out through the door into the spotlight of the sun. It reminded me and resembled a single file of characters stepping right off of a comic strip in the papers, so ridiculous and varied were the combinations and colors and general condition of their clothing.

There was one old fellow who stood out from all the rest He was the last man to leave the place and just one look at him was self explanatory as to why he had waited until the last: His age and infirmity and the amount of paraphernalia he had with him would naturally be an impediment to anyone moving about the country on foot or riding a freight train. How he managed to get around would have been a story in itself.

I asked one of the men that was watching him if he knew who he was and where he came from, but all he knew about him was his name and that he was a "Desert Rat." "Arizona Charlie," they called him he had heard, but he wasn't sure that name was his right one.

When I heard he was a Desert Rat my interest in him was intensified, so I made up my mind that if I could find a way to get acquainted with him and to get him to talk, I might hear some wonderful stories of the desert and his own experiences in that vast tract of sand and mystery. That time spent listening to him (I thought) would be time well spent, for it would come first hand and not out of a book, so before he got away from me, I walked right up to him and said as though I had known him for years, "Hello there, Charlie. How are you? When did you get in, you old son of a gun?"

I might as well have saved my breath and the time for all the attention he paid to my salutations, for he didn't bat an eyelash. He didn't even look my way. He just stood looking straight ahead of him as though undecided as to whether to keep on standing there or to go on up the road.

The only thing I gained for my trouble was a good close look at him and a whiff of body odor that almost stiffed me. It was such a sickening odor, I had to turn my head and step back a pace from him. I don't know of any other odor that I could compare it with to describe it, unless it be that of rotten fish or dead decomposed horses. It seemed to be an odor all its own, so to speak.

We stood there on the sidewalk, he not even noticing and seemingly unaware of any one near him and I taking in every inch of him and his make up, and hoping he would at least mumble a few words to give me an opening for further conversation—but none was forthcoming. It seemed he had closed up like a clam and was not talking, at least not on this morning.

I judged this queer old character to be about sixty years old and perhaps a little older if I took into consideration the senility that was written on his weather-beaten face, and the effort it seemed to cause him to move about. As weather-beaten and creased was his face, so was his neck, but not with age, for I hope to never see again such a dirty neck, caked with dirt and grease. So thick was the dirt and grease it had cracked with the movement and play of the muscles of his neck. It put me in mind of a dirty old "crazy patch" quilt.

His hair was almost turned white and reached all the way down to his shoulders, while on his face he wore a full grown beard, both of which were matted and tangled and no doubt beyond ever getting a comb through it. His mustache and chin whiskers were stained with grease from food and tobacco juice and saliva. It would be a safe bet to risk any amount of money betting that he had not seen the interior of a barber shop for many a year.

I had seen about every conceivable manner of wearing cast off clothing, and the different methods of mending them; from using safety pins to using rope and white wrapping cord and even sticks of wood to hold them together, but this old fellow went them one better in his method of repairing any rips, tears, holes or any other breaks in his wearing apparel. He didn't bother with any pins or needles or string or cord or sticks of wood; he had ways of his own, which I must allow were quite original.

His clothing was made up of three different outfits, none of which fitted him within three sizes. Each was of a different pattern and color and texture, and all pulled over each other in such a manner as to cover the breaks, rips, or tears that might by chance cause any nudity. But there was one part of his clothing that seemed to outwit him in his efforts to close up by simple arrangement, for it seemed that of the three different trousers he had on none of them could boast of an entre solid seat, and here is where the inventive genius of the man showed itself in getting around the difficulty. All he did was to take a gunny sack and cut it in half and then cut or tear it into the shape of a half pair of trousers and then place it in position and hold this by a cord around his waist. By the same method, to keep it from flying rearward like a swallow tail coat, he tied the lower split end to his thighs. And there you have it: One good pair of trousers from three pairs and a piece of gunny sack.

And his hat, ah, that was indeed a work of art. I have seen in my time any number of shapes and contraptions used in making up the various styles of hats, but for originality in something different in hats, this old fellow had them all beat and then some. So odd was this creation of a hat, I took the trouble to make a sketch of it with the intention of submitting it to some milliner for the benefit of those ladies who dote on feminine head gear. One would have to see this original creation in reality to appreciate it, for being made up from three old hats it would be quite difficult to describe it in order to get a perfect picture of it in one's mind.

An old straw hat with the top cut out was used as a base or frame for the brimless crown of an old Stetson to sit on. This had the top cut out as well, while stuffed inside these two was the crown of an old black Derby. And then to keep all three in place, or to hold it on in case of a strong wind or perhaps while riding on top of a freight, he had an old Army hat cord attached to the brim and this extended down under his chin.

One would think that with an outfit that perhaps needed constant attention to keep it from falling down or from coming apart, he would have enough to do to keep it together, let alone toting around a lot of other paraphernalia that was tied around his waist and hanging from his shoulders by every conceivable kind of rope and even wire. This paraphernalia consisted of old gunny or burlap bags which were discolored by the greasy contents which were no doubt old bacon bits and so forth. In conjunction with all the bags and sacks, there was a small frying pan, a tin cup, and knife, fork, and spoon, all either hanging about his waist or, like the knife, fork, and spoon, tucked down into his trouser waist band like a "old buccaneer" would carry his scimitar or dagger.

After taking this quaint old character in inch for inch, I got to thinking that after all, perhaps I wasn't inspecting an old Desert Rat as he was believed to be, but instead I had been only observing an old "Pack Rat." But whether he was one or the other, I would have gladly given plenty to possess a camera on that morning, for I know I would have to travel many a mile to see the likes of him again. If ever there was embodied in one individual a counterpart or some little characteristic of all the other boys of the "Road," here it was, I thought, standing before me on the sidewalk in front of that "hellhole" I had slept in while standing on my feet. He was a combination of hobo, tramp, bum, bindle stiff[1], desert rat, and pack rat. I certainly would treasure a photograph of him greatly.

As far as the city of Tucson itself is concerned, I would judge it to be a nice place to stop over in; that is of course if you are paying your way. The accommodations for tourists are many and varied and I imagine quite reasonable, due no doubt to the competition that exists between the numerous tourist camps and hotels.

The population no doubt fluctuates considerably with the opening and closing of the tourist season. But like El Paso, it has a large percentage of people who have come there for their health.

The sanatoriums and hospitals are not quite as numerous as in the vicinity of El Paso, but Tucson is compensated by its loss in that respect by the heavy traffic of tourists and the business derived from the various government projects nearby. Too, Tucson is at the junction

---

1. A hobo or tramp, especially one carrying a bedroll or other bundle on his back.

of two lines of the Southern Railroad, one which goes direct west to the coast and the other via Phoenix, Arizona. This perhaps accounts for the great number of itinerant travelers that congregate and pass through it which naturally puts an extra burden on the police.

The climate is quite healthful during the great part of the year, but in the evening it gets cool and in the winter months, the nights at times are almost unbearable with their intense damp and cold. Of all things, they have some heavy fogs; some are as heavy as those one sees along any seaboard.

I wouldn't care to take up a residence in Tucson. I don't like the quality of hospitality that its people extend to visitors or tourists. It looks genuine on the surface but underneath it lies plenty of ulterior motives, especially so in the manner they have of trying to get all they can out of you and that runs all the way down to taking the last cent even from a poor wayfarer.

They are especially adept on calling the police on the slightest provocation and that is all I can say for Tucson, Arizona.

Chapter Fourteen

On to L.A.

The next freight out of Tucson will pull out around four pm and from what information I have on hand it is a hard job getting out of the Tucson Yards, but like a lot of other places there are ways of getting around the authorities.

Now there is an ice house and an ice conveyor under which all refrigerator cars that are destined for California are iced before they reach there. This is done to get the temperature down to a minimum by the time they reach there, before any perishable merchandise is loaded on its way east.

It is while the cars are under this conveyor and out of sight of the officers most of the boys get on and secrete themselves until the freight has cleared Tucson. After that you can crawl all over it while enroute for all the crew cares, or gives a damn.

Having some time on my hands, I walked a short way out of the city limits and got a fire going, made some coffee, and then took a snooze in the sun and came damn near oversleeping. I just made the yards in time and had to catch the freight on the fly at one of the crossings. That was the first time I ever tried hopping a freight while going at a pretty good clip. I saw the officer watching me; he was standing about half way down in the yard and I suppose he was only waiting to see me going flying through the air. I had my own misgivings about making it, but somehow or other I did it right, and from that time on I never worried about catching a freight on the fly. There is quite a knack in catching a freight on the fly but there is a limit to the speed at which you can accomplish it. I have witnessed men who had misjudged the speed go flying through the air—fifty feet or more—and some don't live to tell the tale.

There is a stop between Tucson and Yuma, Arizona, called Gila Bend and it is here where most all the boys stop over and clean up, or "boil up" as they call it. By "boiling up" is meant the process you go through in washing all your clothing to rid it of vermin and so forth. So not to be any different than the rest, I plan to stop there and do likewise, whether I need it or not. This place, so I am told, is the only place now left where there are any facilities. Here, I am informed, is a small-sized river and plenty of space for fifty men to light up fires and so forth.

Despite the sun being out the wind is quite cold and I, in comparison to some of the men on this freight, can consider myself very fortunate in having an overcoat. And still I feel somewhat chilly, which no doubt is due to inactivity.

We rolled along through vast sandy wastes, picking up sand and leaving it behind as though we had just passed through a fog or bank of heavy mist.

There were several small hamlets through which we passed and left in a cloud of dust, for this was another "Manifest" I was riding, and it seems the farther west I got they made better time than those in the East.

I grew tired of looking at the same old terrain for, as far as the eye could see, there was nothing but sand and more sand, so I rolled up in a corner and fell asleep. When I finally awakened I found I had slept all through the shifting of cars and now I am on one of the side-tracks in Yuma railroad yards and damn it all I had passed Gila Bend and missed the general clean up I wanted before I entered Los Angeles, California.

The Yuma Yards are practically within the city limits of Yuma, so I had very little trouble on finding the "Main Stem," as all itinerant travelers call the main street of any town or city.

Now Yuma is one of those cities that has very little accommodations that are within the reach of the average man who is out of work or on the Road, and its restaurants are somewhat prohibitive in their price. So after walking practically all over Yuma seeking a place to stay in and a restaurant that I could afford and finding none, I went back to the station. There I learned that right across from the station is a restaurant where most of the boys stop at going through Yuma.

So I hie[1] me hither and find it to be a little old shed or shack which on passing I took for a workshop. This place was run by a Negro and I must allow he was very reasonable. Here all the railway workers eat and congregate in between shifts and the incoming and outgoing trains.

I hung around in this restaurant as long as decency would allow me, and then returned to the station where the rest of the men were waiting for the next one out.

Yuma, I learned from bits of conversation I listened to and overheard, is one place and about the only place along the whole length of the Southern Pacific Railroad that puts thumbs down on any kind of itinerant traveler. Here they are all rated as common bums and treated as such even though they have the price to get by on. They are not wanted and they show their resentment in the crudest and most rude way.

---

1. Hasten

One fellow related to me an occasion of one restaurant proprietor refusing him service, telling him quite bluntly that, "He would sooner he and his kind wouldn't come in his restaurant and that he didn't want his money."

It is said that there is an understanding between all business houses to the effect that none of them are to help those who pass through Yuma such as hitchhikers and all the rest of those who could be classed as hobos, bums, bindle stiffs, and the general run of floaters. From all appearances they sure live up to it.

In a way the Yuma authorities cannot be blamed, for I had taken special note of a peculiar breed of floater that seems to hang around Yuma. To me they looked more like a band of bandits, yet on the surface they appeared to be just ordinary floaters, so perhaps there is good reason for their resentment.

Having four hours to wait for a freight and not wanting to hang around one place too long, I took a walk along the tracks. In my wanderings I noticed small fires down in a ravine and, wondering just what small fires would be used for at that time of the night, I started down the bank. Just as I got to the foot of it I tripped on something and went head first into a mess of pot holes. Luckily they were dry. I finally got clear of them and made for those fires. Surprise of surprises, I walked into the midst of a tribe of Gypsies. I excused myself and beat a hasty retreat and got back to the station and spent about two hours cleaning the stickers and burrs from my clothing.

There was a Jungle along the tracks in Yuma but I am told that it often happens that the Yuma River goes wild and erratic in its course. It has been known to rise so swiftly and suddenly that it is almost impossible to get out of this Jungle without being drowned, so it was used very little. When I passed it, it was overgrown with weeds and other vegetation one generally finds in wet or boggy regions.

Well I am nearing my goal and on my last lap of a trip across the continent and my own country and I am as excited about it as a boy would be on being told he could go and see the circus. So when I notice the rest of the boys easing their way into the yards one by one, I surmise it's train time. Not wanting to miss getting out of Yuma on this night I follow suit and soon I am on my way with the rest of those California-bound.

I rode out in the open. Why, I don't know. Perhaps it was just one of those times that some guiding hand picks out certain persons to steer them clear of trouble or gives them the benefit of their "one good deed a day." However, whatever it was, a guiding hand or some other unknown reason, it was well I did.

At the first stop I see from my perch the whole crew running along the train and stop at a box car near the end of it to order all of its occupants out. And then one of the shacks[2] climbs in and out comes a lot of fire and sparks. I suppose after being sure all was safe, he closes the door and gives a signal for the train to go ahead a little. Just as the caboose clears both the men and those who had started the fire, they hop on and leave them stranded, I should judge about twenty miles from any habitation.

This was the second time I had witnessed a lot of men stranded. It seems to be the method used by most all train crews as a punishment for taking advantage of a train crew's good nature.

After seeing that, I stuck to my place and rode all that night through all kinds of weather; from fog to rain, sleet, and little snow flurries, and if ever I wished I was sitting by some cozy fireside it was on that night.

---

2. Slang for Brakeman

The visions or even the very thought of a warm bed actually gave me the ague.[3]

I was riding on top of a car loaded with strips of steel that were not tied together and no one can imagine the discomfort caused by the constant vibration of the car and the shifting of that steel and the racket caused by the slapping and flapping of the ends that overhung the shorter pieces. It was two days before that racket ceased ringing in my ears: flap, flap, slap, slap, swish up and down. Gee, I was overjoyed when we finally pulled into a yard along which ran a highway. Believe me, I'll bet no railroad man in that section ever saw a man get off a freight and get onto that highway as quick as I did. Nor did he ever see a man walk like I did in making it, for, if ever a man had a sore seat, it was yours truly. It felt like as if there wasn't an inch of skin left, and when I finally got into a restaurant I couldn't sit down. I had to drink my coffee standing up.

This yard was in Indio, California. And here everyone I met told me I had better take a bus the rest of the way into Los Angeles. Rest assured it didn't take much talking for me to decide that would be the best thing to do, especially when they told me that it was almost impossible to get by a place called Riverside. That would be the place where the Los Angeles Police gets all who are foolish enough to attempt running the gauntlet of cops who wait for them. This I learned to be the truth, for about one month after I arrived in Los Angeles, I met one of the men who had rode that freight. As a result of sticking to it he spent thirty days in the Highland County Jail.

And so I spent one dollar and thirty five cents on the bus. After almost a month to the day I left New York City, I stepped out of the bus in Los Angeles, California, with four dollars in my pockets and

---

3. A fever or shivering fit.

in possession of a lot of experience and knowledge that changed my views of life in general. It was worth the time and trouble to obtain it.

Chapter Fifteen

Daytime Los Angeles

Well, so this is Los Angeles California. Now what? Will this be the place where I shall find a job? Will this be the place where I shall spend the rest of my days? Will this be the place that I shall learn to like as well as my own hometown? And most important of all, will it like me? Well, no matter whether those questions will be answered, there was one thing certain—this was new tramping grounds and it was bound to be interesting if only for that. Well, we shall see.

As I stepped from the bus, the clocks on the bus informed me it was just 4:30 pm; time for me to look for a place to get under cover. So I follow my nose and by watching the street signs I was going against the numbers. When I reached Fifth Street and Main Street I knew by looking down Fifth Street to my left I was in the right vicinity for such as I am, an itinerant traveler.

After I actually got down Fifth Street and looked around, I saw so many places to select from I didn't know which one to take. So instead of taking a room on Fifth Street, I finally selected one on a street a little removed from the main "Skidway," for Fifth Street was, I was told, the one and only "Skid Row" in Los Angeles. No one needed to tell me that, but I was too tired and hungry to take in any sights, so after I checked in a fairly clean "Flop House" and had a bath, I went out and ate and then went to bed and didn't wake up until ten o'clock the next morning.

The following morning was as beautiful a morning as one would want in their first day in a strange city. The sky was absolutely cloudless, the sun was balmy, and to one who had spent a month on the road, putting up with all kinds of inconveniences and hardships, it seemed as though I had just burst out of a shell like a butterfly just newly born.

The flop house I was staying in was only a half a block from Fifth Street and right in the middle of the district that harbors the majority of the riff-raff that stop over, or that have come to stay, in Los Angeles. By that I do not mean that all who live in this district can be rated as riff-raff, for just across the street from the hotel I observed some upright families.

As I mentioned, the flop house I was staying in was only a half-block from Fifth Street. I had but a few steps to walk when I was in the midst of the crowd and I had not turned the corner when someone walked along side of me and said, "Say, Bud, how about it? Are you carrying anything?" Meaning of course did I have any money on me. I don't like to refuse any down-and-outer a lift, but I thought he was asking too much when he asked if I was carrying any money, so I told him to get going. It would have profited him more if he had asked right out for a stipulated amount, but such is the boldness some men develop from years of panhandling.

I kept on walking on down Fifth Street until I came to the Southern Railroad Station and went in and sat down for a minute or two. It was while I was in there that I saw a man walking in between two other men (who had police written all over them) with one of those "Oregon Boots"[1] that they put on prisoners enroute to prisons.

I made a note of the fact and then started up the other side of the skid row. Then I really started to see the real skidway and its real habitués and their tactics. Fast workers all, they let no grass grow under their feet. They know when a strange face appears and for proof of their presence I noticed one of them wink at another as I passed.

I had always thought, having been born within a stone's throw of the Bowery, I knew the ways of slick and shady gentry. But in a day or two of observation on this street, I soon learned I didn't know the half of it. The old timers (and even those now) who practice their nefarious ways on the Bowery and Broadway in New York City couldn't hold a candle to these boys here in Los Angeles.

Talk about high pressure and the rush act. These boys are past masters at it and it doesn't matter whether the stake is one cent or larger amounts, the same system is used. It's a quick take. Easy money is their dream.

I thought too that New York City was about the only dumping ground in the country, but after seeing the mixed mass of humanity on this skid row and a few other streets, I'll have to admit New York City is pure American in comparison to Los Angeles.

I counted about fourteen different nationalities in as many minutes while standing on the corner of Fifth and Main Streets, and if you like the ladies, all you have to do is just mumble your wants and bingo you have five or six pimps at your service. Believe it or not, they have competitive prices. In other words, they put their women on the block.

---

1. A 50 pound metal collar locked around a prisoner's ankle. The prisoner could walk, albeit with great effort, but any attempt to run would break their ankle.

These are the ones who abide in a whore house. The street walkers were plying their trade as openly as if they were selling newspapers. I asked one fellow with whom I struck up one of those momentary acquaintances one often makes in the course of a walk how come there were so many of them in Los Angeles. His solution to it was he thought it was the subtropical climate that made them that way.

I suppose he was trying to tell me that a subtropical climate brought out a stronger sexual propensity than did a more temperate one.

The beggars, panhandlers, lush workers[2], and confidence men were on the make by the hundreds. I thought for a while they were holding a convention in Los Angeles, for they seemed to have the run of the town. The only place I didn't see them was in the middle of the street where the trolleys stood. That, and the trolleys seemed to be reserved for the pickpockets and there are some good ones here. They could take the laces out of your shoes while you were talking to them.

I was told I ought to go up to Pershing Park[3] to see the real thing. That was the place to go and see the cream of all the fast workers do their stuff. The League of Nations they call this park, so my informant told me.

That park would be some place to see if such was the case, so leaving Main and Fifth Street for another day, I hie me to this "League of Nations" as they called it. After an hour's observation, I feel amply repaid for my trouble, for I had only been seated about ten minutes when a pickpocket started to work on me.

I was always curious about just how one of these fellows really went about filching anybody's pockets, so I let this fellow proceed with

---

2. Petty thieves

3. A small park in Los Angeles formally known as Pershing Square

his operations and, when he finally found I had nothing in my back pocket, I leaned over and asked him how he made out, or did he get anything. I'll never forget how quick he jumped up and beat it out of the park like as if a thousand devils were at his heels.

If this pickpocket was one of the top notchers in that particular line, I thought he was very crude, for the instant his fingers touched me I felt them.

I remained seated and in an hour's time I was propositioned by no less than ten women and two men. Degenerates, and it was the last man (if you can call them men) that held my interest more than the ten women and the first man, for he was so insistent in his talk and the inducements were of a peculiar nature for one of his species (the male) to offer.

The first man I knew, from the crude manner of his talk, was addicted to cunnilingus, a most disgusting form of degeneracy. But this second man's inducements certainly sounded to me like those I had often heard were advanced by homosexuals. He was very well educated and stylishly dressed and lived in one of the best hotels and had plenty of money. According to him and his inducements, I wouldn't have to worry from then on. Seeing I wasn't falling for his line of talk, he started to get quite irritable and abusive, so I told him to get the hell away from me. That didn't see to bother him, so I had to get up and find another seat to get away from him, but changing my seat didn't help much, for not five minutes after I did, the man beside me struck up a conversation and gradually he drifted into making lewd remarks about women and fat boys.

I listened to him for about fifteen minutes and then I stopped him and asked him why he was telling me all that kind of stuff for. "Oh, I thought perhaps you would like a good time with the girls," said he.

"Ah, so you are one of those "pimps." Eh, well, I'll do my own selecting of women so get going," I said in a warning tone of voice.

This park was alive with prostitutes, degenerates, bums, tramps, pickpockets, snatchers, stews[4] and sharks and lush workers. But it seemed the degenerates were in the majority and most of the degenerates seemed to be very well educated, some to a high degree and well dressed, nicely mannered, and interesting talkers and well supplied with money. To those who might be ignorant of such things, certainly they would accept them as highly cultured people. Some no doubt are from very nice families. By that I do not mean that degeneracy is found particularly among the intelligentsia. It is also found among the uneducated as well and as practiced by them you will find it is of the lewdest and lowest in character.

This indeed was an interesting spot. It reminded me greatly of weeds in a flower bed, for the park was really beautiful in its way and nicely laid out or I might be more correct in saying, "The devil's own boys have taken over the Garden of Eden."

I saw some dope fiends pass by, some several times, all shaking and jerking for a shot or from just getting over a debauch. Their shifty eyes and erratic steps and nervousness gave them away to the knowing; all ready to kill if necessary to sate their cravings.

It was getting around suppertime and the sun was sinking and a chill was in the air, so I left my observation post or seat and started to leave this park that was so restful in its subtropical beauty, yet so base in its revelations of the extent to which some human beings can become so depraved.

As I emerged from the park my attention was attracted by a strange sight. An old woman was coming down the street with a pet rabbit on

---

4. Probably a reference to stew bums - habitual alcoholics

a leash and not far in the rear of her was another woman with a pet monkey also being led by a leash.

It was the pet rabbit that made me pause, for it was the largest rabbit I had ever seen in captivity. Too, the fact it was a pet struck me as being quite novel. Its ears were extremely long and its color that of a Belgian Hare. If I am not mistaken, judging from its size, it might have come from Australia or some other foreign land.

When the woman with the monkey came abreast the one with the rabbit, I was looking forward to a skirmish but no, instead of showing any animosity towards each other, they began to romp around and play like two kittens! A smart monkey and a very intelligent rabbit, I thought.

I retraced my footsteps back to Fifth Street and stopped on the corner of the street I was staying on and went into the restaurant and had my supper. There was quite a crowd at the counter and all the tables were in use, which kept the help pretty busy waiting on the customers. Naturally they couldn't have their eyes everywhere, so taking advantage of that fact, everybody was helping themselves to all the cakes and pie that were displayed on the counter somewhere, putting it in their pockets. If they had to pay for what they filched, the amount would have been greater than what they had ordered legitimately.

I certainly would not like to see what would happen to anyone who took it into his head to report any one of those who had helped themselves. It certainly wouldn't be well for them. It might be another one of those unsolved murders we read so often about in the papers.

Before I turned in I took another walk along Fifth Street and some of the streets crossing it. It was just as I was turning one corner I saw two young fellows trying to get a woman's bag away from her. One was holding her while the other one was beating her and pulling on the arm that she had the bag under. Apparently the job was taking them longer than they thought it would, so the one that was holding her pulled an empty beer bottle from his back pocket and started to beat her over the head. Finally down she went and down the street went the two men. The distance was too far for me to get to her to do her any good, so seeing the woman was not exactly knocked out, I crossed over on the other side and proceeded on about my business. I had seen enough in the last twenty four hours to know it's best to mind and tend strictly to my own affairs. I stayed off of side streets at night thereafter as much as I could, especially near the "Skid Row."

I circled back to the corner from which I had witnessed the woman being held up, and I picked up from the general conversation of those congregated there that she perhaps was only another whore who perhaps had been holding out on her pimps, so they took what they thought was theirs away from her. When I heard that, and knowing what kind of parasites pimps are, I couldn't imagine pimps giving a prostitute even a ghost of a chance of holding out on them. But I could, without even any stretch of imagination, believe they would hold up anybody—man, woman or child, if they got the chance with everything in their favor. For this form of making a living is in my opinion the lowest that can be followed. It's only a yellow cur of a man that lives off of women.

I left this crowd of people standing there and sauntered on down Fifth Street and went to my hotel—I mean flophouse—and called it a day. I turned in and fell immediately to sleep but not without a thought or two to the events of my first full day in Los Angeles.

On the following morning I tried one of those cheap restaurants where you can obtain breakfast for the small sum of ten cents. At first the food tastes savory but about an hour after, it starts to work on you and generally you are troubled with gastric disturbances for the rest of the day.

Fifth Street and South Main Street are lined with this quality of restaurant, and for the life of me I don't see how they get by the health authorities, for there seems to be no attempt at keeping these places sanitary. This doesn't exist only in Los Angeles, it exists in most all of the large metropolitan districts all over the country.

No one is forced to eat in these places, it is true, but that is no alibi for such neglect on the part of the health departments. Nor is the fact these restaurants have cut-throat prices any excuse for keeping their counters, food containers, kitchens, and even their employees in an unsanitary condition. I have been in restaurants where ants and cockroaches were running all over the counters and seats. In one place a waiter attempted to pass off on me a half cup of coffee that had been left by a customer. All he did was to warm it up by putting in some hot fresh coffee and that was the day I came near going to jail, for I let that waiter have the full cup right smack in his dirty tobacco-stained face. The only thing that saved me was there happened to be a five-cent movie next door into which I ducked after I left that restaurant.

And speaking of five-cent movies, this was the first city I had ever run across in which its movie houses offered such cheap entertainment. Here was a price certainly within the reach of all.

I had in mind to visit one of these five-cent movies later on in the day, but the events of my experience in that restaurant forced upon me a change in my plans.

Here again I was to experience the same unsanitary conditions as one meets in a cheap restaurant. Here one meets the same element that patronizes all of these cheap, chiseling establishments and, like the flop houses, all are not conducive to a hygienic existence. None created any incentive to try to live oneself a more abundant life. They exist only to catch those few pennies or nickel or dime that the very poor or the itinerant traveler or transient might by chance have to spare. Worst of all, they are very frequently used by transient or itinerant travelers to flop in, for they are open both day and night. And, too, like I did: For pickpockets and sundry other petty criminals to duck into when they want to get undercover quickly. No questions or scrutiny are bothered with—all they do is scoop that little old nickel in.

Now listen to what I observed in one of these five-cent movies on one night I spent in one of them just out of curiosity and to satisfy myself that the stories I had been hearing were truth or not. Some of them were revelations for boldness and loss of shame, and uncouthness.

First, there are no ushers to keep order and consequently the libertines take over the place to such an extent they show absolutely no regard for the comfort or a view of the picture being shown to any one but themselves. As for instance: I selected a seat about halfway down and in the middle of a row and just at the most interesting part of the picture the young fellow in the rear of me shifted his position and put his foot in between the space in the bottom. Not satisfied with that, he put his other foot up on the back seat in between and against my clothing, and when I remonstrated with him, I got an earful of abusive language to show me he didn't give a damn. And, for spitefulness, he plants the other foot on the other side of me. To argue with a young fellow of his caliber would be like arguing with a dumb animal, so I shifted to another seat in another part of the theater, and right alongside of an old tobacco chewer who used the floor for a spittoon.

When the program had run its full course, I changed seats again and this time near the main exit, for you could smoke in any part of this theater. Observing there was only one exit, I wanted to be sure of getting out in case of fire. This theater was without a doubt a firetrap, and while I sat there, I was disturbed once more by a middle age man asking if I would do him a favor. I told him that depended on what kind of favor it was.

"Just hold this for me a minute or two, please," says he. Then he handed me a small pasteboard box.

I took it and looked it over and I caught the word "syringe" in fairly large large letters. This I handed back quickly, for I am sure it was a hypodermic syringe and all he wanted was to prepare the ingredients preparatory to taking a shot.

"What's the matter?" says he when I passed the box back to him.

"Just this, mister. As far as I am concerned you can do what you want, but as for me, I'll be no nurse maid to a 'dope fiend' and I don't give a damn what you think about it either. That's all."

"OK," says he. And then he gets up and walks all over my feet; stumbles and falls all over me and mumbling something about he "has to have it, he's sick, he's got to have it," finally he manages to get to the aisle and there he crumples up on the floor. Two men pick him up and half-carry him away while his feet are dragging on the floor.

I was just about getting fed up and almost gave up hope of ever seeing an entire picture when something else attracted my attention. I was not the only one distracted by what was going on, for if ever I saw a young couple acting up with so little shame and indifference to those about them, here it was. Everybody around them was more interested in their lewd actions and behavior than the pictures. And this was no love match by any means, everything was there with the exception of the consummation of the actual act.

I managed to see the whole program presented and, having satisfied myself that all I had heard was well grounded on truth, I took one more look around the theater but for the smudge made by the smokers I couldn't get a very clear look at what kind of decorations were on the walls. So, glad to get out in the air and away from the fumes and odor that impregnated the atmosphere of the place, I got up and left the place feeling I certainly got my five cents worth.

It was near noontime when I finally got on the outside once more, so I walked on up Main Street, not so much to look for a restaurant as it was to see or look for more strange and novel sights. For this city of Los Angeles was becoming a gold mine of surprises and strange behaviors, and a paradox to me.

For every block I walked. I was panhandled and propositioned and on one or two occasions I was taken by the arm by girls who stepped from the doorways of barrooms trying to induce me to buy them a drink. They're one of the bar girls, which are called "B" girls for short, or "come-ons"—either one means the same if you fall for their line of honeyed words or their synthetic charms, and some are absolutely repulsive when you get a real close look at their make up in trying to cover up the lines of age and dissipation. Some are really good looking, but of these you will find them in the more swanky grill rooms. To give these girls due credit, those who make a living on percentage of the amount they manage to make a male sucker spend all are not prostitutes by any means. They might lead you to believe they are, and let you take certain liberties and hold you in expectation in the hopes you will stay longer at the bar and squander your money. It is after they find you are busted they either tell you they are not that kind of girl or they are married or it's time for them to knock off work, which is only a run out in a nice way.

South Main Street and Fifth Street are lined with such gyp joints. The liquor and beer is alright, but for being masters at short-changing you money, a government mule[5] couldn't show as much nerve in the open manner and ease with which they do it.

All the information I had received in regards to the "B" girls and the short-change artists in these gyp joints came from just one house observation while I was eating in one of these places at a buffet lunch counter. The meal cost me fifteen cents and I will say this for it—it was good.

---

5. Slang for someone or something pretending to be useful or helpful. From the promise of "40 acres and a mule," made to newly emancipated slaves after the Civil War. The mules provided were swaybacked and useless.

Chapter Sixteen

Los Angeles at Night

I returned to my hotel—I mean flophouse (but you don't like to say to anybody that you are staying in a flophouse, so you call it a hotel)—and took a rest by sleeping until suppertime. I wanted to see Los Angeles at night time. I thought perhaps I would see things going at full speed.

So once more I am sauntering up Fifth Street towards South Main Street and while on my way I am accosted by no less than five men who panhandle me for coffee and this is the term they use for Coffee and Cakes which can be obtained for five cents. I finally reach the corner of Fifth and South Main Street and turn the corner to go on down it when my attention is called to two men who have plainclothesman written in their every action.

They were standing by two pleasure cars[1] and while doing so, they were stopping men as the passed by and ordering them inside the cars. That made me pause for a minute and, as it dawned on me they were taking men right off the street, I turned and ducked around the corner out of sight, saying to myself, "What the hell is the idea of arresting men who seemed to be going along minding their own business? How can they do that?"

I crossed down to the other corner and watched them, and sure enough I had seen right. There they were, picking them out like a farmer would when selecting cattle or hogs or chickens preparatory to taking them to market.

When the two cars were filled, they got in and whizzed away on up S. Main Street. There were several other men watching them as well as I, and I overheard one man say, "The sons a b—s, they are at it again. The poor suckers didn't do anything and for that they get thirty days in Highland County Jail."[2]

It was all Greek to me, so I didn't venture to ask any questions, but I certainly was going to find out somewhere or somehow on what grounds men that were apparently innocent could be arrested on sight and without any preliminary examination or demand of identification. I wanted to know for my own good and safety, for under such police regulations I figured I might be next. And what could I do about it here all alone and with no connections? It suddenly dawned on me then that perhaps that was it. They were picking up men for vagrancy,

---

1. What today would be called a private car; one not displaying police markings.

2. Probably a mangled reference to a jail in Highland, California, a city in San Bernardino County.

or on that old excuse I have often heard the police use as an alibi to cover themselves up with when they take a notion to show they are on their toes by arresting a man or two. They call it "on suspicion" or "a suspicious character."

I gave the riddle up and continued on down S. Main Street, taking in the sights but keeping a wary eye out for plainclothesmen standing on curbs by pleasure cars.

S. Main Street suddenly became N. Main Street—just where, I hadn't noticed in my wanderings along it. However, I kept right on down the street and finally I came to a park and after walking through it, I came upon what looked like the replica of a small village. Then again, it looked like a beer garden. So here, thought I, was something to see that was different. So I crossed over and entered and found I was walking through a bazaar, or a replica of a Mexican village. Everything, I noted, is of Mexican origin.

It really was a bazaar in the strict sense that there were souvenirs of every description on sale of Old Mexico. But its Mexican atmosphere was more interesting to me than the idea of its creation or that of being simply a money making idea.

I could not pass on its many novel displays of pottery, personal apparel, little knick-knacks, souvenirs, and the general makeup or arrangement of the bazaar as being genuine. I wouldn't know, for I have never been in Old Mexico.

I spent about two hours in this place and ate my first tamale and that will be the last one I eat. I don't like them, and besides the pepper they use in seasoning them I think is injurious to one's saliva glands. It was four days before I could get rid of the burning sensation from my mouth. It seemed the more water I used to rinse my mouth out, the greater became the discomfiture.

I left this representation of Old Mexico (genuine or otherwise) and retraced my footsteps back to Fifth Street, but on the opposite side of North and South Main Street. I passed the Post Office and the City Hall and as I glanced up at its Tower I noticed it is considerably out of plumb. This I learned was due to earthquake disturbances.

I got down as far as Fourth Street (or between Third and Fourth Street) and I became a witness to another one of those raids on pedestrians by the same plainclothesmen I had seen operating earlier in the evening. The same sort of procedure was used, but this time they were taking in some pretty seedy looking men of whom I might say needed considerable assistance in the way of getting cleaned up both personal and their clothing. All this was happening right in front of a Mission, in front of which was congregated quite a group of men who no doubt were looking for a free night's lodging and an evening meal.

I put down in my mind that place for future investigation, for I had taken note of several of these places in Los Angeles and, too, they seemed to be pretty well patronized by all the down-and-outers and itinerant travelers. If I didn't find a job I might be looking for one of the places myself. One never knows from one day to the other just how things may go when you are on the Road and in a strange city. That made me think that perhaps I had better be thinking of looking for something to do instead of wasting so much time taking in the sights.

It was now around 10 pm, so the corner of Fifth Street and S. Main Street was going full blast. The winos were feeling pretty good by this time, if I was to try and judge by the number I saw staggering all over the sidewalk or sitting in the doorways or making themselves general nuisances to pedestrians by panhandling.

The "B" girls were working hard and fast and getting plenty of suckers. All the bedrooms were filled to capacity and the noise and din from the music was so loud and harsh on your ears as you passed them you would be led to believe someone was hammering on a lot of anvils instead of playing instruments.

Street hawkers were pushing their wares under your nose, begging you to buy. They were selling everything imaginable and one fellow, by way of getting me interested, stopped me for a match. While he was lighting the stub of a cigarette, he asked me if I was interested in any raincoats. "Three for a quarter—they are good—they are safe. You ought to carry them with you at all times in this town—you can't afford to take a chance. How about it, Bud?" "I can't use any tonight," I told him.

I knew what he was trying to sell me and I had accommodated one of these petty salesmen earlier just to help him out. But, when I came to open the little box or container this article was supposed to be in, I found it to be empty. So, like the cat that sat on a hot stove lid, one experience was enough. The cat wouldn't even sit on a cold one either, and I wouldn't buy any more from such petty gyps. To get stuck once is enough for me.

The pimps and whores and sharks were plentiful and all on the make, but they are easily sidestepped by just not paying much attention to them. If they bother you too much, all you have to say is, "Get going!"

I had reached Fifth Street once more and here I decided I had had enough for my second day in Los Angeles. After sampling that famous coffee and that famous in-between repast that pretty much every itinerant traveler falls back on when he is low in cash, I returned to my hotel and turned in. Before I finally fell asleep, I had made up my mind that on the morrow yours truly would see what this city had to offer a man who was willing to work. I had now only one dollar and a half left.

It was quite a while before I did fall off into slumber. Events and sights of the last two days seemed to be passing before my eyes as I endeavored to go to sleep. But that parade of unfortunates kept coming on and on and the scenes seemed to be appearing more vivid and endless as the minutes flew on. I could not help wondering what it was really all about, and naturally I fell to asking myself why such conditions and such perfidy should exist in these supposedly enlightened times. Then I fell to thinking along different channels: Perhaps, I opined, we are not enlightened as much as we think we are. And then I took to chiding myself for even thinking about it at all.

Still, it would be interesting to hear (or know) the answer to it. I finally grew somewhat sleepy and between fitful dozes I thought of the name of this fair city that had given me these two interesting days. The city of "Los Angeles"—if I am not mistaken, that means in Spanish, the city of "Angels." What a paradox, I thought, it was in comparison to the actual and real atmosphere of the place, for it seem more like Hades than a place of bliss where we have been taught angels only dwell.

Chapter Seventeen

Los Angeles - Obstacles, Red Tape, and Danger

I awoke the next morning to find Los Angeles enveloped in a heavy fog that was so ladened with moisture that every once in a while as you walked through it, it seemed there was small splashes of moisture dropping from it as if it was squeezed from a sponge.

The sidewalks were coated with what seemed to be slime, for as I walked up Fifth Street I had to take short steps like one would have to do while walking on wet ice.

I felt thankful for having an overcoat, for I noticed men all huddled up shivering in the doorways. Some didn't have a suit coat on, and some no doubt would go without breakfast, and there is a possibility some had carried the banner all night, as they call it when forced to stay out all night. You feel sorry and you look at these men and shake your head with sadness and only wish you could do something for them, but you say to yourself you might be in the same fix yourself. Then what? Well, why worry about anything until the time comes?

I had reached the restaurant I had found to be about the best for the money and my pocketbook, and just as I was about to enter, a woman's voice called out to me. I looked around and I saw she had a child by the hand. I turned and faced her and asked her what it was she wanted of me. She stood there looking at me as though undecided what to say. Finally she asked me, kind of stunned like, if I would buy her and her child something to eat.

I don't believe there lives a man who could refuse helping a woman out, especially when there is a child involved. I don't believe it possible they would if it was possible even though the woman didn't deserve it, for to refuse the woman under such circumstances would be to let the child down, and to my way of thinking the man would have to be terribly callous to do that.

I couldn't refuse this woman and child, so that morning I sat and listened to a story of a woman and child who had stuck it out with a man for five years, trying to help him fight his way back to manhood. Morphine was his enemy and nemesis. But just the other day, he cracked up and became violent and to save herself and child from fatal harm she left him. I believed her, for she showed me a diploma certifying she was a college graduate and a certificate proving she was a school teacher.

I was sorry that I couldn't have helped her more than I did, but I looked up the address of a certain organization which I knew would straighten her out. I left her with enough carfare and bid her good luck.

The mist is lifting slowly, so looking forward to as nice a day as I had enjoyed the day before, I start out looking for a job, and in only one hour and a half, I am washing dishes in a restaurant on S. Main Street, but it is only good for three days or, as the chef says, "Until the other man comes back."

This job netted me the munificent sum of $2.10 and my meals. If I was a diabetic in a hospital, my food couldn't have been weighted out to an ounce as close as they were on this job. I caught the chef ordering the cook to take off a half of a potato, saying, "That's all that is allowed; remember next time."

I was told my work was OK and to be sure and drop in once in a while, but I never did. Three days in that Hash House was plenty for me. Its butchery actually stank, and the food was heated over and over again until it fell apart—then it was used in the soups.

I spent the next four days looking for another job but without success. There were jobs but with no pay; the only thing you get is your meals and they fix the hours so you are sure to miss a meal. So for two meals a day you wash dishes or clean up for nine hours a day. You are always told not to come in before ten o'clock and when you do you will find all the dishes left from the breakfast.

My money was getting down to a few cents and I had no other alternative than to appeal to one of the many Missions in Los Angeles that take in itinerant travelers.

If the red tape I had to go through to be admitted into one of these "Bailiwicks" could be an initiation into the ranks of the down-and-outers, the derelicts, and all the rest of the riff-raff, I actually can claim a life membership. It took exactly four hours before they finally decided I was worthy.

The questions to be answered start practically from the cradle and up to your intentions for the future. After all the questions are answered to their satisfaction, such as they are, you can't help asking yourself what any of them have to do or whether they have any bearing on your simple plea for help. To tell the truth, they haven't, for whether you stay in one of these places one night or a month, you cannot find any connection whatsoever between the place and the information you gave.

After going through this four hour ordeal, you may (and you may not) get just one night's lodging, your supper, and your breakfast such as they are. And just let you look cross-eyed or make a remark or even a peep and an officer will be called in and you are out on the street again.

Now this place was one of those places that had been going for years. It was run by an old Englishman and when things went bad and the Depression had put so many on the street, the burden on this place was naturally increased. So, instead of perhaps two or three nights you might get in normal times, you now would get only one night once a month. If you came back again, you would have to go through practically the same ordeal. This no doubt is to find out whether or not you told the truth on your first application for shelter, and if there is the slightest discrepancy between the answers of the first questionnaire and the second one, you are told about it and then it depends upon the person you are talking to as to whether or not you are admitted. Generally you don't get admitted.

This being my first experience, I was more or less at a loss as to the manner in which men are handled, so I got two or three reprimands for one or two slight infractions of the rules of the Mission, but it doesn't take long to get yourself more or less adjusted. There is one thing I know that would never be able to do, and that is to get myself completely acclimated to this mode of living, for I don't care what anybody claims to the contrary, this form of handling men is copied from the system of management of jails, prisons, and institutions. Neither one of them are conducive to any form of uplift, nor is it a very pleasant environment even for a one night stop over. There is no attempt in segregating the sick or disabled; all are tossed into a heap, so to speak.

Some of these places don't require a bath, nor do some of them ask you to have your clothes deloused. Too, you may find the bed sheets have already been slept in, which when you take into consideration the filthiness and the possibility of some of the men who had previously slept in the bed you were given may have an active case of syphilis or tuberculous or other communicable diseases, certainly doesn't make for a very pleasant night's sleep or rest. You naturally will hesitate before you actually get into bed or between such sheets. There is a complication you surely will get in some of these places if you are not careful: Athletes' Feet. But as one old timer said, "These places are better than staying out all night in all kinds of inclement weather, at least. You do get off your feet. Yet, I don't know, it's a chance you take, and what's a poor unfortunate to do? They have you coming and going. The Hell with it! I have ceased worrying about it long ago."

That is the attitude most of the men who are forced to check in to these places generally take, who have spent years on the road in idleness.

It is only the men who have been suddenly thrust on the street by reverses that seem to be conscious of the conditions about them. The confirmed itinerant traveler seems to be immune to any abusive treatment or inconveniences or the unsanitary state of these places. For them, such conditions are everyday occurrences.

In the morning, my name was called out and I was ordered to report to the office. How on earth any organization of this sort had the information on hand that I at one time was connected with the U.S. Army is something I was never able to find out. It was a surprise and sort of had me in a bewildered state of mind.

"We cannot do anything for you from now on. This is no place for you. The U.S. Government has thirteen homes where they take care of veterans, so here is the address which you are to report to. They will take care of you," said the man in charge as he handed me a slip of paper and a business card with the address of the Veterans Division of the Relief Department of Los Angeles on it.

Now, thought I, what more could a man ask for? What a nice thing it was for this man to do—he had solved my greatest problem. Now my troubles were over. There would be no need to apply for or be forced to ask for charity. I was all set.

I managed to find the County Relief Department on the fourth floor of a building not more than ten minutes walk from where I had stayed the night before.

After presenting the note enclosed in a sealed envelope, I am told to be seated. After about a one hour wait, my name is called and I am told to enter a room and ask for Mr. ____.

Mr. ____ simply gave me another address with directions as to what bus to take and where to get off at.

So I find myself standing on Olive Street near Pershing Park waiting for a bus to the Soldiers Home, just fourteen miles away. Finally I arrive and present myself to the Headquarters there and bingo! I am told I should have gone to the Veterans Bureau in Los Angeles. "That," says the officer, "Is where you make your application for admittance here, but," he adds, *"I doubt even though you are eligible we could take you in, for we have no available beds."*

So, back to Los Angeles I rode and just caught the examining doctor and was examined and found eligible but, like the officer said, so said the doctor: "There are no available beds." And, so that was that, and also I was busted flat with the exception of seven cents.

I went back to the County Relief Office and explained and, boy, you should have heard what they would tell that bunch at the Vet. Bureau and those out at the "Home."

I sat there listening to them and thought to myself, trying to figure out how this bunch of loud talkers could possibly tell the U.S. Government where to get off at.

"Well," says the young woman, "I guess that's all we can do for you. Come around tomorrow. Maybe they will change their minds."

Yeah, come back tomorrow you say. Then I went right after her, by asking her, "Where am I to stay and where is that forty or fifty cents you made me spend unnecessarily? Why did that man in there send me out to the Home, when all I had to do was to go to the Vet. Bureau and now you dismiss me like as if my pockets were lined with money?"

She looked at me sort of dumbfounded and then she suddenly got up and called the man out and asked him if all I said was right.

"Yes, yes," said he. "That is right. Where else would I send him?"

"OK," the young woman said to me. "Just sit down and I'll fix you up. That's a darn shame. I'm sorry I can't reimburse you for the money, but here is a three night ticket. And be sure to come back tomorrow. Perhaps I can get you out to the Home. We'll see."

That woman was terribly provoked. I wouldn't be surprised if sometime in the near future a new "contact man" wouldn't be seen around that office, I opined as I hustled back to the Mission and presented my ticket to the manager.

"Three nights!" said he as he turned the ticket over and over. Then kind of grudgingly he said, "Well, OK."

I ate my supper, then took a walk up and down Fifth Street for a while, and then returned and took a bath and went to bed.

For some reason or other I couldn't get to sleep; something seemed to keep me hepped up. Something seemed to be telling me that something was going to happen—it seemed to be in the air. I felt at times (just a moment or two) that there was some impending danger nearby or soon to happen.

I finally fell to sleep, and sound enough to sleep through the talk and noise that is made by one hundred odd men getting bedded down in one of these places.

It was after the lights had been put out I awoke from necessity and got up and returned to the back of the room. On my return I overheard an argument going on down in the lobby, and it was a pretty hot one. That was why I got somewhat suspicious that it might be the police.

I listened for a minute or two more and I heard someone say, "Listen you, you keep your damn mouth shut or you will go along too for interfering with an officer."

That was all I needed, so, not knowing just exactly what this officer was here for (but I had my surmises), I gathered up my things and ducked back into the rear of the room. I raised a window which I had noticed the night before was an exit to the fire escape and crawled through it and then shut it and got on my way and then awaited results.

Suddenly, the whole building was ablaze with light and through the top of the window I heard the officer call out in a loud commanding voice, "Alright you guys, get up and get your clothes on and go on downstairs and make it snappy."

I waited another ten minutes or so before I attempted to re-enter the sleeping quarters. Instead of returning to the bed allotted me, I plopped on the nearest one to the window and finished the night out without any further disturbances.

In the morning I awoke and the place was still empty, so I washed up and went on down to the lobby. As I stood there looking around, someone came out of the office and stood with his arms akimbo looking at me as though I was some ghost or someone that had come back from the dead.

I couldn't help smiling. It looked so comical the way the expression of surprise flitted across his face while his eyes blinked and his lips quivered as though he was trying to blurt out a word or two, but just couldn't get them under control to form them to say anything. He seemed to be tongue-tied.

So, to break the ice and release the tension that seemed to have gripped him, I said in as cheerful a tone as I could, "Good morning, sir."

That salutation seemed to wake him up and after giving another searching look, he says, "Say, how come they didn't get you? I thought they cleaned up last night. Cripes, I tried to stop them!"

Just then, another man came out of the office and he also said, "Yep, we tried our best, but it didn't do any good. But how did you escape them? That's what I want to know."

"Why are you so interested in that one thing? You seem to harp on the fact I was not taken in—why?"

"Well, I don't see how they missed anyone up there. We don't know of any way you could have hidden out on them."

"Well, I'll tell you. I climbed through the window and sat on the fire escape until they were gone."

"On the fire escape? G— damn it, I thought I had that fastened! So, that's it, you sat on the fire escape. Well, I'll see to it that that won't happen again," said he and then retired into his office.

So I said nothing, but I did put two and two together and figured the whole lot of them were in on the raid and let it go at that. I went in and had my oatmeal (no sugar), bread (no butter), and coffee (no milk and no sugar) and then hied me to the open air and the County Relief Office.

It was while sitting in this office I overheard two of the men sitting across from me talking about the raid the "Tree Grabbers"[1] pulled off last night. One of them remarked kind of offhand, "Yeah, they got eight loads. Took them right out of their beds and put them in Highland County Jail."

Why I should be told to come early when it was nine-thirty before the first employee came in, and it wasn't until I called their attention to me (I was there and waiting since eight o'clock) did anyone seem to be aware there was work to be done.

After I explained my case to another woman, I was told that they had been able to get into contact with the Vet. Bureau and they were sorry, nothing could be done.

Well at least they tried, so I am once more at the mercy of the fates and I'll have to figure on a day to day existence. Well, I still have two days left at the Mission, so I'll cast away my worries, so to speak, but I'll be on the lookout for something. And even if it is just for meals I'll grab onto it and trust to luck for shelter.

Such was my line of thought as I sauntered on towards Pershing Square to take it easy with the rest of those who bask in the California sunshine.

It was after I had grown tired of sitting that I decided on a little walk up the street to see what they called the Angels Flight.[2] This is just a trolley car that is pulled up quite a steep grade. There are two cars so when one is up, the other is down. I suppose it is done this way to equalize the weight.

---

1. Unknown slang term.

2. In operation since 1901.

While I was watching this peculiar trolley, I met up with another veteran who claimed Oakland, California, as his home. He intended to go back on this very night. Says he, "There's nothing doing here, so there is no use hanging around."

Now, I happened to have the address of a man who used to room in the same house I once lived in, so I asked him if he knew him and was there such an address in Oakland.

"Yes," says he, "I know where it is." But he didn't know my friend.

We walked on down the street talking about things in general and all the while we were walking along I kept on thinking perhaps my friend might find me something to do. So I asked this fellow if he really was going back home and if he was, would he mind if I came along.

And that is how I found myself traveling along with this fellow towards the Glendale Yards to catch a freight to Oakland and San Francisco and the real Pacific Ocean. And, as I hoped, my old friend, and perhaps a job.

Chapter Eighteen

Oakland and an Old Friend

We jogged along to the outskirts of Los Angeles and on to the Glendale Yards. I noticed by my friend's line of talk and his actions he wasn't what one might call a man of the road. He took too many chances or, I might say, he worked too much in the open or he wasn't very cautious in his approach to a railroad yard.

However, he seemed to know the way, so I let him lead on, but I suggested he be more careful or else our trip might be interrupted by a sojourn in the Highland County Jail.

After watching very carefully for officers of the railroad and the cruising patrol cars of the Los Angeles Police, we managed to slip through the gate and into a boxcar standing on a side track. Here we watched our train being made up and in about a half hour we were given notice of its departure by two blasts of the engine whistle. Soon we were leaving Los Angeles like a shot out of a cannon.

There is a grade a short way from the yards and for anybody who is forced to ride on top in the open they won't fail to remember that grade, especially in the month of December.

Without any exaggeration, we maintained a speed of about sixty-five miles an hour down that grade. The wind resistance was so great I had to lie down full length on top of the car and, the air being quite damp and cold, I soon grew stiff from the cold. I was glad when we started to slacken up as the train started climbing another grade into what appeared to be a low range of hills. It being now dark, I couldn't make the surrounding country out very clearly.

It started to sprinkle a little rain and, in spots along the route it did rain pretty hard, which forced us to ride in between the cars. This is a very dangerous way to ride on freights, for you must straddle the distance between the two cars while standing with practically only a toe-hold on the ladders. And, too, your hand hold isn't any too good. The distance is too great to get a good secure hold for safety, and then you have to contend with the constant jerking and swaying of the cars. It is a style of riding freights I keep away from as much as I can unless necessary, like on this short trip, to keep from getting wet.

We rode the entire distance on top. It took us about ten hours to make it and we got off at the foot of one of Oakland's main thoroughfares.

If ever I make a ride like that again it will be under cover, especially in the Winter months.

Now for my old friend. I hoped he would still be here so, after walking around a little bit and being pretty hungry I suggested to my fellow traveler that he take one side of the street and I another for a couple of hours work.

"Well, OK," said he. "You go ahead and see what you can do, but for me I can't do that in this town. I am known too well here, but I'll meet you here in about an hour. I think I can borrow some money for the both of us, but you go ahead."

I had good luck in the first place I entered.

"Sure", said the man. "Here, take this broom and sweep the place out and then do the sidewalk, then come in and eat."

And I did eat. That meal was a real banquet to me; I was hungry after that cold wet ride of the night.

I met my new-found friend and he had a streak of good luck too. I shall never forget this fellow for being my idea of being a real pal; one that I could bank on and would be willing to travel the world around with. So far in all the many miles I had traveled, this man was the only one that didn't run out on me.

We went into another restaurant and had some coffee and doughnuts and after changing a five dollar bill, this fellow paid the bill and handed me two one dollar bills, saying "You might need this."

We returned to the street and stood there for a while and then my benefactor turned to me and said, "Well, Bud, so long. Hope you find your friend."

We shook hands and that is the last I ever saw of him.

Now for Oakland and San Francisco, California, and to hunt up that address.

This old world of ours truly is, as the old saying has it, a small world after all.

After I bid my fellow traveler from Los Angeles goodbye, I started out immediately to look up the address that my old friend had given me, but I wanted to be sure I was going in the right direction. I felt it wouldn't do any harm in asking the police officer who was directing the traffic for further information. So I stepped off the curb and, as I did, I heard my name called out from the opposite side of the street and lo and behold if I don't see the very man I am looking for—my old friend from New York City.

There is no need to dwell on how happy I was to see my friend looking so well. Apparently from his appearance, he seemed to be getting along, and he gave me quite a welcoming handshake and fired question after question about that "Old Hole," meaning New York City. For some reason or other, he just couldn't get acclimated to New York and the East.

We parted for the time being and he promised me I would live here for a week at least, and I was only too pleased to accept under the circumstances. For I certainly would enjoy getting my feet back under a family table and the environment of a home once more.

Well, I am all fired up for a week and a job, if, as my friend says, "the firm keeps their word." This job will be working for an installment house as a collector of back accounts. Having had some experience at this kind of work my friend recommended me, so I am to report tomorrow. So with that much encouragement to fortify me for a very pleasant first week in Oakland, I relax and proceed to spend an evening going back to when things were good.

I slept the sleep of the just on that first night under the family roof of my friend, and what a treat it was to get up in the morning and not have to go looking up a restaurant to suit my pocketbook.

I got up real early and took the car downtown and reported for work. After a few minutes' conversation I am put to work. On my first day I made a five dollar bill on finding the address of a delinquent customer who had moved and had managed to elude the rest of the collectors. I discovered also that he had a bank account, and on the following days I made from three dollars a day to six dollars a day. This job was only good for two weeks or during the holiday season; this would take me up to the first of January, 1933[1]. After that I would have to go looking for another job, but what is the use of worrying over things that may or may not happen? No one knows their days one day from the other what may happen. That is one lesson I have learned since I started knocking around.

My friend was a tennis enthusiast, so to humor him we played tennis until my feet were sore, but I enjoyed it, for that was the first time I could ever get interested in it. I still believe that a good game of basketball is as beneficial as ten games of tennis.

So the days went on until New Year's Day, which marked my dismissal from my job and the ushering in of the New Year of 1933. And what a New Year's Day that was. There was rain, sleet, and about six inches of slush to make it still more memorable. The cold damp wind that blew in from the Bay darn near froze you.

We walked up and down the main thoroughfare I'll bet twenty five times before the bells and whistles announced it was Nineteen Thirty-Three.

My friend, his wife, and I drank to each other's health and, as the clock told us we were now in Nineteen Thirty-Three, all of us were feeling our oats. That was the first time since World War One that I was under the influence of liquor and I was not alone in this state, for it was hard to tell who was the worst off.

"Well, we had a good time," said my friend in the morning as we ate our breakfast.

"Yes," said his wife. "But oh, my head."

---

1. This portion of the journal contains the only dates clearly stated. The start of the journal is estimated to be late 1932 based on the information given here. However, see the next footnote for difficulties with timing related to the Federal Transient Bureaus.

I didn't have much to say for my head was near splitting open with the headache I had myself.

New Year's Day being a holiday, all three of us went to church and returned. Not much was done but rest up and read and by eight o'clock the house was in darkness and all were sound asleep.

I stayed in Oakland for three weeks, but outside of the job and our New Year's Day celebration, there wasn't much of interest to me there.

The time came to say adieu, so on a cold snowy morning I left and took the ferry and crossed over to see San Francisco proper. I had taken a short trip one day and I saw enough to interest me and from then on wanted to see more of it.

Chapter Nineteen

San Francisco

San Francisco is a pretty busy place day or night. The night life (that is, of the street) is as different as day and night in comparison to Los Angeles. Everybody seemed to be pleasant and friendly. In fact, the contrast between the behavior of the people of San Francisco and Los Angeles is so marked in character, one would imagine he was in a different part of the country instead of still being in the same state.

I liked San Francisco from the day I made that one short trip. I like the people there if for no other reason they mind their own business and will at least bid you the time of the day.

Of all the cities and towns in the west and on the Pacific Coast, the people of San Francisco certainly are proud of their hometown. There seems to be more civic pride among its citizens than in the majority of the many I had passed through.

I had plenty of proof of what one citizen thought of his hometown who was giving a stranger a going over when he started to berate San Francisco.

"Well, I don't know," said the old fellow. "She's good enough for me. And if I didn't like it, I would get out of it. So, my friend, there are a hundred different ways of getting out of it, so why hang around it?"

From that I judged the old man thought San Francisco suited him, and from the actions of most of its citizens it seems to be mutual.

I liked the straightforward answers to your questions. There was none of that evasive manner you often experience in some places and, too, there wasn't one single man or woman I asked for directions but what knew of the place I asked for and all gave me the right directions. They knew their San Francisco.

I saw evidence of what havoc an earthquake can cause. There were some pre-earthquake buildings still standing; out of plumb but still serviceable.

The fortitude of its citizens is to be admired. For to see San Francisco now one would hardly believe there had been an earthquake and, too, it had only recently experienced a devastating storm.

I must have walked fifteen miles or more through its many interesting streets and it had turned dark as I returned to where I had started from. So, after making inquiries as to where to go for reasonable lodging, I was told that I was foolish to be spending any money when there was a good place to sleep in over on a street just five blocks away.

"It won't cost you a cent," says the man quite pleasantly.

I followed his directions and soon I am checked into one of the best Transient Bureaus[1] I believe the authorities ever ran, especially in the West.

---

1. Although John refer here (and earlier) to Transient Bureaus, the Federal Emergency Relief Administration (FERA) did not officially establish them (with the help of states) until late 1933.

I was welcome. That I could see by the words and actions of those who attended me. For efficiency I must admit it beat any other place of its kind.

Cleanliness seemed to be its slogan, for its floors were spotless and the sleeping quarters couldn't have been arranged more carefully if it had been built especially for the purpose. The class of men were so different in character and behavior I could hardly believe I was in a Transient Bureau.

Here in San Francisco a veteran is treated as such and they go to considerable trouble to ascertain whether you are or not. Thus it came about that I was enjoying a few more privileges and better accommodations than I would otherwise.

We didn't have any great amount of work, which gave me practically all day to look over San Francisco and for work. Now I had heard of a place called the White Angel[2], which I was told was in San Francisco some place. I had heard so much about it I wanted to see it, so in the morning I started to look this place up. It was two hours before I found anyone who knew about it and, after following my informant's directions, I finally reached it. But I couldn't get on the inside due to the fact I had no papers to show I had any business with it, so I returned to the metropolitan section and took a car and rode up to Telegraph Hill.

I do not know very much about the history of Telegraph Hill, but I had heard so much about it I thought that a visit to San Francisco

---

2. Probably the White Angel Jungle, the location of a soup kitchen founded by Lois Jordan (the "White Angel") in 1932, which fed over one million during its existence. Dorothea Lange's photographs of White Angel in 1932 helped bring to light the depth of the Depression and its toll on ordinary men and women.

would not be complete if I didn't at least look it over. So I did, and as far as having or seeing anything of interest there, I might as well have saved myself the trouble. However, I can say I was pretty well all over it and the section adjacent to it.

There was one other section of San Francisco I wanted to see and this was another section I had heard and read considerable about. This was the Chinese section, or Chinatown. If what I saw could claim to be Chinatown, I can tell those of San Francisco it doesn't even come up to par with other cities that can boast of a Chinatown. Perhaps the police have cleaned it up or else it was greatly exaggerated in its notoriety. The whole section was as quiet as the proverbial Christmas Mouse who ran up the clock.

About the only thing in San Francisco that held my interest was the two street car lines that run along the main street. It isn't every city that can boast of two different companies or managements. One seems to be controlled by a private company and the other I am told is run by the municipality of San Francisco, so there is created considerable friction and competition between the two. It was this that caused me to take special note of how each other were trying to beat the other to the fares as each company's car ran abreast of each other down the main thoroughfare of metropolitan San Francisco.

At one time I saw four street cars standing together; two on one side and two going the opposite direction. It was quite comical in a way to see one motorman putting on speed to beat the other motorman to a fare that was perhaps a block away. In such a case it was up to the motorman on the outside track to beat or get in front of the inside car if possible.

Some seemed to have preference to using the inside track car rather than the outside car, so if the passenger stood on the outside track waiting for the car on the inside track, the outside track motorman couldn't do anything but stop and let the passenger get on the car of his choice. And so it went on for the two hours I watched them, and perhaps has been going on for years.

There is perhaps a political aspect to this. Perhaps the competition is brought about to keep fares at a minimum and, too, perhaps the city has its line running so that when the charter of the private line runs out, the city line will just take over the city's transportation system and as a political issue use the low fare as bait for votes.

What ever caused the existence of the dual transportation system was not what interested me. It was the petty competition that they were resorting to. It looked much like the methods used on Bayard Street on which is sold considerable second hand clothing.[3] One can use his imagination for the rest.

It is now one week since I checked in the Transient Bureau. So not to wear out my welcome I decide to try Oakland once more for a job.

I couldn't even get a promise of one in San Francisco, there was nothing doing for one not a citizen, and in a way I admired them for that.

The following morning I checked out of the Transient Bureau and crossed over to Oakland on the ferry and applied at the office of an organization of which I belonged for work. This organization took care of veterans by running a small employment office and sometimes you do run across some pretty nice jobs.

"Yes," said the young lady behind the desk. "I think I have the very job for you." At the same time she reached for the telephone and called someone up and after a few words back and forth I was told to wait.

The party must have been in the building or very close by for not ten minutes elapsed when a woman came bustling in as though her life

---

3. Bayard Street is located in Manhattan's Chinatown district.

depended on getting in on time. I thought at first she was an employee, but when she walked right over to me and said, "Well are you ready? If you are, we will leave immediately. I must get back to the ranch right now," I didn't know just what to say. She didn't even mention a single thing about what kind of job or how much she paid or anything pertaining to the job. All she seemed worried about was she wanted help. The rest could or would take care of itself.

But after a minute's thought and after I got over the effect of her rush act, I had entirely different ideas. I wanted to know more about the job—how much pay there was in it, and what kind of work it was for. What was the use of going blindly into something you weren't sure you could do? And if on finding you are not satisfactory in the performance of the work you may find yourself perhaps fifty or sixty miles back in a county that would take you a week to get out of. According to stories I had heard, I wouldn't be the first man to have such an experience.

So when I asked for particulars in regards to this job I was told there will be no pay and the nature of the work would be such that it wouldn't take much to figure out the hours I would have to put in for no pay. It undoubtedly was a sunrise to sunset job as far as the hours and work was concerned.

What amazed me was that, in spite of having a thirteen room house, eight boarders, two hundred and fifty orange trees, fifty milk cows, two automobiles, and I don't know how many acres of land, the most of which was now being cut (alfalfa being the crop), for which she claimed she didn't get very much for (so she claimed), there was no pay. From the revenue of the above sources I felt she could at least pay something, but she claimed she couldn't so I told her I was sorry I didn't want a job like that.

She was quite put out and left the place in a huff, slamming the door as she went out and got into her Packard and looked back in my direction with a sneer, as though to say, "Just like all you men."

The clerk asked me for an explanation of her actions, so I told her and the clerk said, "I don't blame you, and she need not ask for any more help here. The very idea of asking a man to work only for bed and board."

There was an awful lot of this sort of business all along the line, especially along the route starting from New Orleans, Louisiana and on to Los Angeles, California, but not quite so bad further on near the locality I was now in.

I just can't get the idea why people should ask anyone to work for no remuneration unless perhaps they are taking advantage of the scarcity of work and the person's destitution. It seems anyone doing so must have to be quite petty in their minds and business deals.

I felt there was no use of hanging around Oakland or San Francisco any longer, so I made one more call on my friend and his family and on the following morning I caught a freight back to Los Angeles.

Well, I certainly cannot complain in regards the fruits of my visit to Oakland. Everybody was very kind and more than willing to help me out if they had any way of doing so. My pocketbook could show plenty of evidence to the fact. I had more money to fall back on for shelter and subsistence and certainly fifty times more than when I started out from New York City now more than a month ago.

Chapter Twenty

A Coastal Trip and An Escape

This short trip back to Los Angeles could be classed as a pleasure trip in comparison to any other. I had the means of subsistence, so I was riding a freight like a rich uncle in the disguise of a hobo, so to speak.

As luck would have it, I caught a freight that was to take the coast route to Los Angeles, but I was unaware of it until we stopped on the summit of a range of mountains from which I could just make out in the distance the vast expanse of the Pacific Ocean.

It was at this point or summit where all freights are rearranged preparatory to making the descent to sea level. This is done by dividing the train into two parts and inserting an extra engine in the middle, then another extra engine on the tail end. Thus you have a freight train that can't run wild or buckle as it descends on down the steep grade to the sea.

To say the least of this railroad, I think it was a fine piece of railroad engineering. There were places that all you had to do to see both ends at the same time was just to peep outside the door of the car you were riding in. At one place I'll swear the curve was half an arc in degrees, and at another place I think we ran under our own track. This I am not sure of for it might have been another railroad line.

The scenery was worth coming thousands of miles to see, for to me it was nothing short of marvelous and awe inspiring. The valleys and ravines through which we traveled and rolled over were so deep they made me dizzy as I looked down into their depths. I gasped for breath and a feeling of fear gripped me as I gave thought to a possibility that the train might by chance be derailed and hurled through the air and down into their depths. Then again I felt that sensation one feels in the stomach when one descends in an elevator, for at times it seems the box car I was riding in was suspended in midair like some airship.

There were times too that the hair on the back of my neck came near standing straight up, for going around some of the curves, I thought the speed was too fast for safe riding. But nothing alarming happened; we just rolled and rolled on down through that gorgeous scenery until suddenly we shot out of the mountains into the open like as if we were emerging from an arbor covered and overhung with verdant vines.

That short descent through that glorious bit of scenery was worth more to me than any or all of the scenery I had seen in the thousands of miles I had so far traveled.

We are now back to sea level and traveling on the shore of the sea. The Pacific Ocean is calm; not a ripple is on its surface. It looks like a mirror covered (or sprinkled) with powdered sugar. The sun is gradually sinking down into it like a ball of molten metal into a puddle of quicksilver. And as to give the whole scene a touch of life, a flock of seagulls are flying low over its surface. But as they pass, they look as though they were pasted on it like silhouettes on orange-colored glass.

I was somewhat disappointed in this scene of a setting sun. There seemed to be an absolute lack of color (or combination of colors) that, according to all the descriptions I had ever read, should accompany such a scene. There was no purples or blues or magenta or cerise.[1] All I could make out for color was the fury red of the sun itself. And yet the sky was cloudless.

After the freight was back to its normal arrangement, we pulled out of the small yard (or set of tracks) and proceeded on down the coast.

It was dark before we reached any habitation where the freight stopped for any length of time. At the first stop, I ate my supper with the crew of the freight. But I naturally kept my distance for, while a crew may shut their eyes to anyone riding, that doesn't mean they are not aware of your presence, so it's best not to show any friendliness even when off railroad property. There may be inspectors around.

I was surprised by the few men that were riding on this freight. I don't believe there were more than six all told, and every one of us seemed to keep to ourselves, which was another reason I was enjoying this return trip to Los Angeles.

If I am not mistaken, this first stop was at San Jose. We tarried here about half an hour or just time enough to grab a bite to eat, as I related a line or two ago.

I had heard considerable about this city, but a half hour is hardly time enough to get one's bearings, let alone get any idea of what a place looks like. This city, if I am not mistaken, is the site of a cult or philosophical society known as the Rosicrucians, of which at one time I was interested in.

I felt sorry and considerably disappointed this trip had to be finished under darkness, for along this famous sea coast are some of the

---

1. A deep reddish pink.

old points of habitation in this country. The history of this particular section of California dates back to the early 1700s. It was then that this part of the coast was opened up by Catholic priests and some of the old mission churches still stand. It was these I wanted to see very much. I had half a mind once or twice to get off and make this trip in relays, with the idea of seeing the entire route, mission and all, and be done with it. But I gave up the idea on second thought, leaving this part I was covering under darkness for some other time. And I was rather anxious to get back to Los Angeles and give the Soldiers' Home another try, and from there I could take side trips to places such as I was passing on this night. It would give me something to do, I thought.

We continued on towards Los Angeles at a fair rate of speed, weaving in and out according to the shore line. There were times we seemed to be riding over the sea and in due time we finally came to another stop called San Lucas.[2]

It was while we were standing here my attention was called to another (and an entirely different) scene formed by the reflection of the moon on the sea. Now instead of that dull leaden look it had when the sun was setting, it now looked like a silver mirror or a glass reflector, which threw almost enough light to enable me to read a railroad map. The most interesting part of this night scene was the ever changing effect the action of the water gave to its surface—from a solid disc of silver to one of black and silver and then breaking up into grotesque patterns of all sorts and too at times giving off an effect of a gigantic picture puzzle of the "Man in the Moon."

Once more we are rolling along the sea and according to my map a place called Paso Robles Hot Springs is the next stop.

---

2. A stop on the Southern Pacific Railroad located in Monterey County.

It was between San Lucas and our next station I observed oil wells quite a distance from shore. These oil wells I had read about and from reports and statistics were producing to the satisfaction of their owners.

All along the route I had taken note of some elaborate yachts and yacht clubs. There were more motorboats than sailboats moored to their buoys or tied up to runways that run out to sea.[3]

We are now going along a very narrow strip of shore and the hills on my left are casting their shadows so far out on the water everything seems to be obliterated by darkness. It is almost pitch dark.

We passed through Paso Robles and on to San Luis Obispo.

As we approach it, I can see off in the distance lights on the opposite shore that seem to twinkle like little stars on a frosty night. I can't make out any objects so I am not sure whether they belong on shore or on ships or harbor craft.

San Luis Obispo is another place we just sailed through as though it was a place to be avoided. I saw its lights as we approached it. I saw only a blur as we went through it. And then once more, I saw them disappearing in our rear.

Apparently we had made all the stops this freight had on its schedule, for we just picked up speed and more speed, until I finally saw the reflection of the electric signs of Los Angeles in the sky. In spite of the wonderful day I had on this trip, I was quite pleased to be so near its end.

The only unpleasant part of this trip was now at hand, for at this end of the route was the most dangerous to an itinerant traveler than

---

3. Obviously John was not familiar with piers. His two sons would have much more familiarity with the sea.

all the rest of the railroad yards in California. This spot was really "hot."

So yours truly will have to be damn careful and then some if he don't want to see the inside of that "tank" in the Highland County Jail.

The freight is slacking up in speed so I prepare to drop off before we enter the yard. It is pitch dark on the side I must get off, so I don't know whether I will land in an irrigation ditch or a batch of thistle, or just plain road bed. But it is a chance you must take or get caught in a trap, for this yard is enclosed with a seven or eight foot wire fence and there is only one way out and that point is right on the main highway.

Well, here goes.

It was a ditch alright, but not a wet one. This gave me a soft path to walk on as I watch along the tracks for a fence I can climb over into someone's backyard. Here I stop to listen and, not hearing even the bark or whine of a dog, I hasten by the house along their driveway on the soft grass onto the street. Well, so far so good. Now for a trolley and all will be OK.

I don't believe there was ever a person who had walked along this particular highway but what sometime or other they are either watched or stopped by the ever-present police. The highway seems to be their pet tramping grounds and on this night they didn't miss me, as careful as I was.

I had only walked fifty feet along the sidewalk when one of those Highway Patrol cars edged up to the curb and, as it slid to a stop, one of the officers stuck his head out and said, "Hey, you! Come over here. Where do you think you're going?"

I didn't know just what to do, whether to heed his command or turn about and run back through a yard into the railroad yard again. The only thing that stopped me was, I believe, a little thought that suddenly ran through my mind. I had visions of being shot and in that case, if I was, it wouldn't be worth the chance. So I walked over to him and said, "Hello there. Say, what time is it, please? I've got to get to work. I'm late now."

The officer looked at his watch and informed me it is exactly nine-fifteen.

On hearing the time I said, "Holy Mackerel! Damn! I'll have to hustle. So long. Thanks!" And then I heard the trolley coming and, looking ahead of me, I saw a car stop and I ran to it and just got there in time.

These two officers were not so easily shaken off as I thought they were, for after I got on the car and had got nicely seated, I notice them riding right alongside the car. One kept watching the exit at every stop, the other scanning the windows. I was sure they were trailing me to see if I really was going to work as I said. In substantiation of my fears, they kept right after the car and when I stepped off it near the city hall they were parked right at the curb.

Right near the city hall a block aways is a daily newspaper office, so to keep them thinking I really was going to work, I made a beeline for it. Sure enough, I saw the car trailing me on up the street. Boy, I was glad the door was open in the office building, for I fairly knocked it off its hinges as I lunged through it and ran at a half trot up a pair of stars, listening every second to hear that door swing open. But after ascending two flights, I heard nothing, so I stopped and started to come on down cautiously, and, seeing the coast was clear, I looked around and found another door that opened on an alley and through it I ducked to safety.

That was one night I escaped doing thirty days for vagrancy and thirty additional days in jail for trespassing on private property, and saved the fifty odd dollars I had in my pockets.

You should have seen me hotfooting it down one of Los Angeles' main thoroughfares that night, heading for that hotel (or flop house) to get under cover and off the street. I didn't even stop for the traffic lights, I was so occupied with the thought of completing my escape and to make sure I was really safe.

I was wringing wet with perspiration and so exhausted from exertion and anxiety by the time I reached the room I was given, I had to lay down immediately on entering it. It was two hours before I felt able to get up and go out and eat.

Boy, what a day this has been, I thought as I lay there thinking over the events of the past ten or twelve hours.

Beautiful mountain scenery, marvelous sunsets, and equally spectacular moon-lit seas, oil wells out on the sea, missions hundreds of years old. Money in my pocket. No worry about shelter or food. Riding alone—no "gimmes" or "have you"s from every rider on the train. And to bring the day to a climax, I am challenged by the police, for whom I managed to stay out of their clutches by a little subterfuge; they have suspicions, so I am trailed and once more I escape them, and here I am. Well, here's to a thousand more such days in the future. I could go on living quite happily if all the rest of my days were to be like this one. Gee! What a wonderful day!

Chapter Twenty-One

A Very Close Call

It was almost ten o'clock when I awoke on the following morning, feeling better than I had felt for years. It seemed I had awakened into a different world; everything seemed to be just right. I felt thankful for having such good luck as I had experienced on my trip to Oakland and back here once more to Los Angeles.

Even when I emerged from the hotel, the sun seemed so warm and soothing. As I sauntered on towards Fifth Street, everybody seemed to have a smile on their face.

As I entered a restaurant for my breakfast, the cashier even said, "Good Morning, Sir."

But, through all this good feeling, there was just a little discordant strain running through it all. It sounded like little voices whispering something I just couldn't make out clearly. They were jarring sort of sounds and then suddenly something made me think of New York City. Then the little whispering voices became more clear and then took full concord when the word "Home" ran through my mind. So that was it, thought I.

Thus it was I decided that if I couldn't, on this day, find some way of getting admitted to the Soldier's Home, I would start back on a return trip for good old New York City in a day or two.

I had one important thing to do above all others. I must pay back that two dollars that was so kindly loaned to me by that fellow in Oakland. So, after eating, I started out to look around Fifth Street for my friend who left me so suddenly in Oakland. After about an hour's hunt around some of the places I thought he might be, I gave it up. So now my mind was at ease. I just couldn't go ahead before I tried at least to find him, for when you are on the road you can never tell where you may be one day from the other. So I wanted to meet him, pay him, and thank him for his kindness.

I am now free to follow up the business I would have by trying once more to get in the Home. So, after making a few inquiries about where the American Legion had their headquarters in Los Angeles, I am informed I would find them in the Patriot Hall on South Figueroa Street. I follow directions given as to how I would get there. I step out as it is getting towards noon and I want to catch who ever happened to be in before they left for their dinner.

I arrived there in good time and soon was talking to the contact man, who by the way was very courteous and attentive in every respect. I presented my membership card and from then on he did his level best to get me in that home, but with no success. Well, I couldn't ask for any more effort on his part. These men can only go so far.

Well, that was that. As I was preparing to leave the office, he called me back and handed me a card for one week's lodging and meals. The funny part of it was the lodging was made out to the very place I had always stayed at since I came to Los Angeles. The meal ticket was made out to the restaurant right on the next corner.

Well, I am now all set for one week more if I care to use it.

I handed the lodging ticket in as I checked in that night and got credit for it. I didn't have to do that with the meal ticket, for it was punched out as I used it. Well, now for another try for a job.

My experience has been that looking for a job is one of the most trying experiences anyone can possibly go through. The climbing and walking and talking and being turned away is tiring and discouraging. You start out with high hopes. You even will plan this and that if you get one, only to finish the day and return to your hotel pretty well done up and worried. So it was after I canvassed Los Angeles pretty well all over it for three days. I gave it up as useless and packed up what I had and prepared to leave on the fourth day, and went to bed out of sorts and a little disgusted with myself and Los Angeles.

I am feeling better about things.

I ate breakfast on my meal card and then looked around for some other veteran who might be down and out. I found one who seemed OK to me, so I took him into the restaurant and talked to the manager and told him to let this veteran eat on the card. He agreed, for if he didn't he would lose just that much business. As far as he was concerned it made no difference who ate on it. I couldn't make any headway with the hotel manager, so I called up the contact man to charge on the hotel for one night only. He thanked me and claimed that if every veteran did that a lot of money would be saved in favor of the American Legion.

Well, I am all set now for the return trip back to New York City.

I walked out to where all the hobos hang out, and by 3 o'clock pm I was on my first lap of my return trip. The "Fee Grabbers"[1] were around and tried to keep us moving away and off railroad property in the hope we wouldn't be able to catch that freight. Most of us did keep on the go, but none of us moved too far away. The freight finally came down the line and all of us made a run for it. Most all of that gang got on. It being a local, it was short and from the time I got onto it, it stopped at about every telegraph pole, all the sidings, and small towns. We passed through the small station of Alhambra and, when just outside of town, it went into a side track and stopped. What I couldn't figure out was that no passenger went by on the main track. No fast freight came along either. I suppose that train crew had so many hours to put in and they were in no hurry. We stood there for one hour.

This line of track ran right through that part of the countryside I missed when I changed from the railroad line to a bus when I first arrived here. So now I had a chance to see it. There were orange and walnut and lemon groves all around us. Here and there I could make out the ranch houses among the trees. All seemed to be painted white and green which made them blend well with their surroundings. The driveways and walks to the groves and outhouses and highway were lined with palm and eucalyptus trees. I didn't see any ripe fruit in any of the groves, so I just sat in the door of the freight train taking it all in.

Well, the freight is on its way again, but it only creeps along.

I wished now I had waited a little longer for a faster one, but as is often heard among the hobos, "We have no particular place to go, so what is the hurry?" We finally arrived in Ontario and here we

---

1. Probably a term for non-railroad law enforcement.

were chased off by an officer who, by his uniform, looked to be from Ontario itself. I got off right in front of him. He gave me one look and said to me, "Do you see that row of eucalyptus trees along that street over there?"

"Yes sir, I do," I answered back in my most respectful tone.

"Well, if you want to be helping the rest of the bums we took in yesterday who got 90 days each for riding this very freight, why just let me see you around here when I come back. So get and get pronto, or else you will be trimming them too."

So I got and as fast as I could, for 90 days out here means 90 days and how. From what some of the boys tell me who have had that experience, I wouldn't relish it under any circumstances whatsoever.

Now, here is one time that a police officer did me a favor and perhaps saved my life. If I ever go through there again, I am going to look him up and thank him.

I found the highway and started to walk around the end of the town with the idea of trying to catch a passenger (and ride it blind[2]) that one of the boys informed me would be along in a few minutes. We planned to catch it as she left the station, but when we got near the station there was that officer coming right along to keep anyone off who might try it. He didn't see us, but I heeded his warning and made sure he didn't see.

So, back to the highway again, and this time I stayed there. It was dark by now, and it was no use trying to signal for a ride. I plodded along and, after a couple of miles of walking, I stopped to rest in a little waiting station in a vineyard. I hadn't got seated for more than ten minutes when I noticed an ambulance going by with a doctor's car

---

2. Riding between the baggage car and tender where one couldn't be seen.

following. I thought nothing of it until I saw the highway was getting pretty well crowded with all kinds of cars, all going by at a dangerous speed, I thought. It wasn't long before the ambulance came back at top speed, so I stepped out on the highway and looked on down the road to see what had happened. I could see not even two blocks away the highway was jammed with cars.

I walked on down towards them and as I got closer I noticed a few cars coming out of a side road that ran through the vineyard. I finally came abreast of the side road and waited until a line of cars passed, then I crossed over and proceeded down the side road and after a short distance I ran onto a scene that gave me somewhat of a shock, believe me.

For there I saw piled into the sand the passenger train I tried to catch and ride blind only an hour or two ago. She was late, so I was told, and of course trying to make up time. The engine and tender were doubled up like a jackknife. The express car was buried head on into a sand bank to the depth of about ten feet. The rest of the train was strewn along the way, off the track in the sand. The rail was ripped up for about four hundred feet and some were bent straight upwards. As nice a mess as any wrecking crew would care to entangle. I am sure it took some time to clean it up. The only ones killed were the engineer and fireman. The passengers were only shook up and piled out of their seats. None were injured.

I left there quickly, for I saw the very officer who had chased me out of town and by his vigilance he kept me off this very passenger train. I was on the point of going over to him and thanking him, but on second thought I figured it was better not to, for his last words came back to me with double force. So I got out on that highway again "toot sweet" and then some...

I started out once more. It was daylight by this time, so when I came to the first auto camp[3] I went in and bought some sandwiches and a small package of doughnuts. I went on a little farther and then crossed over a patch of sand and into a small clump of trees and started a fire to make some coffee for my breakfast. Breakfast over, I packed up and went back to the highway again, and this time I tried to get a lift as far as Colton, which would be the next place I would have a chance to pick up a freight. I was lucky; a traveling salesman picked me up and it wasn't long before I was in Colton.

I just cannot get that wreck out of mind; all morning it comes before my eyes. And every time it does, I can see myself standing in between the tender and the baggage car. It makes me shudder to think what would have happened if that officer hadn't appeared as he did. I cannot help but offer up a prayer of thankfulness that I am now sitting where I am. I cannot help but think that officer must have been a medium used by some unseen power to guide me away from that passenger train. The more I think about it, the more convincing it becomes that there is—there must be—some mighty and all-seeing power guiding all of us along the pathway of life, using everything or anybody that may be close at hand as its servant to help it in its aims and endeavors. I cannot give to that officer the entire credit for the fact I escaped death so closely. But I do give him credit for responding so readily to whatever it was that brought him in contact with me at the time. Call it what you care to or call me foolish for thinking as I do. But in spite of all you may say or even scoff at the idea, I am thoroughly convinced there is some mighty and powerful force working with us at all times.

It is a part of us, we a part of it, and both must work and respond to each other in harmony. If we don't, then it is the time things go wrong.

---

3. Roughly equivalent to an RV Camp.

For witness the fact that when that officer told me to get out of Ontario pronto, I did what I was told. Consequently I am alive, but if I took the bull by the horns and insisted on getting out of there on that passenger train, I am sure I wouldn't be here. So what better proof would anyone want than that? And for better proof, I saw that heap of wreckage, with that baggage car buried in the sandbank!

Chapter Twenty-Two

From Colton to Tucson

*C*olton is seventy miles from Los Angeles and the first division on the Southern Pacific Railroad from that city. I will have to wait until almost noon for the next freight out. So until that time, I will have to find a place to lay low in, out of sight of the Fee Grabbers.

So I started up the track, peering into this place and that, when and where. I didn't see any likely place—until I ran onto a shack across a fairly wide stream. A man appeared at the door and beckoned me over, pointing out the way across. I crossed over and found the path to the shack without much trouble. After I finally reached the shack, the man went inside and brought out two large pails and handed them to me. I took them and looked at them and then at him. I just didn't catch on for a second, but he pointed to a full pail standing inside of the door. It was then I came out of it.

So, I retraced my steps and crossed over and up on the road bordering the stream, looking for water. I finally spied a barn a little way down the road. So down to the barn I went and found a good sized well where I filled my pails. I went and placed the pails just outside the door of the shack and then sat down on a bench close by. Soon the man reached out and grabbed the pails and disappeared once more inside. I sat there thinking of nothing in particular. I looked the site over on all sides. I scanned the doorway for the man to appear again. I gave a glance at the shack and found it is built of every kind of material imaginable. There was wood sides; the roof was made of corrugated sheets of iron, the cracks stuffed and filled with old newspaper. The door was part screen and part wood. And, tucked in between the roof and the ends of the boards were long bundles of straw. All no doubt found in and around the place or in some dump. Even with all this combination of different materials it was firmly built.

I note by this time smoke rising out of the stove pipe stuck through the roof and I smell the savory aroma of coffee and bacon. And that makes me think of my bundle and what I have left from the small stores after making breakfast this morning.

I reached down to pick it up, thinking I might as well eat here and now as any other time or place, but I didn't no more than get it up in my lap when the man appeared again in the doorway and beckoned me in. Well, to say the least, I could not resist his invitation, for the aroma of that bacon and coffee egged me on. So I arose and entered, not knowing whether it's for another two pails of water, but hoping it is to have some of that coffee and bacon. After I got inside he pointed to a chair and table. I sat down while he went over to a small sized cooking range and then returned with a plate filled with fried potatoes, bacon, and eggs, after which he reached over the table and from a shelf he got a cup and saucer, knife, fork, and spoon. Then back to the stove for a pot of coffee and, of all things, toast.

I ate my dinner in total silence and I must admit I enjoyed that dinner immensely. I wasn't so very hungry but this man's cooking was as good as any I had ever tasted. Everything was seasoned just right and the toast was done to a "T," tender and crisp. I certainly couldn't help but admire him for his culinary art. He was good, and his cooking better than any I ever ate. As I mentioned, I ate in silence; not once did this man utter a single word all this time I was there. Not even as much as a smile did he give. I thought at first he was deaf and dumb. I tried to get him into a conversation, but he only looked at me and would turn his face away and go about his chores around the shack.

Anyhow, I knew he could hear and I am sure he wasn't dumb, for he did not have the earmarks of that affliction. Even when I helped him wash up the dishes and brought another pail of water and gathered up some wood, not even then did he utter a sound. So I gave it up and gave him a salute as I picked up my bundle and left. He returned the salute, but said nothing. "Huh," thought I, "That guy sure doesn't like to talk, and I don't know but what he has the right idea." As a rule we all talk too much and when we do talk, we don't say anything most of the time anyhow.

Well, here comes the freight and I walk on down a little ways into the yard to get in a better position to jump her. The freights coming out of this yard are sometimes short and in a case of that kind they pick up speed quickly, so by the time it hits the end of the yard, they are stepping along at a good speed, and it is then you must have a little running space to get on. Only those real experts can get on from a stand still, and I am no expert yet. So, I take it easy and let them go by if they go out too fast. Better to wait than get killed or maimed for life.

I made this one, and we are on our way to the next division which, according to the railroad schedule, is Indio, California. We passed through Redlands and Palm Springs, both of which are in the midst of the orange district. All the way from Colton to Indio you can see about every kind of fruit that California is famous for: limes, dates, lemons, oranges, English walnuts, pecans, Japanese persimmons, and I saw a few avocado trees. Grapes abound in this section. In this district somewhere is the largest vineyard in the world. It covers five thousand acres of land and I am told it stretches along one highway for five miles. It is owned by five brothers—Chianti Brothers, I think is the name the vineyards are known by.

It is getting cold and I am feeling it very keenly, more so than at any time since I have been out here. I suppose from the grade we are slowly climbing we are getting into a higher altitude, which no doubt accounts for such a sudden change in the temperature.

It is only about seventy miles from Colton to Indio, so we arrived there about 6 pm, and of course it being a division point, I had to pile off, for here at Indio the railroad officers are rather hostile at times. I got off before the end of the freight was actually in the yard and walked the rest of the way to the other side of the yard.

If all those who travel "a la hobo" would get off before the freights entered each yard and caught them as they left on the opposite end, they would eliminate an awful lot of friction between themselves and the railroad officers. Not only that, if when they do get on they would only keep under cover while riding, they wouldn't be bothered as much as they generally are. Nothing riles a railroad officer so easy as to see a whole trainload of Hobos and what not come riding right into the middle of the yard in full view of the whole yard and town or city. If that was all they did, it wouldn't be so bad, but just as soon as they get off, they start to wander all over the yard, getting in the way of the train crews and right of way, causing no end of worry on the part of the yard crews and officers. I have seen times when they were so many, work had to be stopped for fear of killing some of them until the railroad officers ran them out, and that is some job in any yard, especially for only one officer. They seem to enjoy poking here and there. They seem to be happy making it more difficult for those who respect the officers and the law. The truth of the matter is they know it is against the law to trespass on railroad property, yet when the officers chase them off, they will berate them and just double their efforts to make things just a little bit harder to ride day or night.

Indio seems to be a concentration point for a large number of crop pickers. It is not any too large and of course any influx of any number would be very noticeable. At this writing, the season is pretty well over, but when the crops are ready for harvest, I am told the place is overrun with pickers. They come from all parts of the south and west, with a sprinkling of beginners from anywhere and everywhere. No one crop seems to draw any more pickers than the other. They come on the freights or hitchhike it; some come instead in their own cars—these generally have the whole family, baby and all, with paraphernalia hanging or tied on all sides and top of their cars for making a camp right on the job. I imagine having a car to travel from one crop to the other has its advantages and I wouldn't be surprised if this sort of employment wouldn't be a good way to pay for and have a very nice vacation. I am sure it would be a change from the ordinary hum-drum routine of the business world and consequently one would come back greatly benefited, both mentally and physically. I certainly would recommend it highly.

Indio seems to be the chief shipping and receiving point for all the cotton grown in its vicinity. Long staple cotton is, I am told, the chief grade grown. This grade of cotton is chiefly used in the manufacture of automobile tires and other fibroid products, and I suppose it is used also in the manufacture of cloth. In its season the pickers flock here, some even leave other crops where the pay is low and harder to make.

Long cotton is bulkier and naturally one can pick it faster and easier than fruit or short cotton. The cotton growers pay from three quarters of a cent to one cent every hundred pounds, and I am told a good picker can pick from five hundred to one thousand pounds a day, and the average picker can average $3.00 a day. Good pickers will average from $5.00 to $10.00 per day. There are two ways in which a cotton picker can hire out. One, he can work for the cotton grower and keep himself. The other way, he can work for so much a hundred and live under arrangements offered by the cotton grower. I was told by some who have picked cotton that the cotton growers charge from 75 to 90 cents a day for room and board. Whether one arrangement is better than the other I am not able to state. However, many—in fact I inclined to think, the majority—pay the cotton grower for room and board.

Whole families pool their earnings and I imagine no matter how easy they may work, they couldn't help but make a fair day's wages. They no doubt get more out of it by the fact they keep themselves and live camp style. Further than what I have already wrote in regards to cotton picking, I am unable to furnish any more information for I have never had any experience working in the cotton fields. I hope to, though, sometime.

Towards evening it grew pretty cold further back on the line from Colton so by the time a freight was made up (about 8 pm), it was real cold. In fact I was thinking of stopping here in Indio, thinking it might be too cold to ride. For when it gets cold out here it seems to get right into your bones and no amount of exercise seems to help keep you warm. A heavy mist was starting, which only added to one's discomfort.

Well, here she comes, and on I go with about fifty others. I am off again.

We wheeled out of the lighted yards into the darkness. Now I was getting the full blast of the cold, damp wind. I was riding on top with no hopes of getting under cover unless I broke into one of the ice compartments (or Reefers) that are built at each end of boxcars used in transporting perishable merchandise or fruit and other produce. I walked along the top of four of five boxcars and found the hatches battened down and sealed. I climbed down into an empty gondola—a type of car for carrying coal or other material that doesn't need protection. I rode this into the next division, which is Yuma, Arizona. There I hopped off at the risk of breaking my neck. I was so stiff from that ride I let her slow down a bit though before I did.

Believe me, I made a beeline for a little restaurant I noticed near the railroad station the first time I was here. It is run by an old colored man but that is not the reason I didn't patronize it before, I just didn't notice it, it being so small as it is and so ill lit it didn't look much like an eating place. So as I ate up town before, I passed it close on my way back to the yards. I entered it in somewhat of a hurry and when I did I saw the old colored man reach for a cup and draw me a hot cup of coffee and set it on the counter. He knew what I wanted without me even asking for it. Did I drink that coffee? I'll say I did! I had another and a couple of sandwiches with it and then another cup of coffee. I felt better after that meal. I got up and paid him and started for the door and was just about to open it to go out and back to the yards again as I didn't want to miss any chance of getting out of Yuma as soon as I could.

At that moment he called out and said, "Here, you, White boy! Where do you think you're going now?"

"Oh, over around the station until the next one pulls out," I answered.

"Well, you have a long wait ahead of you. You can stay here where it is warm if you want to. There isn't another freight until early in the morning", he advised me with a smile.

"Gee, thanks, old man. If that's the case, I'll be glad to, for it is kind of raw out at that," I said, and then ordered another cup of coffee.

He drew a cup for himself and came over and sat down beside me.

We talked about things in general until a few of the yard crew came in to eat. He wasn't long waiting on them. They talked and kidded each other about things that happened in the yard during the night. They all got up together and as one of them started out, I noticed the colored man called him to one side and spoke to him in a low tone, pointing me out as he talked. I noticed the railroad man nodding his head as if to say, "OK."

The railroad man came over to me and said, "Come along boy and follow me. But don't let on you are with me."

I followed him at a distance. We crossed the street and through the park and on up past the railroad station onto the tracks of the yard, and then on over the tracks to a line of cars. We walked along them until we stopped by one of the cars. He then reached up and opened the side door. He looked around as though he thought someone was watching us.

"Get in there and be still and everything will be OK. She will pull out in about five minutes," he said just above a whisper.

I thanked him and said, "This sure is mighty fine of you, Old Timer. So long!"

This visit to Yuma was certainly different in every respect than the previous one. Yet I still don't like it. Perhaps if I made an extended visit I might. It is perhaps unfair to judge a place by first impressions. So I may be entirely wrong.

We are backing up now in order to get on the main line and right of way, and then be on our way. In this yard it is rather hard to tell a live string of cars from a string standing dead on a storage track.

WAITING FOR THE TRAIN

We are underway at last and if I am not mistaken, I am the only hobo on this train. I didn't see anyone else get on. I will know if there is when we stop. Being the only one on helps considerable, if I keep under cover and out of sight, or if I get off at stops while the railroad officers go over her, I am sure I will not not be molested or interfered with at all.

This freight is one of the many fast freights that run over the Southern Pacific Railroad. They call them "manifests," and they carry produce and other perishable goods and valuable material. So this kind of freight doesn't stop at every little hamlet and village along the way. About the only thing that stops her is for coal, water, and at each division, a change of engines and train crew. Sometimes there is some changes in her make up, perhaps adding more or taking off some cars destined for towns off the main line. So this style of train is out to make time. They are even run on scheduled times. I have seen passenger trains side tracked to let them pass.

We are stepping on it in grand style and if we keep the rate up I would be in Tucson sooner than I expect. It is about 300 miles between Yuma and Tucson. But there are any number of small places between. There are: Walton, Dome, Sentinel, and Maricopa; here we made our first stop, I think for water. It was only a few minutes, though. We were soon on our way again and she stepped on it a little faster and faster until she struck a small grade. After we got over that and started on down the other side of the same grade didn't she go—and then some! I am not exaggerating when I claim for her a speed of 75 miles an hour.

Well, being as it is night time I can make nothing out as far as scenery is concerned. Everything is a blur on account of the speed and darkness. So I just sit in the darkness and listen to the roar of the train, the rattle of the wheels and click of the rails as we go on into the night, trusting we will arrive there safe.

We pass through another town, Casa Grande, I think is the name of it. We didn't even slacken any speed as we tear through it; the lights of the little station looked like a streak of light. Picacho is next and then Tucson, Arizona.

The dawn is breaking. I am glad for the light. So, I get up and scan once more the scenes in and around Tucson. I see automobiles going towards the city, no doubt people going to work or on business. I look out and peer ahead and make out the tall poles that hold the yard lights. I am about to enter Tucson once more.

Now I've got to be real careful, for I have no business on this train, no how. So I watch for just one second's slack in her speed. Ah, she slacks up and off I tumble and roll into the ditch alongside of the track. I lay there for a minute and then get up and thank my stars that I didn't get hurt—not even a scratch. I think to myself that was some ride!

I got off just outside of the yards, so when the caboose went by, the conductor and the railroad officer saluted me as they went by. I saw both of them smile at each other. The railroad officer pointed off to one side that that was the best way to enter the town, so I took the tip and crossed a sandy patch of land and soon was walking on the highway with a better feeling than ever towards railroad officers and railroad men in general, for what better treatment could I ask for on this trip? I am inclined to think that they are OK, even the railroad officers included, if you respect them.

Now, the last time I was in this city of Tucson, I came in rather low in finances. I did have some money, but I was conserving it for emergencies at the end, mainly in Los Angeles. But on this visit I have just about three times as much, so I didn't bother around with no Salvation Army. I found a nice room for the day and night, if I cared to use it that long, for no one knows whether one is sure of getting out soon or later.

I met a fellow here who seemed to know Tucson pretty well. That was the impression I got from the way we talked. You will meet up with people very easy sometimes, especially in a strange city or town. Every one of them had its hangers-on who seem to be the only ones who know anything and everything about the place, and of course if they are courteous and decent looking, you are glad to have someone to talk to like that. You will find it hard to give them the go by; you don't like to seem rude or discourteous. In other words, you fall for their line of bull. Now these fellows after a half hour's conversation about things in general hint about a nice place to eat and close by is a nice poolroom for a nice sociable game. "How about taking a walk over and seeing the place?" is the next suggestion, and so on and so on until, if you're easily led and don't know the breed, you are following them like a lamb for a shearing.

Now, I don't claim to be an expert at playing pool, but I do know enough about it to know when—and if—there is any funny business being pulled off. So I don't know what possessed me to get real chummy with him, but anyhow we started to talk about pool and billiards. I found in him a ready subject on the game and from what I could make out, he was a pool shark of the highest rank. Maybe he was, but I took a chance and asked him was it very far to this poolroom. He told me where it was and I promised him I would call around there this evening as I had some money coming from a rancher who I was to meet.

He got up and started over through the railroad station park. I got up also and turned about in the opposite direction and went on down the street to a little restaurant on a corner. Here I ate a pretty good supper and bought a paper and sat there killing time reading it. I scanned the headlines and read a few articles of local interest, and then glanced up at the clock to find it is within the time I promised to be at the poolroom. So I pay my bill and start out to keep that date.

Did you ever have a feeling that all was not right? Well, just that sort of a feeling came over me like a bolt of lightning out of the sky. And still, I didn't stop to heed it. I just kept on going in the direction I was supposed to find that poolroom. I got near the locality and just as I really saw the place I saw my new-found friend standing outside of the building.

We shook hands and talked a little while about nothing of much interest. After a few moments he said, "Well, let's go in and have a sociable game of pool to kill the time. It gets monotonous hanging around here."

So we started for the door and just then I see out of the corner of my eye someone peeking around the corner of the building, and that stops me right there. In so doing he gets ahead of me, and opens the door. I got one glimpse of the inside and couldn't see nothing but a large vacant room, and that stops me once more. I don't know to this day why I did what I did next. All I did was to step to a window and peer through that window, and there it was again: an empty room. Besides that I see my nice courteous friend climbing out of one of the rear windows. I ran to the corner of the building just in time to see the guy who was peeking around it meet the other one, and when they both saw me standing there, boy didn't they go, and that was the last I saw of them.

Well, that's that, I thought as I sauntered on back to the hotel to turn in for the night. I turned in and tried to go to sleep, but the events of the day kept running through my mind. I couldn't help but give thanks I wasn't nursing a nice sore head right now, for I couldn't figure no other way about what they were up to other than to bat me over the head for what I had on me. Another close call—that's the second one—and so from now on I'll have to be more careful if I want to finish this return trip to New York City.

I was up real early the next morning, feeling refreshed from the night's rest and the warmth of about six blankets, for I was experiencing some more of that penetrating cold that seems to be only felt in this section of the desert country.

On my first visit to Tucson, I tied this intense cold to just one of those spells of weather that comes occasionally in the winter months. But now after a month's absence I found it the same. So one can perhaps figure on such weather here as being quite a regular weather condition in the winter months. So unless your car isn't heated, or if you are not staying over in a nice warm hotel, be sure you have plenty of woolen clothing or blankets for use at night. If you don't take such precautions, I'll guarantee you will wish you had, for I don't remember when it had been that I had ever suffered from the most penetrating cold than I had experienced on those two occasions of going through Tucson. The hell of it is it sticks to you almost half a day after you have left this area.

Well, so much for the desert nights in and around Tucson in the months of December and January.

I ate breakfast in one of those Mexican "Chili Con Carne" establishments that abound in this section of the country for a change and mostly for the experience and the novelty. There are as many different kinds and styles of restaurants in the West as there are souvenirs of it. A "Chili Con Carne" restaurant was one that I had not as yet visited. So, thinks I, I'll try one for perhaps I may never be this way again.

This restaurant was fitted out in real Western style and I imagine the cost must have run into the thousands of dollars and perhaps far in excess of what it might have cost for ordinary restaurant fittings or decorations.

About every known decoration: saddle spurs, lariats, Stetson hats, branding irons; and the pistols represented would have turned any museum or collector of firearms green with envy. On the walls hung pictures in lithograph and real photographs of most of the old Western celebrities: Wild Bill Hickock, Billy the Kid, Daniel Boone, Custer, Calamity Jane, and a hundred others of greater or lesser fame. And don't let me forget an extremely large painting of "Custer's Last Stand." This was the best and largest one that I had ever looked at of that famed battle.

I was so engrossed in looking at this array of the "West that used to be," I wasn't taking much interest in what I was eating, other than the fact I had ordered a bowl of chili con carne and a cup of coffee.

I guess about everyone has gone through the same experience, but instead of a display of relics it perhaps would be some interesting talker who was holding their interest rather than to that of what they were eating. So it was I took a sip of coffee or a spoonful of chili con carne in between my inspection of this Western atmosphere until I had finished—and not five minutes after the fun began.

When that food started to really go to work, I knew there were two places I had to get to, and right "pronto" as they say out West. I couldn't very well be in two places at the same time, so I dived to the curb, that being the nearest, and fomented the food off my stomach, but for the other necessity I was out of luck.

Oh, shades of my childhood. If ever I had complained about wearing diapers, please do forgive me. I'll take it all back. For if I had a pair on now they certainly would have come in handy. At least they would have helped considerable in keeping the mess I was in a little more centralized or in one place. Amen.

I am positive if I didn't have one of those stomachs that rebels against impurities in food I certainly would have had a serious case of ptomaine poisoning[1]. How was it that I didn't notice the food was bad?

Well it is an old trick, one as old as the hills to a certain grade of restaurant, but the thing that fooled me was the fact that this had been the first time I had ever eaten chili con carne. So the heavy sage flavor was, I thought, part of the proper seasoning. But really it was used to cover the rancidness of the food. And ever since, just a mention or even the thought of chili con carne and I get sick.

Don't ask me how I ever managed to get back to the railroad yards. I don't remember myself, but I did and got cleaned up the best way I could in one of the outhouses used by the railroad employees. Was I weak—a kitten could have tripped me over, my legs were so wobbly.

It was getting late in the afternoon by the time I felt able to do any traveling, so after being informed by one of the "shacks" in the railroad yard that there would be a freight ready to leave around 4 pm, I sauntered on down the road to where all the boys generally go and hang around until train time.

I watch the train crew make up the train and scan its length for a possible empty box car, as I will be riding some of the distance by night. Well, here comes the engine down over on the other side to a switchback, here she backs up and is connected to the line of cars. The brakies[2] are giving it a final going over, and the car inspectors connecting the air lines—it won't be long before you will see the conductor give the high sign. Then the engineer reaches for the whistle, you hear two short blasts of the whistle and she gives a little jump to try the brakes. Now is the time to

---

1. Ptomaine was previously thought to cause food poisoning; thus, an obsolete term for the affliction.

2. Slang for brakeman.

get your position to catch the car you have picked out to ride in, or take your choice. All is set now. So I cross over, keeping my eyes pricked for the railroad officer. I see none and then I take her just as she starts to get under way and in a few moments we are clear of the yard.

Who says, "There isn't a thrill in railroading?" Who is it that has been on the road hoboing that doesn't get a kick out of it too?

There is a certain knack to hopping a freight as they call it. It takes considerable experience and practice to hop one at the right time and in the right place. I have observed "Old Timers" on many occasions hop them from a stand still while they were rolling by at fifteen or twenty miles an hour, and do it with as much ease and form and grace as a seasoned athlete going off a hurdle.

Well, I bid Tucson, Arizona goodbye for the second time, but with certain regrets and a none too affectionate feeling towards it or "Chili Con Carne" restaurants.

It took every bit of my remaining strength to hop this freight and get on top. I still was feeling somewhat weak from my experience from eating that damn swill they served me in that "Chili Con Carne" restaurant.

If ever I was pleased to get out of a city it was right now, for this was the second time I thought that Tucson had treated me pretty rough. The first time I visited this city and my experiences are elsewhere related a few chapters back. I swore this would be the last time I would ever set foot within its limits.

I don't know of any other city in this country of ours that has within its environs such a class of people whose one idea in life is to bamboozle everyone who stops or goes through it. They even try it on each other. They use some of the most petty subterfuges and it is a wonder to me the city itself hasn't a small "civil war" on its hands.

The City of Takers, it might be more correctly named rather than its present one.

One or two of its citizens that I had talked to were of the same opinion and there wasn't a single man on the road but what didn't curse the place and every one who lived within its limits. I can only express the average itinerant traveler's opinion of it in their own words: "It's lousy."

Chapter Twenty-Three

An Owl Named Peter

This freight is what they call a Mixed Freight, so it is subject to more stops than if it was a Manifest. So, as it worked its way east, we stopped here and there, dropping off cars and taking them on.

Bowie, Arizona, really is the first place of much consequence between Tucson and Lordsburg, New Mexico. It is here where a line of tracks comes down out of the hills from Globe, where copper ore is mined.

Bowie is also a water and fuel stop for freights going east. It was while they were shifting cars and refueling I took the chance of missing it by stopping in the nearest restaurant for a cup of hot coffee. The queerest thing happened, or, you might say, came about, while I sat there waiting for my coffee and listening for the signal of two blasts of the engine whistle announcing its departure.

As I entered this restaurant I found it empty. Not a soul was around. But after a moment or two, I discovered I was not quite alone, for, from the depths of the restaurant came a sound that I knew to be the cry of an owl.

"Whoo. Whoo. Hoot. Hoot," it came. "Hoot Hoot" again, and then I heard the flutter of wings coming through the air and of all things it dived straight at me! Naturally, I jumped from my seat and ducked, but try as I might, the owl kept fluttering about me until by some bird strategy it found an opening through my uplifted arms and came to rest on my right shoulder. There it clutched my overcoat with its talons and refused to be shook off.

Some one—it sounded like a young woman speaking—called out, "Don't be afraid, he is harmless. Don't bother him."

It was a minute or two before the young woman came out and when she saw me sitting there with the owl perched on my shoulders she gave an exclamation of surprise and said, "Well, of all the things, I never saw that owl do that before. How queer!" Then she reached out to take the owl off my shoulders. But the owl had different ideas about that, for if ever I had anything screech in my ears, that old bird sure gave me a good example of sitting right alongside of a locomotive whistle. I thought my ear drums would split open!

"Of all the funny things. I wonder what has got into him? Why, Peter, I am surprised at you." And then she tried to coax him by saying, "Come. Come over here, Peter. Come. Don't bother the man."

But old Peter might have been deaf and blind for all he paid attention to her. So I advised her to leave him alone while she got me a cup of coffee and a small cake, thinking that perhaps the owl might of his own accord fly back to nest or roost. And besides, I didn't want to be slashed up with those powerful talons that he had sunk into my overcoat.

I drank my coffee and ate my cake, trying to think of the best way of getting the bird off, but in spite of all the tricks I tried, he refused to be budged from his roost. So, as a last resort, I tried to coax him down to the counter by putting my shoulder on the level of the counter, thinking he might just step off onto it. But all Peter did was to take my hat off with his beak and it went rolling to the floor.

The young lady got a good laugh at that prank and finally, after she watched him, she said, "Well, I guess Peter has found someone he likes." Peter, as though he understood what she had said, gave a little screech and a couple of "Whoo Whoos" and then I could feel him kind of getting himself permanently settled on my shoulder—for keeps.

"Well, lady," I said, "evidently Peter seems to be content where he is, but I have to catch that freight or else I'll be stranded here in Bowie overnight and I am not so well fixed with money to be stopping every four hundred miles, spending my money for hotels. For I have considerable distance to travel before I get home."

Just as I had finished explaining the why and wherefore of my anxiety to get going and rid of the bird, the exhaust of the engine of my freight gave off warning that she was on her way out. So right then I decided bird or no bird I was going to take it. So I jumped up from my seat and made for the door, but Mr. Peter the Owl had different ideas about that, too.

I never knew a bird the size of an owl could raise such a fuss. He slapped me in the back of my neck, he boxed my ears, he flipped me across the face, and then almost enveloped my head with his wings. Then, not satisfied he had his way, he smacked my hat off again and all the while, through this apparent chastisement, he was screeching and Hooting and Whooing. And not until I retreated back to the seat I had occupied did he cease. The queerest thing about his assault was, not once did he scratch me or really hurt me, but he did one thing and that was—he caused me to miss my freight.

"What the hell was this all about, lady?" I was getting pissed. I felt put out on account of missing that freight. It was a hold up of almost a day. I felt like wringing the bird's neck.

To tell the truth, I came near doing it too, but something seemed to stay my hand. *Perhaps there is a reason, who knows?*, I thought. I didn't know just what to make of the bird's actions, nor did its owner, and I couldn't make myself believe it was just a matter of any personal attraction, nor could I believe that this bird had any particular or sudden affection for someone who had never been in contact with him before. It couldn't be. What—an owl? Impossible! What—a night bird? No, it's something else. And I didn't know until the morning how much I had to thank that bird for holding me up in Bowie that night.

After sitting there trying to think what best to do, with the owl still perched on my shoulder, the young lady said, "That's certainly queer and I am sorry that bird held you up, but there seems nothing we can do about it." Then she leaned against the counter, as though in deep thought. And then as though she was struck with a happy thought, she suddenly said, "Say, come to think of it, my father was remarking this morning he wished some needy man would come along and help him with some work he has to do. He's old now and can't do heavy work any more. So, I'll tell you what I'll do, I'll let you sleep in one of our tourist houses and perhaps he might hire you tomorrow."

"Well, that's mighty kind of you, ma'am. I'll take a chance on any kind of work at any time," I said.

I tried once more to dislodge the owl from my shoulders, but I couldn't, so I gave up and told the woman to please show me that cabin.

I must have looked funny following her to the cabin with that darn old bird trying to keep his balance as I stumbled along the path to the cabin. But he made the grade and, of all things that bird did, his next behavior was the queerest. When I entered the cabin, he gave one more of his "Hoot Hoots," left my shoulder and took roost on the head of the bed I was going to occupy that night.

"Now," said the young lady, "perhaps I can get him back to the restaurant."

But, when she attempted to get ahold of him, the owl by his actions let her know in no uncertain terms he was staying right where he was. He made a dive at her, flew a couple of times over my bed, sort of wobbly like, and then went after the young lady again and practically chased her out of the cabin.

That bird, I thought to myself as I was preparing to retire, *certainly knows what he wants, and he is mine if I want to bother taking him along*—and I had half a mind to do so. But in this last thought I was wrong, as I was to discover on the following morning.

I put the light out and rolled into bed and fell immediately asleep. But not for long did I enjoy my good luck, for suddenly the screeching of the owl woke me up out of my slumbers deep.

He was making another of those fusses and he wasn't the only thing making a racket, for on the outside I could hear the hiss of sand and wind as it hit my cabin. Then came a sound like as if hail or small pebbles were being shot from pea shooters of my boyhood days up against the walls and windows. And then suddenly the wind died down a bit and then came the rain, And how it did rain. It sounded like the roar of Niagara Falls as it came down from the sky.

Then all of a sudden the wind picked up in velocity and, with the force of the wind and the weight of what sounded like a wall of water, it lifted the cabin up on one side and I thought sure it was going on its side, but it returned to its original position with a thump, but the rain still kept coming down in torrents.

I happened to look down to the floor and to my amazement I discovered it was covered with six inches of water. Over in the corner, there, was my one and only pair of shoes floating and bobbing up and down like as if they were pieces of wood trying to get out of an eddy into the current of a stream.

I was lucky in the fact that I had left them as I did, and with my socks rolled up inside of them, for outside of the soles being wet, no other harm was done.

I looked up behind me to see how my companion the owl was taking the tempest that was raging outside, but outside of sitting there, and occasionally a Hoot or two, or a blink of his eyes, he wasn't showing much anxiety about anything.

The storm stopped as sudden as it seemed to have started, so I rolled over and went to sleep again. When I awoke in the morning, the sun was shining as though there hadn't been a storm there for years, and the owl was still perched on the head of the bed, looking as wise and solemn as owls generally do.

It was while I was eating breakfast that the young lady remarked about the storm and the washout all along the highways and the railroad and says she:

"That freight you missed just about piled up in the sand down the line from here somewheres. At least that is what I heard the yard man telling old Burns at the station."

I wasn't surprised to hear such a report, for this part of the country is famous for sudden storms and washouts, so I said nothing. But I did do a deal of thinking, as it was I had escaped another wreck and also a terrific rain storm. That's a part of what I have been getting at, but

I can't as yet say there is anything queer or strange, or that it has any connection with the strange behavior of that owl.

The picture is not complete. I will have to see what the young lady's father has to offer in the way of employment, for far greater events may crop up that might be more significant than just a repetition of what happened to me back in Ontario, California, when a policeman was the means or cause of my good fortune in escaping a passenger train wreck.

I was introduced to the young lady's father and I was hired on the spot and started my first day's work cleaning up the debris that was strewn all over his property by the previous night's storm. There wasn't much pay, $1.25 per day, my meals, and the cabin I had slept in the night before. Which, by the way, wasn't such bad pay considering the conditions throughout the country at that time.

I was here for about three weeks and they were the loneliest three weeks I ever spent in one place. I didn't leave Bowie once in those three weeks and nobody else did. It was just get up, eat, and work, and eat again, then return to work and then eat and then turn the lights out and go to bed.

I got my instructions at the breakfast table and from then on I didn't see the boss until the next morning came, when I had occasion to pass by his window where he sat reading the paper.

In all those three weeks he didn't lift his hand to a thing, not even in the restaurant, where I could always find his daughter ever busy doing something.

How that restaurant paid expenses was a problem I gave up trying to figure out just one week after I was there, for I never saw more than six or seven customers in at one time. Save for a few steady men who work on the railroad, there were no others, but yet, at each Saturday noon, my pay was there to the red cent.

At the expiration of those three weeks I had about everything cleaned up and repaired, so I left one afternoon, but, instead of taking a freight, I hitch-hiked to Lordsburg, New Mexico.

Now for the incident of the strange behavior of the owl, I have only this to say: From the time I started to work the owl went back to his old roost in the restaurant and never much as looked at me, which to me only made his behavior on that first night I entered the restaurant still stranger. And the young lady too was of the same opinion. On the day I left she said,

"I'll never forget how Peter fussed up as he did that night you tried to leave."

I asked her if she had any explanation for his strange action, but she had none, except that he perhaps was trying to tell us something. For she claimed in all the six or seven years they had him, all he ever did was to sit on his roost all day and eat. And Hoot Hoot once in awhile.

I think the young lady came as near as anything I could think of by way of explanation when she said he was trying to tell us something. What that something was I honestly and truthfully don't know, unless it was the terrific rain, sand, and hail storm and the subsequent train wreck. Or was it he knew his master needed a man to help him?

Well, have it your own way. He wasn't doing no such thing and I guess one guess is as good as another, but I did miss a train wreck and I did miss being in one of the worst rain storms in this section. And I did get work for three weeks.

We have all heard of some faithful old dog who, in the middle of the night, woke up the family of the house warning them of a fire that was raging, or of that same animal howling when there is going to be a death or howling after one in the neighborhood. So why couldn't an owl who is just as lowly be accredited with the same mystic propensities?

I have always given animals a little more credit for knowing more than perhaps the average person ever gave them credit for. At least in comparison to some people I have had dealings with and others by way of behavior and other things not fit for print. I don't know but what I'd sooner live with them or have them for companions instead. I would trust them far sooner at least.

So I salute you, Peter—you wise old owl.

Well, this is no treatise on the relative intelligence of animal life; but in knocking around, one does run across some things that are a little out of the ordinary and worthy of attention. Consequently, as I said, it's not a treatise, but it can't help but be a little bit of everything.

So as I write this I am sitting on a little bank just off from the end of the Lordsburg, New Mexico, railroad yards, waiting, as the boys of the road say, "for the next one out."

Chapter Twenty-Four

New Mexico

I had always heard that Lordsburg, New Mexico, was "hot,"[1] especially at night. Why it is not so in the daytime is perhaps just one of those conditions or variations that is caused in many instances by the difference in the dispositions of two different people. One in this case was a little bit more "hard-boiled" than the other, or perhaps he took his job a little bit more serious, which by the way generally made him the object of considerable ridicule and too, it made his job a little harder. In other words, these "hard-boiled" railroad officers don't keep down the traffic of itinerant travelers any more than the one who hardly pays much attention to them, and neither does he keep down the destruction or theft of property to any greater degree than any others. In fact, I have observed that some of the habitual freight train riders are never so happy when they are making things harder

---

1. By hot, John is referring to the increased danger of being caught and arrested.

for them. While in the case of where the railroad officer is somewhat more lenient and sympathetic, they actually respect him to the extent of reporting a great many irregularities, such as reporting a theft or a hot box or a defective rail, etc. But in spite of whether the officer is okayed by the "Gentry of the Road," it wouldn't go well with the ones who were seen talking too much to them or caught reporting anybody, for that would be breaking one of the strictest codes of the road. You will be judged as reporting your brethren to officers who are not "right" as well. In other words, if you snitch to one, you are just as apt to snitch to all. "A snitch is a snitch, no matter which way you look at it, and under all circumstances, no matter what," was the way an old timer expressed it to me one day.

So to be on the safe side, I am waiting here to catch the freight I see now standing ready to leave. So for a few minutes I put my notebook away and adjust my clothing and bundle over my shoulder, preparatory to try my luck on hopping her.

I don't know what happened. Perhaps it was a change of orders that caused the hold up of the freight, for all of a sudden I note the engine is disconnected and pulls away and switches back onto another line of tracks and returns to the roundhouse.

I waited for another hour or so, but I couldn't see any activity that would indicate the possibility of a freight leaving that morning, so I left and sought a restaurant and had my dinner.

It was while I ate my dinner I learned there wouldn't be a freight out of Lordsburg until late that night, due to the fact they didn't have enough cars to make up a proscribed number of cars, or tonnage, to bother making a run.

Having a few hours to wait, I sought out a place where I might stretch out in the sun to get a nap. For, if I did have to ride at night,

I most likely will have company, and that generally means I'll have to keep awake most of the night.

I had just got settled and thought I would at least be able to rest without anybody interfering. But no, here comes a young fellow who looks as though he hadn't had a change of clothing for months, nor did he bother much in keeping his face or neck clean. Everything about him spoke of laziness.

"Gee," says he, "I am hungry and I haven't had anything to eat for two days."

"How does that come? You look pretty good. You don't look hungry to me," I said, and then added, "Maybe if you cleaned yourself up, maybe you would eat better."

"How am I going to get cleaned up along this line? There's no place to wash up along here," he answered, looking rather hurt.

"Yeah. Well, I'll tell you what I'll do. I'll buy you supper if you get cleaned up. Now, go ahead and let me see what you can do. And I mean *clean*."

"Okay," says he, and off he goes.

I called to him, saying, "We got until eight o'clock tonight! So you have lots of time, so take it easy."

It was two or three hours before he came back, but he was cleaned up, even to a shave. When he sat down, he says, "How do I look? Gee, it feels good. Now, how about that supper?"

"Okay boy, you'll get your supper. Don't worry about that. But tell me, how did you manage to get cleaned up along this line? I thought you couldn't."

So he relates to me how he went right up to a woman and asked her, and that was all there was to it. She said, "Sure, my son, there's the pump, and there's the soap."

"Alright, come on and we will eat."

And from the way that fellow ate, I must have misjudged him, for he ate what I bought for him and the restaurant man gave us two extra cups of coffee. And of the two extra cups I had, he drank one of them.

When we got outside, this fellow turned to me and started to thank me, and I thought I detected somewhat of an emotional tone to what he was saying. I don't think it would have taken much to bring the tears flowing.

There were thousands of young fellows on the road just like this one, many of them roaming around of their own accord and choice. But there were others, who by force of circumstances, were not to be blamed for seeking some way out and had taken to the road, hoping against tremendous odds to rehabilitate themselves. These young fellows should be admired.[2]

After I heard this young fellow's story, I couldn't help feel sorry for him and I was sure he was truthful and honest about his freight time. I more than admired him when he told me he had to leave home, for says he, "That would only give those left at home just that much more to eat."

He took to eating and living in Transient Bureaus, and then he started traveling from one to the other, but he got so sick of them. But now says he, "I guess they were not so bad after all."

We had reached the railroad yards by this time, so we got settled out of sight and waited for a freight.

---

2. The subject of youth riding the rails during this time is covered well in Riding the Rails: Teenagers on the Move During the Great Depression, Errol Lincoln Uys, T. E. Winter & Sons, Boston, 2014.

According to my Ingersoll,[3] *it is now eight o'clock, and true to reports, we are elated to see a big road engine pulling out of its hold near the roundhouse and back to a line of cars. We also see the railroad officer going over the entire length of the train, and when he is at the end of it, we ease our way along the opposite side, for he will no doubt come on down the other. And by the time he does get back to the engine, the freight will be on her way out.*

We found an empty car and got inside and remained quiet. I was pleased my companion was more or less of the quiet kind, so I figured we would get away without this "hard-boiled" officer knowing we were ever around.

Well, we are off, and leaving the yard as though the engineer's life depended on getting the caboose clear of the yard. As far as I know, we are the only riders on this freight, but one never knows for sure, especially at such yards that are considered "hot." But one thing is sure—we are lucky to have a box car to ourselves and still more fortunate to be in one because it is gradually getting cooler.

My companion I note has rode before, and for proof of that fact, he had gathered all the loose paper and has it arranged for both of us on the floor of the car. And as a courtesy to another fellow traveler, he has given me more than my share. I accept the courtesy with thanks, and up goes this fellow's rating about another twenty-five percent. But it remains still to be seen if he has another fifty percent of real comradeship in him. His percentage has not gone up just because it was I that was receiving the benefit of his good will—far from it. It is the caliber of the man I am interested in. If he is on the up and up, he will get my full support and help.

---

3. Ingersoll was famous for the "Dollar Watch," a price point made possible by mass production.

We sat back out of the cold desert wind, but not so far that I couldn't get a glance at the darkened countryside we were riding through. I really can't make out any objects very clearly, but once in a while the moon peeps through the rifts in the clouds and lights up the desert. In its dim light, the Mesquite and Chapparal cast gruesome and skeleton-like shadows, giving the whole scene an eerie and ghost-like effect, or like some cemetery—old cemetery—that the winds of a thousand ages had uncovered and the dead that had been buried now stood up like like petrified skeletons with their arms extended, as if in a mute appeal to be sent back to their earthly beds again.

As I look upon this eerie scene of what was once a sea, flashes of its history run through my mind. And I don't have to stretch my imagination much to see visions of men going around in circles in their madness from the unmerciful sun—the monotony of the nature of the country, and the hopelessness of their release from its cruel grip, and whose bones since have been bared by the vultures, and now are a part of the desert's dust and sand.

My thoughts are suddenly jerked from the past back to my present surroundings by a group of low buildings which are indicative of some town or city. Perhaps, I thought, it might be Deming, New Mexico, which I recall is the next division.

My companion has evidently noticed the signs too, for he is standing by the doorway of the car looking ahead, and suddenly he announces we are pulling into some yard.

"I think this is Deming, New Mexico, if I am not mistaken. If it is, I am getting off before we ride right into it and get tangled up with some 'Bull.' How about you?" said he, turning towards me expectantly.

"Yessir, my boy. I'll be right behind you, see if I don't," I said as I got to my feet.

The freight slackened its speed and we slid off to the ground, one on top of the other. We got to our feet and made for a small bank, on top of which we saw a tree, under which we brushed ourselves off and then awaited results.

It was well we did so, for we saw someone running along the top of the train with a flashlight, focusing it here and there. And when he finally got to the last car, we both noticed he was flourishing a pistol through the air as if he had really come upon someone riding and was threatening them with it.

My companion remarked something to the effect that he sure was a live one.

I had to agree with him, but I wasn't so much interested in the fact of being a live one as I was as to whether he could keep us from getting on this freight again.

The train rolled on into the yard and, after it was out of sight, we followed it on down the track, keeping in the shadows as much as we could.

This officer must have known someone was on that freight or else he was looking for someone in particular, for he went over the freight once more and then started a tour of the yard, poking into every nook and cranny and building with his flashlight.

We eased our way towards the end of the train until we got within about three car lengths of it or within a distance that would give us a chance to make it on the run. It was lucky we were as close as we were for all the work that was done on this freight was a change of engines.

My companion says, "Come on, that 'bull' is busy down at the other end. Now is our chance!"

Chapter Twenty-Five

Traveling in Style to El Paso

You never know one minute from the other what is going to happen when one is knocking around. Events seem to just drop out of the sky like shooting stars, and so it was with what happened as we were easing our way along the track. When we came abreast of the caboose, one of the trainmen who had been standing in the shadow of the caboose stopped us and said, "You fellows had not better go any further. For if you do, this 'bull' will shoot the hell out of you. Besides, he is looking for an escaped convict; reward, you know, and he is after that reward."

Then he held his lantern up and looked us over and then looked in the direction of the engine, and finally he says, "Here, climb into the caboose and be damn quiet."

I hesitated a little but my companion had by this time reached the steps, so I thought one way or another if the railroad officer did run across us, it wouldn't make much difference where he found us. And too, if this trainman, or "shack," turned out to be dirty, well, I'd do my best to make him remember me.

We pulled out of Deming, New Mexico, very slow and watching through the door of the caboose. I noticed that instead of pulling out straight ahead, we were easing over to our left and finally we came to a stop. This sort of worried me, for I still didn't know just whether or not we were in a trap, and now there would be a general shakedown by the officer. But we were only on a side track and waiting for a passenger train to pass by. There was only about a ten minute wait here.

After the passenger cleared and we had the right of way, we continued on our way and clear of all danger.

After the trainman was through with his lights and had closed the door, he sat down and asked us our names and where we lived and where we were headed for and when we ate last.

I answered him honestly and then he asked sort of sudden like, "Which one of you two fellows can cook?"

My companion spoke right up and said, "Show me your stuff and the stove."

"OK, young fellow, come with me," and my companion followed him into the forward end of the caboose. I soon heard him puttering about and in about an hour, the shack, conductor, my companion and I were munching sandwiches and drinking what I thought was the best coffee I ever drank.

We sat there talking about conditions all over the country and the political situation and things in general, and then finished up by having a good laugh over how all of us had fooled the officer.

After cleaning up our supper, all of us found a place to sit back and rest.

El Paso, Texas, is our next stop and there I would hang around a bit or rather, that was what I was planning on, hoping that perhaps I might find another job to bolster up my finances a little more. I was trying hard to get a hundred dollars together before I entered my old hometown again.

This trainman certainly was very sympathetic and considerate to most all the boys and the road, and I certainly learned alot from him as regards what he termed as "real brotherhood."

While his beliefs had a religious trend, he couldn't be judged as having turned religious; but many of his ideas had a religious origin. And as he claimed, "If everyone lived up to the Ten Commandments, things wouldn't be so bad as they are. There is no need of anybody going hungry or without shelter in any country."

One couldn't doubt his own sincerity. Especially when, by his kindness, he was running a big risk of losing his job if it ever was brought to the attention of the railroad he had allowed two wayfarers to ride with the crew of a freight train. For such treatment is not generally extended to even hobos.

With the comfort and warmth and this interesting man's pleasant conversation, the time and the miles seemed to have had wings. It didn't seem hardly an hour had passed before he told me we were within fifteen miles of El Paso.

My companion had fallen asleep and I was loath to wake him up, but I did and told him we would have to get off soon, as we were pretty close to El Paso.

When the caboose was abreast of the Texas and Pacific Railroad station we dropped off, but not before we thanked our kind friend.

Well, here I am once more in El Paso again and here I expect my companion will leave me, or at least that is what I am led to believe by his remarks.

It is rather late and so we part, at a suggestion from me as a precaution, just in case we are stopped and questioned by the police. And so, right in front of the YMCA, we agree to meet at a designated place down on the skid row, where we had something to eat.

It was there I shook hands with him and both of us wished each other good luck. And with a few more words of no consequence, he went on his way to look up a place to stay and I returned to the Army and Navy YMCA and turned in for the night.

I was tired, even though I had rode in style, so I dropped off to sleep soon after I had retired. But along towards midnight I was disturbed by someone opening the door of the dormitory in which I was sleeping. Who do I see standing between me and the light in the hall, but my companion of but an hour ago.

Now this place charged forty cents for a bed in this dormitory, and naturally I wondered where he could have raised that much in El Paso at this time of the night. He sure must have struck it mighty lucky, I thought to myself, but I didn't envy the boy's good luck. No doubt out of courtesy he would have some good explanation—at least I hoped so. And if he didn't, I couldn't say a word for we had parted and from then on each was on his own, so it was none of my business.

I was up bright and early the next morning, as I wanted to give El Paso a good canvas for a job, but after tramping that city from stem to stern, as the sailors say, I couldn't even find a bed and board job.

It was pretty hard to get jobs in the face of such keen competition as exists near the Mexican border. There, an American wouldn't and doesn't have much of a chance, what with the extremely low wages they pay. Most of the menial jobs are given to Mexicans, who will work for almost nothing and sometimes for just their meals. Some live across the Rio Grande river in their own country while working in this country. It doesn't seem to make much difference to some employers in El Paso whether those they hire are bonafide citizens or not. So it follows if an American does get hired, he will have to work for very low wages.

I got disgusted with the situation in El Paso and decided there was no use of trying any more, so I gradually eased my way to the park and rested up. It was here I found my late companion sitting off to one side by himself taking it easy.

"Hello there," said he. "How did you make out today?"

I related to him my experiences of the day, but he made no remarks about it in return.

We sat there taking in the people who were sitting around and telling each other about, or rather comparing each other's experiences while on the road. We must have sat there for about two hours, when he remarks something about how he felt hungry. I took that as a hint for me to invite him once more to supper, but this time I didn't fall so readily as I did the day before. I did remark to him that he hadn't ought to have any trouble in making his supper in El Paso. So I got up and bid him a "so long" and went and ate mine alone. It struck me funny how he could get the price of a forty-cent bed, but he couldn't make the grade when it came to his meals. I always found El Paso one of those places where you get plenty to eat, but a hard place to get any shelter. There were hand-outs galore in regards to meals, if only you care to go after them, so I figured this fellow wasn't much of a hand at hustling for himself. And from all appearances, he wouldn't work. I was disappointed in him, so his percentage still remains at twenty-five percent. And that was the last time I ever laid eyes on him.

If El Paso is the "Gateway to the Golden West," then it must follow it is the gateway to the East. Heretofore I have expressed myself in regards it as being neither one or the other, and since then I have formed still another opinion: That the term "Gateway to the West" is merely a phrase used only to draw tourist trade directly to El Paso. In other words, it is an advertising slogan.

El Paso, Texas, I here reiterate, is not the real "Gateway to the West." Neither is it the gateway to the East, and, believe it or not, there is no more "Golden West."

Well, now that I have given El Paso a good going over and finding nothing here in the way of employment and being solely on my own once more, I have decided to be on my way east again with good old San Antonio, Texas, as my next stop. So, here I am, sitting under a short trestle just on the fringe of the railroad yard, keeping a wary eye for the bulls (both railroad and city) and a freight I see just about ready to pull out.

El Paso has always been an easy place to get out of (in fact, sometimes you are encouraged to do so), so, to respect those who might have any authority, I am keeping out of sight—for what they don't see won't bother them. And what little they might see of you while you are making a run for a freight would be plenty enough, as one old colored hobo expressed it.

I am leaving El Paso with only one regret. I would have liked very much to see Juarez, Mexico, a city over the border. I had heard considerable about this place being one that affords a good time at little cost and all the señoritas and their boys (punks) and the hilarious nights in "Number One" and "Number Two," the American bars.

I doubted the truth of most of what I heard, but I was more than curious and would like to see if it could be possible.

It is about seven hundred odd miles between El Paso and San Antonio, so instead of taking the freight that was now ready, I let it go by for another one that would pass it. For there is no use of traveling perhaps two days to a given place, if you can do it on one.

So I have until 8:15 to saunter around El Paso, and eat and perhaps in that intervening time I might run into a job. One never knows what might be around the corner, so to speak.

Chapter Twenty-Six

A Reefer to San Antonio

*W**ell, it is train time, so I ease my way back towards the railroad yard and catch this Manifest just as though the trains and I agreed on a scheduled time to meet each other.*

In that whole train of cars I couldn't find an open car, nor was there even a gondola on which I could get down on or between two box cars to break the cold wind. So I had to walk the whole length of the train on top, hounding up a "Reefer," or else ride it out on top and freeze.

I wasn't aware there were so many riders until I started to look for an empty Reefer. Practically every one had an occupant, and it was a toss up as to which one to take. I finally selected one after sort of asking permission or whether it was OK to drop down into it from its occupant. You don't like to thrust yourself on someone's company, and too, you wouldn't like to be an unwelcome comrade in one of those Reefers, so you in general ask. So, at about the fifth one, I lean over and go through the usual code and I am told, "Sure, come on down."

Perhaps I had better explain just what is a Reefer.

A Reefer is that part of a refrigerator car that is situated at the extreme ends of the car. It is partitioned off by a strong wire screen and it is in this small space that the ice is packed in to keep the car cool, so that whatever perishable goods it is loaded with are kept from spoiling by the heat from hot weather. Or, as in some cases, where perishable goods spoil from their own heat, especially when packed tightly, such as bulk oranges, apples, melons, etc., etc. In the winter months the car is not generally iced, but by keeping the trap doors on top of the cars open, there is sufficient frigidity from the cold air.

So, that is a Reefer, and one of which I will have to spend at least eighteen or twenty hours in if I stick to it, before I reach San Antonio.

If there is any place on a freight train that is more uncomfortable to ride in than a Reefer, I have never found it, unless it might be underneath on the wheel tracks. If you want to add to the discomfiture, just double up with another rider, especially one that has no principles or decorum and insists on taking up three quarters of the space for themselves.

It is bad enough to ride in a car where there is plenty of room in which you do have half a chance to at least move around in, but it is worse when you are cooped up in a space about nine feet long, five feet wide, with a fellow who might perhaps be lousy and smell with body odor and clothes that stink with the odors of a hundred mission flop houses, and whose language is anything but decent, and who is so lazy and unprincipled that he urinates down between the grating of a Reefer. And I have seen them attempt to defecate in the same manner and would have done so, if someone hadn't raised hell about it.

Many and many a time I have had to vacate one of these Reefers and finish the journey riding on top. For it is far preferable to me to get a freezing out than to stand some of the men you by chance have to associate with. And too, when I had been the first man to be lucky enough to beat any one else to an empty Reefer, I have prevented others from forcing themselves on my privacy. I do this especially when they look exceptionally dirty and don't observe the code or etiquette they should.

I was particularly fortunate on this trip to have doubled up with a very sociable fellow who showed more consideration for the next fellow and who seemed to have a fairly good education. But I had only to look at him once to realize he was a pretty sick man.

It would have to be a pretty fussy person who couldn't stand a sick man, even though he might look pretty seedy, so I felt satisfied with my lot and prepared to make the best of it, but I hoped he wouldn't get sick on my hands.

There was no doubt he was suffering from tuberculosis, for during a short conversation we had, he had to stop several times on account of the severe coughing spells that seemed to take all his strength to conquer. On one occasion, I noted he coughed up blood, which is an indication of an active and very advanced degree of Tuberculosis.

After an exchange of personal history, I learned he is a veteran, only two days out of a hospital and on his way home. He claimed he couldn't stand the monotony of a hospital and he didn't feel there was anything more could be done, so he felt he might as well die at home, where at least he was among his own people and friends.

I thought that was a very foolish way to look at things, for what could his people and friends do to help him to recover or how could they help make death any easier? Too, why ask his folks to care for him and run the risk of contracting the disease? And too, there were children, for he claimed to have two young children at home.

Well, I am a veteran myself, and out of respect to another comrade in arms, I'll have to help him all I can if he gets too sick to handle himself, so I proceed to make things as comfortable and as pleasant as I could by keeping up a conversation about things I thought would be of interest to both of us. He seemed to respond to my efforts. If anyone happened to be listening, they perhaps would have heard the World War going on again, and of course won again. It is this kind of recreation (that is, pleasant conversation) that makes for a pleasant ride and the time passes on, for it isn't often you will meet up with a man who can hold a conversation and argue certain points without getting personal or insulting while traveling a la Hobo.

I had two blankets that I bought in Oakland, California, and which I managed to hang onto without having them stolen. I had rolled within them some food and a little contraption of a stove I had made out of an old tomato can, and so we had sandwiches and hot coffee, after which we stretched out and tried to get some sleep.

Now, I don't know how many people there are that might read this account of my wanderings, that have ever had the experience of trying to get any sleep in one of these Reefers. If they have, they will bear me out if I say, "It's an experience one will not forget for quite some time after."

Sleeping on a flat surface, whether it be on the ground or on the floor of a boxcar or any other contrivance is one thing, but trying to get a comfortable position and to sleep on a galvanized iron V-shaped floor with the narrow part of the V upwards which are about four inches apart—that is still another thing. Anyone who can sleep on that must be as hard as nails or built (or born) with corrugated ridges.

Such is the kind of a floor one has to contend with in a Reefer. And one of the many inconveniences one must contend with while riding freights.

There is an element of serious danger too in using a Reefer. Being situated at the end of a car, they are the first part to receive the brunt of an end-on collision. In that case, anyone in one would most likely be trapped like rats and crushed to death. The other dangerous element is suffocation, for there are cargoes that require that all the vents be closed. If it should happen that the top door, which is bound around the edge with felt insulation, should accidentally fall closed and you should happen to fall asleep for any length of time after being closed in such an airtight compartment...well, it's a hundred to one chance if you do awaken to discover your predicament. You wouldn't have the strength to open the closed trap door, for these doors are fitted and made in a wedged shape. I know how hard one is to open and if I ever was close to being scared to death, it was on one occasion when a shack closed both doors on account of a heavy rain storm, but he didn't know anybody was inside. He undoubtedly would have ordered us out instead of shutting us in as he did.

But to go back to where I left off, neither one of us could get any rest laying stretched out, so I doubled my blankets up. We sat side by side like two tired soldiers sitting in a "shell hole" on a battlefield, the one wounded and the other holding him up so that the pressure on his back didn't hurt him.

My sick companion was complaining somewhat and had had two severe coughing spells once we had our coffee. We had sort of dropped off in a doze when we were suddenly brought to our full senses by someone walking along the top of the car. They suddenly stopped and poked a flashlight in the Reefer and commanded us to come up on top.

"I want to get a look at you," says he.

I told my companion to remain where he was so I got on top and I found I was answering questions in regards to who we were and our citizenships.

Before I returned to the Reefer, I looked around to find I am in a town called Alpine, Texas. Here is where is maintained an Emigration

Station and it was an Emigration Officer who was shaking the train down for possible unlawful entrants that might be slipping into the interior.

I returned to my companion's side and explained matters. Just as I got nicely settled, someone came along and hollers down, saying "Don't any of you fellers get off here."

I waited a minute or two after his footsteps faded out of hearing and climbed up and peeked over the edge. I saw silhouetted against a street light a man about six feet tall with riding breeches and a ten gallon hat on and he grasped two heavy Colt pistols. While he stood with his feet spread apart, he reminded me of one of those Western moving picture heroes. While I am on the subject, this officer was the closest approach or semblance of a real He-man, hell-shooting wild cowboy, and general all around "Terror of the Western Plains" I saw in all my wanderings to and from California.

This freight was making marvelous time, which in fact should bring us in to San Antonio on scheduled time. My companion had another coughing spell and this time I thought he would pass out from the severity of the attack, but he finally got control of himself and had to lay down from exhaustion.

I was getting worried but I didn't let on to him my opinion in regards to the seriousness of his condition, so I tried to get into a position to sit down. Try hard as I might, any position I got into was too uncomfortable, so I stood up and once more I actually fell asleep on my feet.

My partner seemed to have fallen asleep, for I could hear his heavy breathing above the rumble of the train. It was a rasping kind of a noise, which led me to think that San Antonio would be as far as he could go. I let him sleep on, for while he was asleep I figured he would get some of his strength back. He remarked once or twice that he was more or less worried as to whether he could get back up on top. He wasn't sure he could make it, but I told him not to worry as I would help him all I could.

There is a code I shall never depart from or violate as long as I live and have the strength or means to uphold. It is one that every veteran should follow. He should do his best at all times to help his comrade in arms when he is sick or hungry or in trouble.

As we rolled on towards San Antonio, it seemed to be getting colder and colder and my companion was awakened by the chill, so I asked him if he could stand another cup of coffee.

"Gee, boy I sure could! It seems to be getting real cold." This he said between chattering teeth.

I supposed he had a fever, so naturally he felt the cold much more readily than I, and besides he didn't have as heavy an overcoat on as I did.

I made some more coffee and after we got to feeling the effects of its heat, we both felt better.

I never was so thankful for making that little tomato can stove than I was on this particular part of my trip back. I might claim without much boasting that that contraption of an improvised little stove, whose only fuel was two tallow candles, might have been the cause of this fellow's ability to hold up as well as he did. I do know he felt as thankful as I did.

My Ingersoll had stopped, so I didn't know the time. So I climbed up to look around, to get some idea as to just where we are. I soon ducked back from the cold air for we certainly were stepping on it through this part of Texas, much of which was just wastelands of sand and cactus.

After about an hour's ride through this wasteland, the air seemed to get much warmer. It seemed as though we had emerged from a cold room into a moderately warm one. The effects of it could be felt even down in the depths of the Reefer.

I took advantage of this warmer spell, or current of air, by sitting on top. It felt good to get the desert chill out of my bones. It seemed to be so soft and balmy and with it came that earthy smell one gets while aboard some ship as they near land, or perhaps might smell while passing some tropical island.

It was a terribly dark night; so dark I could barely make out objects close by the right of way and still the sky didn't seem to be overcast so very heavily. If it was not for the rumble and creaking (and occasional screeching) of the train and its wheels, and the feel of the car under me to assure me I was still in reality, I might well imagine I was sailing or floating through a void rather than skimming across the face of the good old Earth, so stark and static was the inky darkness that seemed to surround me.

The freight is slowing, slacking in its speed and as we round a curve, we suddenly emerge into a small railroad yard and come to a stop. The freight is half in and half out, trailing beyond its limits like some gigantic centipede whose tail is lost in the inky gloom.

I took advantage of this stop to get a respite from the constant vibration and sway of the freight and to get my circulation back to normal and to stretch my legs. It felt good to feel the solid earth on the soles of my feet. It was a respite from standing on those narrow ridges of galvanized iron on the floor of that Reefer.

I had covered about half the length of the forward end on my walk when I caught up with the car knocker[1] who was inspecting

---

1. Railroad slang for car inspector.

the wheels for hot boxes[2] or other defects, and inquired as to where we were. I must have surprised him, for he swung around sharply and held his lantern up to the level of my face as though he had recognized in my voice the voice of someone he knew. After scanning my face and (I suppose) satisfied he didn't know me or that I wasn't some railroad officer or official, he informed me we are in Dryden, and he also informed me I had better get back on again. For, says he, "The freight will pull out right away and it's too dangerous a place to attempt hopping it, so you had better make it snappy," and then he proceeded with his inspection.

When I returned to my car I found two men sitting near the entrance of the Reefer and when I came over the top and dropped down inside I heard one of them remark, "Can you beat that! What a hell of nerve, taking our Reefer."

I made no answer to their remarks. My companion was asleep so I did not disturb him.

Just as the train started, the two men started to come down, so I told them to keep on staying right where they were, but one of them paid no heed to me and said, "Hello, Bo, where are you bound for?"

My pardner now was awake and got to his feet and the both of us just looked at the man. I could see he didn't like the looks of the man, so I answered him by saying, "We are bound in the same direction you are bound for right now, when we get to the end of this run, and that is up through that hole over you. The only difference is, you will reach that opening long before we do, so get going right pronto!"

The man looked at me in surprise and no doubt he was peeved, for he said, "Why, what is the matter? I can ride in here if I want to, can't I?"

---

2. A defect in the devices used to lubricate the axles.

"No sir, you can't ride in this Reefer—not tonight, at least. So get up through there like I told you," putting as much emphasis on the get as I could.

He finally started to climb on out, but when he got clear of the entrance, he leaned over and hollers down, shaking his fist. "Wait until I see you in San Antonio. I'll fix you!"

"OK, pal, I'll see you right near the ice plant any time you say or just as soon as I get there. And don't you forget the date, either!" I hollered back at him.

I climbed up to see if he was still around, for I was afraid he might get nasty and dirty and slam the door down on us, a trick I have seen on one or two occasions by damn punks, but he had disappeared.

This fellow was really a punk, or one perfectly vicious bum in the making. Their "ace in the hole" is making you think they are regular hobos by using a hobo's salutation in order to get acquainted. Then, after they are in, they start to butt into everybody and everything. After that, he starts to bum everybody and everything that anybody has or brings to light. He never gives but he always takes. He never has anything and he never works, and the rest of the time he is either stealing off his fellow man or sleeping a drunk off.

It is he who breaks through the screens on the Reefers, filching everything and anything he can, thus making it harder and harder for other riders who try to respect the authorities and other people's property.

I put the skids under everyone like him every time I get the opportunity—and I have had plenty of opportunities since I hit the road. I give them my special attention.

Dawn is breaking. We can see evidence of it when we glance skyward through the open door way over us. I feel much relieved that it is, for now I know the sun will soon be up and also I know it will not be long before this part of the trip will be over. Too, it will help my pardner to recover a little of his strength he no doubt has lost through coughing due to the night air and the rough traveling.

We were traveling faster now than we had been for the past hour or so, which generally is the way most freights seem to do when near the end of a run or nearing a railroad yard.

Just to get an idea as to what kind of country we were rolling through, I climbed up through the doorway and sat on its edge.

All I see is desolation.

Mile after mile it was nothing but sand, cactus, Mesquite, Chaparral, and here and there a Giant Cactus which really was about the only things in that vast expanse of country that held my interest. I couldn't make out a living thing—not even a buzzard.

Suddenly, the countryside began to take on a different color. It reminded me of a color scheme that starts with the lighter shades and then graduates on up through the darker shades until finally it has run into the solids.

Off to my right, small groups of buildings appear and as the train rounds a low range of hillocks, I see the real outskirts of San Antonio, Texas.

I announced the fact that we are pretty close to San Antonio and advised him he had better get ready to leave soon, but he didn't pay much attention. He acted as if it was an hourly occurrence to him, so I descended once more into the Reefer and told him if he didn't want to get knocked off by the Bulls, both of us would have to get off before we got into the yards.

That seemed to wake him up, so he got to his feet and tried to get up on top, but he couldn't make it, even with my help.

Well. here's where this man and yours truly certainly will have a run in, but there is no use of worrying and too, I can't very well run out on the man now. So let come what might, I said to myself, as the train came near and nearer to the yards. The train has come to a stop and there they are, three of them (officers) shaking the train down, but I keep my seat.

When the first officer reached me, I got on my feet and, pointing down into the Reefer, I said, "I've got a pretty sick veteran in there. I wonder if you would help me get him out in order that I might get him to some hospital."

He looked down into the Reefer and looked the man over and said, "OK. You get him on his feet and help lift him and I'll pull him up. I am a veteran myself."

The officer and another man pulled him up and helped me get him down on the ground and over to one side of the track and then he had a coughing spell that I thought would be his last.

The officer shook his head and looked at me as if to say, "It won't be long now."

I managed to get him out of the yards and on down to a restaurant and then called up an organization both of us belonged to and they came and took him with them in their car.

And once more I am on my own.

Chapter Twenty-Seven

San Antonio to Houston

San Antonio is my pet city in that great state of Texas. It seems like home to me. I feel as I walk along its streets I am among friends. No one interferes with you and no overzealous officer stops you, wanting to know your whole history. When you speak to someone you get a civil answer, and whether you are in overalls or have a fifty-dollar suit, you are treated with the same courtesy and receive the same service and with just as genial a smile. You feel free and a part of the city and it seems as though you have lived there all your life. It seems you have known everybody you speak to for years. It is a great city, I think.

When I came through this city of San Antonio on my westward journey, I stayed at an Army Post, but I felt to ask any more of them would sort of be an imposition. So I am going to try the Transient Bureau this time. Perhaps I might just by chance scare up a job and if I did, I hoped it might be something worthwhile. If it was, it might come about that I could stay on here indefinitely. Such were the thoughts that occupied my mind as I scanned the buildings along San Antonio's main street on the lookout for the Transient Bureau.

This Transient Bureau was like the city of San Antonio itself—it was good. Clean, quiet and well managed as it was, I wouldn't know it was a Transient Bureau if it wasn't that I had to give the officer my pedigree. After that, you were not bothered from then on, as long as you lived up to the rules and regulations.

I spoke of this place being clean and quiet. But when I sat down to breakfast on the following morning my praise mounted to noble heights when I saw the food that was on the table. The menu: Oatmeal, Toast, Pork Sausages, Fried Potatoes, all the Soda Biscuits you cared to eat; plenty of Milk and Butter, and Maple Syrup. And first class Coffee.

If I ever I thanked God I was an American, it was on this first morning I ate breakfast here in the Transient Bureau in good old San Antonio. I might add too, that I came near committing murder when I heard one man at the end of the table I was eating at complaining about the kind of s— they served in this place.

"I wouldn't ask pigs to eat such stuff," says he.

But we all got a good laugh when one of the other men said to him, "No, well, we don't like pigs eating at our table, so it's OK with me if you excuse yourself and be on your way. And please don't slam the door on your way out."

Then several of the men started to imitate a pig grunting. The complainant stood it as long as he could, then got up and left. I never saw him around after that.

The imitating of a pig was to my way of thinking a cheap sort of business, but such is the way of the element that you generally find roaming from one Transient Bureau to the other. But there is one thing about them—they don't hash words when things are bad. Generally it doesn't do them much good to complain; still, it helps to keep things or conditions at a minimum.

I stayed over in San Antonio for three days and got a good rest and refitted for what I intended to be a dash for New York City. I knew I would have some pretty tough traveling when I got up above Washington D.C., for now it is in the middle of February. I had read one of the weather reports and from the temperatures recorded I judged I had plenty of cold weather ahead of me.

I could have stayed over here in San Antonio indefinitely if I cared to accept a very small paying job in the Transient Bureau. The pay was so small I figured it wasn't worth the time and trouble, and, too, it was too much like living as a Mission Staffer to suit me. The duties that I had to perform were such that if I carried them out conscientiously I would become a marked man from one end of the country to the other.

It is surprising how fast news travels along the routes that are traversed by the gentry of the road. I have listened with much interest about this fellow and that fellow who have been long since outcast from the "regular guys," as one is called who tries to help a poor wayfarer or who overlooks certain irregularities.

Using the term "fellow" or "guy" or "man" when referring to some of the men who have any authority or upon whom they come in contact with when asking for shelter is certainly highly complimentary, if I was to believe all I had heard of them.

I later found that nine times out of ten, most of the stories were in most part true. In fact, some of the stories were just an outline of the truth in comparison to what I found when I had any dealings with some of them. For being downright contemptible curs they have no equal, especially if they at one time had been a bum and now were connected to a Mission Staff and have gone "religious." Some actually became fanatical in their cussedness.

I had heard of how easy it would be to hitchhike from here to Washington, D.C. To listen to some there was nothing to it. All one had to do would be to stand at some advantageous point or at a crossroad and anybody would pick you up. Especially, it was easy down in this part of the country. One fellow told me he made eight hundred miles on one hitch.

I tried hitchhiking once when I first started out from New York City (Newark to Philadelphia) and my experience on that occasion wasn't so hot. But of course that doesn't prove that it can't be done, so I am going to give it another try down here where it is easy.

I have always been more or less curious about the why and wherefore of things and generally give most things and fellow man the benefit of the doubt.

So here I stand on the fourth day of arriving in San Antonio on one of the highways leading north, trying to get a hitchhike in that direction.

Whether it was my appearance or whether the drivers and owners of cars and trucks of the whole country had decided they were not picking up any more hitchhikers on this particular day, I am sure I don't know. But one thing was certain: I wasn't having any luck. I wasted four precious hours and finally gave it up and returned to San Antonio and ate my dinner.

Without any exaggeration, a thousand cars with license plates from all parts of the country passed and whizzed by without even the drivers looking at me.

After my second experience with hitchhiking, I fell back on the good old railroad and around three or four o'clock I was on my way to Houston, Texas and arrived there quite late in the evening.

If you haven't the fare, you have a five mile walk before you really get into Houston, Texas.

I stopped at the YMCA here and as one of those queer coincidences that pop up once in a while I received the same room that I had occupied when I was here on my way West.

On the following day I paid a visit to the restaurant where I had received my first real job after leaving New York City, and I was told I had just missed a steady job by two days.

"Perhaps," says he, "I might have something for you in a couple of days if you are around Houston. This fellow may not make good, but don't count on it."

I didn't count on it. Instead I took the balance of the day looking for work in other restaurants and a few print shops, but all I found was two jobs which netted me one dollar and a half and two meals. This more than covered my expenses so far. I gave Houston another day of canvassing and found nothing, so on the following day I was on my way again.

It had turned quite cold over night and now it is snowing. The wind is coming from the North and with these sort of weather conditions this far South, I no doubt will run into worse as I progress farther North. So from now on, I will have to ride day and night if I am to reach New York City before any real Winter sets in.

There was no freight until late in the afternoon, so I wandered around Houston and finally eased my way towards the railroad yards. The freight wasn't made up completely when I arrived there, so I climbed to a nearby boxcar and waited until she was ready to pull out. I didn't have long to wait.

It was pretty cloudy all day, so I expected before the night was over I would see some more snow or rain.

Chapter Twenty-Eight

Leaving Texas

I finally notice a road engine back down through the yard, so I jump down and follow it.

If I had not I would have been stuck in Houston for another night, for, instead of the line of cars I thought was to be my freight, the engine started out immediately with an entirely different one. I had to hustle to get it. I was doubly fortunate, for it had started to rain and I found an open boxcar and had just got nicely in it when the rain came down in torrents for almost two hours. Then it started to get cold.

We stepped along at a fair rate of speed. I didn't bother much with the scenery for, due to the damp cold that was setting in, I stayed pretty well in the end of the car out of the wind. It was real raw and bitter.

I saw glimpses of a few small stations as we went through them without hardly slacking any speed. We rolled on, only slacking speed here and there, and before I knew it we were rolling into Beaumont.

I didn't even get off here, for now it was dark and I had heard of hard boiled railroad officers that were the bane of all the hobos. So I stayed on and under cover as much as I could. I saw one railroad officer around and I also saw him pull a few off and march them towards a couple of cars parked near the engine and take them with him, but I didn't see him pull off any hard boiled stuff.

The train crew got through with their shifting and soon we were on our way once more towards New Orleans. It was really cold—damn cold, if I may use the word. I was looking for snow before we reached New Orleans. I didn't have long to wait before we reached another place. We had some light snow flurries and that just about knocked in the head all one hears about the "Sunny South" and the wonderful climate one may enjoy during the winter months. Yeah, come down to the "Sunny South" and go in bathing all the year round. Maybe so, but they will have to show me. It sure isn't along this route.

We kept moving along through small towns and hamlets, over small patches of sand, then over small bodies of water that looked like swamps. I could make out along the tracks and off a short distance away the outline of buildings or Sugar Cane Plantations. And once in a while, as the fireman opened his fire box door (which casts a reflection on a small patch of countryside), I could make out evidence we were passing some cotton land, shorn of its crop and now almost barren of even the stalks.

Our next stop should be Lake Charles. This is a place I didn't even know we went through on my way West. So I know very little about it, other than it seems to be a division point. When we finally reached there sometime early in the morning, I didn't get out of the boxcar I was riding.

There was the usual activity when a freight pulls into a division: changing engines and shifting of cars, inspecting and so forth. And, last but not least, the usual shaking down of the freight for hobos, bums, and other riders.

You get to know just about how long a freight will be in such a place by the type of freight you are riding or by the size of the division you stop at. So, in Lake Charles we only shifted a few cars and soon were on our way.

Lake Charles is a pretty good sized place, for there seemed to be quite a few waiting for her to pull in. We now had about sixty men on this train. We picked up some in Beaumont; I overheard some talking about how cold it had been. Those who it seemed had been living in shacks along the water had to leave on that account so no doubt they were heading either for warmer quarters or perhaps Florida.

As luck would have it, none took advantage of the car I was riding in, so I have been alone so far from Houston, which was OK with me. I like company but not the company one might pick up along a freight line. You are panhandled from start to finish. I defy anyone riding among a lot of men in a boxcar to pull out a package of cigarettes or bag of tobacco that someone won't beg of you the makings. If that was all that they would ask you (and it makes no difference whether the bag has enough for one making or fifty), you can consider yourself real lucky. No sir. No such luck, for every man jack on that car would make you for the same as the first one. I did this once to my sorrow. It wasn't the amount of tobacco I gave out. I was glad to do it. But it was the last bag I had, and I did not have the wherewithal to buy another. Well, one must expect this sort of thing, but one experience learns you to keep to yourself and also not to pull out anything and show it like cigarettes, money, or a bag of tobacco, or anything to eat; for, if you do, you might as well lay it down in the middle of the boxcar and say, "Help yourself, boys."

So every time I go on a trip, I take with me a bag of cheap tobacco I can buy for just such emergencies. Would you believe me, I was soon known and treated fine by all who ever met me or knew me, from

Washington, DC to Los Angeles, California. I never had to ask but once for a lift or any direction or where the best place was to stop. The code of the road is that way.

Well, here we go, and for some reason or other we came to as sudden a stop as ever I had the experience to go through on anything with wheels. It stopped so sudden the door of the boxcar banged shut. I thought for sure I was trapped, but as luck would have it the fixtures on the outside were broke. It was a good thing too I was away from that door, for as sure as fate I wouldn't be here telling about it. I have heard of men being almost decapitated by boxcar doors shutting suddenly.

I opened the door up and looked down the length of the train and did I get a laugh at the way some of the hobos and so forth were piling off and running across the tracks off of railroad property. They were falling off the train like leaves falling from a tree in the fall. The trainmen were getting a kick out of it too.

What happened was, one of the air connections came loose, so naturally the brakes were set against the wheels to their fullest braking power. The crew cut out the car where the brake was, and soon we were rolling out of Lake Charles, but a good many of the men who jumped off were left behind to wait for the next freight out. Well, I guess they had a bad case of the "Bull Horrors" or heebee-jeebees.

The next stop will be Jennings, Louisiana, so I hope I can stay on as I did in Lake Charles. It certainly saves a lot of trouble ducking about, and besides, it is dangerous walking about railroad yards in the dark.

Well, after we pulled out of Lake Charles, I tried to get some sleep, but for awhile it was useless. So, I paced up and down that car for almost an hour. I tried laying down on the other side of the car and finally I fell fast asleep and didn't wake up until we were pulling into Jennings.

Here the trainman came along looking into every empty car. When he came to the one I was in he called in, saying, "Stay where you are and be still. The Bull just got a nice load, but I'm sure he won't be back this far. He had all he could get in his car, so I don't think he will be back in time for more."

He went on back to the caboose and when he disappeared inside, I just slid down to the ground easy and as still as I could and stepped over into the shadows. Did I use my head that time!

That trainman certainly tried to put it over on me for fair. I don't know what it was, but his tone of voice just didn't ring true when he was telling me about what the railroad officer was doing

In about five minutes I notice a strong light flashing up and down on the other side of the train, so I just step to one end of the car I was riding in and let the wheels help to keep me out of view. I then watched and listened until he was pretty near the end of the train and about to go around the caboose. Down the other side he comes, but in the meanwhile I had climbed up and over between the ends of two cars and let myself down on the other side. One door was opened only and wedged on one side of my car, so when he came to it he flashed his light inside and of course found no one. I heard him mumble something to himself and then flash his light around and, finding nothing or anybody around, he continued on down towards the engine. Just as soon as I saw he was clear, I crawled back over and into the car.

This was only one instance of ducking and playing hide and seek one goes through with the railroad officers. I really think they don't try half as hard as they might and also I am of the opinion they don't worry much about anything they don't see. So if anyone riding on freights keeps well out of sight, they have a fairly good chance of keeping entirely out of all jails, as far as trespassing on railroad property is concerned.

At this place I didn't see any working being done. We just sat there. Perhaps the crew was eating. Whatever it was, we were here for almost an hour.

Every few minutes I looked out, watching for that railroad officer, but I guess he was satisfied that there was no one else on board.

I sat down a little back from the door and fell into a doze, only to be awakened by a jerk of the train which rolled me over on my side. We seemed to be having a lot of trouble getting underway. The train would start and then come to a sudden stop. After a half a dozen such starts and stops we finally got out of Jennings. I sure was thankful, too.

We picked up speed rapidly and after a few miles out of Jennings, we were sailing along at a good clip.

"Well," I thought to myself, "She can fly for all I care. The sooner this stage of the trip is over, the better I'll feel."

After knocking about, you soon learn there are a lot of inconveniences you will have to put up with that you don't like, and one of them is sleeping on the ground or floors or whatever surface you can find. I was getting pretty used to such inconveniences so I didn't have much trouble or any bad effect when I slept some of the time on the floor of boxcars while enroute between stops or division points.

So, soon after leaving Jennings, I lay down at the end of the car I was riding and fell fast asleep and didn't wake up until we reached a place called Crowley, Louisiana. I must have slept right through all the time we were there. I don't know whether we stopped there or not. All I do know is I woke up and peered through the darkness and just caught the name on a sign board which read "Crowley," so perhaps for all I know we may not have stopped there.

The weather or cold seems to have moderated a bit since we left Lake Charles, so I sat up feeling somewhat better for that fact and the sleep I had obtained.

I didn't pay much attention to what sort of country we were passing through. So I just sat there listening to the roar of the train and the screech of the wheels as she rounded a curve here and there. Once in a while we hit a fairly good stretch of track with no turnings in it and through level country. When we did, about all you could make out was the click of the wheels over the rails, as she seemed to take advantage of the level road bed.

I was getting hungry, so I retreated into the car and started making some hot coffee and by the time I was finished we were just pulling into Lafayette, Louisiana. Here I had to get off, for this seemed to be a pretty large place, so I jumped down and walked up and down to get the circulation back into my legs. It is surprising how stiff one can become even though you have the whole car to yourself to walk from one end to the other. There seems to be a different reaction from exercise taken on *terra firma* than that obtained in a small enclosure.

This trip from San Antonio to New Orleans seemed to be the most monotonous of the whole distance I had already covered from Los Angeles. Perhaps it was due to being entirely alone and riding at night. It only brings out the truth to a saying some people believe in, viz., "It is not good for Man to be alone."[1] It would be hard to apply this (and live up to it) to the mode of living I was now in, for it seems the old "Brotherhood of the Road" has either died out, or else I haven't as yet met any of the real old timers I have often heard of.

I killed the time walking up and down in the shadows. I didn't see any activity on the part of the railroad officers, so I grew a little more confident as I kept lengthening my walk as I took my exercise on down towards the engine. At one point I had lengthened my walk to almost within two car lengths of the engine. I stood there for a minute and

---

1. Genesis 2:18b.

was about to return back to my car when someone called out, "Where the hell do you think you're going?"

I said nothing and continued on as though no one had called to me. I didn't see anyone following me, nor did I see the usual flashlight stabbing the darkness you generally see when a railroad officer is around a yard. I didn't even hear a soul about. So, I just laid it to one of the trainmen having his little joke; perhaps he had a couple of shots uptown and was feeling his oats and by now he was having his little laugh to himself.

"Well," I thought to myself, "It takes all kinds of people to make a world, and railroad men were no exception to the rule in making it worthwhile living in. For better or worse."

I welcomed that call out of the darkness, for I was feeling somewhat lonely from the monotony of this portion of my return trip. It sort of brought me back to life and more pleasant thoughts. There is a kind of loneliness that will come over you even in the midst of a crowd of people or in the midst of extreme hilarity or din. So it was with me, walking up and down in that railroad yard and while close at hand was the city of Lafayette with its people—while on the other hand, here was the banging of cars, the hissing of steam, the screeching of the car wheels, and creaking of the cars as they settled into position in their respective places in the yard. It is a loneliness hard to analyze. You would think it impossible to become so when you have everything around you that ought to be of interest: People, humor, industrial activity, travel, and so many other things that ought to have influence enough to keep you from moodiness and loneliness.

I didn't give the subject much more thought other than, "It was beyond me to solve the reason or cause of it," and to leave it to others who are students of such subjects.

WAITING FOR THE TRAIN

From the map of the Southern Pacific Railroad, I note Lafayette seems to be a point where, if you are on a passenger bound for New Orleans and you care to go to Baton Rouge, you can change here. No doubt that applies to freight also, but it made no difference to me one way or another, so I didn't make any inquiries. New Orleans wasn't so important that I had to go that way back to New York City. Then again, I didn't care to advertise my presence in the yard. That ordinarily would initiate trouble, so I ducked back into my car and trusted to luck for a safe arrival in either one: Baton Rouge or New Orleans.

The freight was kept for almost two hours. It stood there for almost an hour after it was made up. No doubt it was run on scheduled time and had its specified hour to leave. I was pleased in a way, for it gave me a chance to limber up and a change from the close quarters of the car I was riding.

At last I see the crew coming on; the knockers are going over her, and the inspectors going along trying the air lines and seeing that everything is as it should be.

And, wonder of wonders, I didn't see any railroad officers. This must be their night off, thought I.

Ah! There goes the whistle and we are off.

We must be going down a grade, for she started without one exhaust from the stack of the engine, so easy did she roll out of the yard. She kept up top speed until we reached another division, which was at New Iberia, a place we only took on oil and water. It was still dark so I tried to get some more sleep, but for some reason or other I couldn't dim the roar of the train as she sped on down the rails and into the night. I had no other thing to do but just sit there and await the oncoming dawn, which shouldn't be so far from breaking.

I am sorry in a way I didn't stop off for the night at Lafayette, for this was the second time I have been over this same route and both times at night. I imagine I missed seeing some very nice country. Well, in a way, perhaps by riding at night I escaped a lot of worry and bother and also I was making a speedier trip.

I notice a few streaks of light in the sky and that informs me broad daylight isn't so many hours away. But with it seems to be a dense fog coming up. So heavy it becomes that I can't see my hand in front of my face.

I could detect the odor of salt air and the smell of some dank swamp in the air. My clothes began to get real soggy from the moisture. The fog was so heavily addled with moisture.

We slackened speed and at times we just merely moved along. How the engineer was able to see any lights is beyond me, unless he was figuring by the speed to know where he was. Anyhow, he kept the train moving along slowly, with here and there a little spurt of speed. I don't know how long we were between New Iberia and the next stop which should be Franklin. We moved along, creeping now at about a 30 mile gait. The engineer perhaps was taking a chance of perhaps getting through the fog into better conditions.

We were going through some town, but didn't stop. The fog was still heavy and the air very warm and muggy. So I took my overcoat off and sat on it, enjoying a soft seat and the warm air, even though it was damp. I gave thought to that for a few moments, thinking it peculiar it should be so nice and warm with all the dampness, whereas my experience had been to feel rather chilly and sometimes real cold in a fog. This was the case with fogs in and around Los Angeles and San Francisco, California.

We finally came to a standstill and I got out of the car and started to walk towards the head end. On my way I ran smack into one of the crew. He excused himself and stopped and remarked, "This is some fog, eh, boy?"

I answered back in consternation by saying, "I'll say so. Just like pea soup, the kind they have in England."

He continued on but stopped a short distance away and shouted to me through the fog, "If you came in on this freight and intend to go all the way through with it, you'd better get back on, for we are only stopping here for orders."

Boy, did I turn around when he imparted to me that piece of information and friendly advice. I found my car and none too soon, for we started to move out of there pretty quickly.

I stood at the doorway as we got underway, trying to make out where we were. I couldn't make out anything, for the fog was as thick as ever and damper than since it came up. So, seeing nothing, I turned around to look for a place to sit down. As I was about to do so, I heard footsteps at the other end of the car. No one came out so I sat down and kept myself ready and alert for any monkey business that might be about to happen. No one came out for a few moments and when they did I found I had for a pardner a real little old man. He wasn't more than five feet tall. I looked at him and he returned the look, but said nothing.

After looking him over I find he is dressed in a good suit and overcoat. He wore a real natty cap, a clean shirt, and a bright red tie. When I came to his shoes I looked in amazement for he had the largest pair of feet I ever saw on a man, or woman for that matter. He saw the surprised look and said, "I know how they look, but I can't help it. I was born that way," his voice quavering.

"Then you haven't any reason to be ashamed of them, my friend. You certainly can't help that," I answered in as friendly a tone as I could.

From then on, I tried not to notice them when he was really looking at me, but between times I got a good look. I'll swear his shoes were made to order and their size wasn't any less than size 16. Some understanding, thought I.

I was more than pleased we were the only ones in that boxcar for I was thinking of obscene remarks that would be made about his red neck tie from some of the younger element that you sometimes meet up with on the road.

I rather liked the old gent for he was soft spoken and apparently pretty well educated. From some of his conversation he at one time had owned considerable property somewhere near New Orleans. I tried to bring him out in regards to his nationality and his ancestors but he evaded my attempts very cleverly by changing the subject on which we might be talking.

I am of the opinion he was a pensioner, by birth an old resident of New Orleans, and by nationality he was a Creole, although he didn't have the complexion of one. At least not like those I had already seen in New Orleans.

It was he who told me the last place we stopped at was Morgan City. To say the least I was much pleased we were really on our last lap to New Orleans.

The fog still hung low and had not lessened in its density, so as far as seeing this part of Louisiana I was just out of luck. I took advantage of the lull in sightseeing by sitting down and dozing while the old gent sort of kept watch.

Every mile brought us nearer to our destination. I gave thought to what I wouldn't do to a good dinner and how long I could sleep when I got to the end of this stage of the trip. The old gent paced up and down most of the time, stopping now and then to peer out into the thick fog, but he didn't disturb me while I dozed off into a sound sleep.

WAITING FOR THE TRAIN

I must have been pretty near dead to the world for the old gent had to shake me before I finally came to life. I looked up at him and asked him, "Are we here at last?" in a sleepy voice.

"Yep, We are here, but this fog I am afraid is going to force us to go all the way into the yards," he said with a little fear and doubt in his voice.

"Oh, I don't think we have anything to fear if we do. The fog is still thick and I am sure no one will see us unless they are right on top of us," I said, trying to encourage him.

"Maybe," was all he said in answer to my words.

We started to slow down and I gathered up my belongings preparatory to leaving on a moment's notice. We still kept moving on and for just one moment there came a break in that dense fog. I saw then where we were—*and off I go!* The old gent called, "Here you! Come back here you. Come back here young fellow—I got something for you. I owe it to you. Wait for me."

It was too late now, for by the time I got up and straightened out and got my clothes brushed off, the freight had disappeared in the fog. And that was the last I ever saw of him.

I floundered around in the fog for almost an hour before I found the ferryboat landing and when I did I could have leaped with joy when I was aboard it and across the river and in New Orleans at last.

Chapter Twenty-Nine

New Orleans, Again

Now for that restaurant I ate in when I first landed here. Now for a good meal and a good cup of that coffee that is only obtainable in New Orleans, and then to bed.

Never was I so pleased I was here and through with that much of my return trip.

I slept most of the first day I arrived in New Orleans. It must have been around 3 pm when I finally checked out of the hotel. It was real warm now; the fog had lifted during the day and the sun was out in all its glory. I took advantage of the few hours of daylight left and started to walk out to the railroad yards. The first time I arrived here on my westward trip I had one grand time finding my way out of the Chantilly Yards. I rode in on the Louisville & Nashville Railroad and I arrived there real early in the morning. This time I wasn't going to get caught by wandering into a swamp like the first time.

It is eleven miles from the center of New Orleans to the Chantilly Yards. There is a trolley line that will take you within a mile of it, but while I had the time to spare I walked it, hoping I might run across something out of the ordinary run of things. There is also a transfer line or track running from the Chantilly Yards to the center of New Orleans, so when I had covered half the distance a short transfer caught up with me and I noticed the brakeman waving his arms to me to jump on. I took his hint and rode the rest of the way to the yards.

There is somewhat of a Jungle just off the road bordering the yards. When I arrived there I found about ten or fifteen other men hanging around it, no doubt going east as I was. I didn't mix with them much, and neither did I speak to any of them other than to say, "Hello, boys."

Some of them were busy washing clothes and many of the other little things a hobo generally putters around with while waiting for train time.

When I arrived in the vicinity of the yard, I noticed an odor coming from across the tracks of the yard. I say "odor" but that wasn't what one could really call it. I should have said "stench." When the breeze came across the track of course it was a little stronger. Once in a while I could detect the smell of creosote too, and then occasionally there came the dank musty smell of a swamp.

But most of the time I got the smell of a combination of the three: creosote, the dank swamp, and whatever it was that made the stench almost unbearable.

I looked across the track trying to make out where the third and strongest odor came from. There were three refrigerator cars standing on a side track on the other side of the yard and, after looking over the yard pretty well, I noticed a pile of debris piled up on the ground on the other side of the refrigerator cars. So, being curious as to what was making that stench, I thought perhaps it was that pile of debris. And it was. For when I finally got the courage up to really hunt the source of awful stench I found this pile to be a pile of decomposed bananas. Boy, when I got real near it the smell near knocked me over.

Now when I got around the end of the three refrigerated cars, what would you suppose I saw? I couldn't believe my eyes, for there I observed two or three men poking about that awful mess and stench for a stray good banana. "Gee," I thought to myself, "Those guys must be awful hungry!"

Well, they say "travel and see things," but who in hell would expect to see men poking around through a pile of rotting bananas for something to eat.

I couldn't stand the stench any longer, so I left and got back and to one side of it where the breeze didn't pass over it.

If anyone wants to smell a real nice stench, just let him get where there is a combination of creosote, a dank swamp, and a pile of rotting bananas. There you have something in the way of a stench you won't forget.

It was late afternoon before we finally saw any evidence of a freight being made up, so I just walked up and down to kill the time.

The sun was starting to set and the wind was getting real chilly so some of the men in the Jungle had started a fire. I sauntered on down towards them and gave the whole lot of them the once over. What I was looking for was one amongst them I thought might be too old and in need of some real assistance. After looking them over I noticed a middle-aged man sitting off to one side leaning over his little fire. The fire didn't seem to be warming him up and I noticed, too, he didn't have the usual can of coffee going on his fire. By the fact he was keeping to himself, I picked him out and finally got his eye and I beckoned him over to the tracks.

He caught my signal and acknowledged it by a nod of his head, but he didn't get up immediately. I walked up and down looking for some wood to start a fire of my own and to look for a stray can to get some water to make some coffee. The man got up and came over and said, "OK, pard, I'll get the water for you."

He came back and we exchanged a few words about the gang in the Jungle and the weather. He called them "a fine bunch of punks" and added, "There isn't any more good hobos on the road."

I answered back, "Yep, it seems that way. Well, don't worry, we'll have them over here when we start to eat, and then we will tell them to shove off."

We soon were sitting alongside a good fire, drinking our coffee and eating the sandwiches I brought with me. No sooner did we get started when I noticed a couple of them easing their way towards us. So I said to my pardner, "You just leave these guys to me," and with that I got up in case they tried to chisel in on our fire.

They came on and when they got abreast of us one of them says, "Hello Bo, how's things?"

I called back to them in a questioning voice, "Well, how do they look and what do you think or wouldn't you know?"

They stood a little distance away as though waiting for an invitation to come near the fire. And when they saw nor heard any coming, they went on further up the track mumbling something in an undertone.

I turned to my pardner who, all though my strategy of keeping them from chiseling in on our fire and eats, was chuckling to himself and munching on a crust of bread. So, with his mouth full, he looked up at me and said, "Yep, I guess they are right."

"What? Who are right?" I said shakily.

"Oh," said he. Then he fell into a study for a few seconds and then he turned to me and said solemnly and slowly, "The laws of retribution sure catch up with some people damn quick."

Such a remark coming from a hobo sure took me off my feet, and I had doubts in my mind as to whether he really understood just what he said. In the incident of the two men trying to chisel in on us I couldn't see where those words could be applied to and have very much sense to them. I was curious just why and how he intended they be applied to any incident or circumstance since he was in my company, so I put the question to him.

"Well, I'll tell you, pard," he said, and then he gave me his reasons by explaining that when he had first entered the Jungles I saw him in, he started a fire and then rustled up a can to make some coffee out of the last handful of grains he had. When he finally got everything going in proper shape, he stepped away from the fire to gather a few more sticks of wood to keep the fire going. When he returned to his fire he found his can of coffee gone, so he being an old hand and a real hobo, he didn't say anything. All he did was to look around at all the fires going for his can, and he wasn't long discovering just where it was and who had taken it. But the funny part of the whole occurrence of the stolen can of coffee was that after they had got it to boiling and about fit to drink, someone accidentally kicked it over, spilling the contents of the can over onto the fire, putting it also out of commission too.

The accidental loss of the coffee and the loss of the fire they were using to cook the coffee with and then the incident of my not accepting their advances of trying to chisel in on our food and water was in all one of the many ways the laws of retribution has of penalizing those who go around committing offenses against the law and innocent law-abiding people.

It is not my belief to be the cause of anyone losing faith in so beautiful a creed. I wouldn't even show the least bit of disagreement by word or action. So I let the fellow alone in his belief and faith, by expressing no opinion for or against his belief in the existence of such a thing as the "Laws of Retribution," although it did coincide in part with an idea of my own; in regards the retaliations that ensue after one commits such offences against mankind in general or any against nature or an established law.

"Well, I guess this fellow and I will get along," I thought as I looked him over with interest. Here was a man who no doubt had some real schooling some time or other and also must have seen better days, perhaps, than I would ever dream of having. Here he was in a Jungle without any money, food, or decent clothing. Queer, then, his remarks about someone being right about retribution came back to me. Was he speaking from personal experience? Was he here and suffering from privation and cold and hunger and many other things one must put up with on the road? Was he a social outcast brought on by the "Laws of Retribution" for something he himself did against society?

I wondered, and then gave it up as being his own business. He was doing the suffering, not I. It was for him alone to carry the burden and from what I already knew of him, he sure was taking it like a man and had learned his lesson, if such be he was guilty.

We sat around the fire in silence, for a cold wind was coming up and when one gets to feeling the chill you don't feel so much like wasting any energy even by talking and also there wasn't anything much to talk about.

It was after a silence of about a quarter of an hour when his voice broke the stillness by saying, "You didn't ask me who it was of all these guys in the jungle that took my coffee."

"No, I didn't to be sure," I answered, then continued with, "Who was it, pard?"

"Those two guys you chased away," he said, with satisfaction ringing in his voice.

Silence prevailed again and it was only broken by a freight engine giving two short blasts, ready to pull out.

"Let's go, pard," he said.

"OK, pard," I answered back.

So up the short bank to the track we climb then over to the moving freight and on it and we are on our way and out of the Chantilly Yards.

My pardner got on first. After he did he peered over the side of the car (which was a gondola) and watched me get on, and after I did and was standing beside him he says to me, "I guess you will do, pard. You made her neat."

We rode in this car until we went onto a side track to let another freight go by. So, while we were here we decided to change to an empty box car if we could find one. Riding outside at night is not as comfortable as riding inside, especially when it is windy or cold, and besides that you advertise yourself.

We found one and a lucky one too for it was full of nice clean paper and that means comfort. I don't know of anything else that will protect you and keep you warmer than paper. We gathered it up and piled it all in one corner and then each took his share of space and stretched out full length, with a feeling on my part that all's well in this World and I am sure he was the kind to feel thankful too.

My pardner immediately fell asleep and as for myself I would have done the same if I didn't have an awful headache. I had been suffering from it since I woke up that afternoon and I was berating myself for not stepping into a drug store to get something to relieve it. I lay stretched out gazing up at the ceiling of the car and getting all the rest

I could. For, anyone riding freights around the country never knows what may happen that might force him to get off where he might have a nice walk back to where he started from or keep on ahead to the next town, city, or whichever may be the nearest. So headache or no headache I was resting anyhow.

Mobile is the next stop of any importance. Here I decided to stop regardless of where my pardner was going. He didn't say where he was going and I didn't ask him and to do so perhaps would bring an answer which I would deserve.

Chapter Thirty

Back to Mobile

We rolled along as all L&N frieghts do. I like that line for its steady and smooth speed. Its freights seem to keep up for every mile from start to stop. So I lay there praising their engineers for knowing how to handle a throttle. On this road too I have witnessed passengers side tracked for freights carrying perishable and valuable merchandise. It is without a doubt one of the fastest freight lines in America.

It was dark when we left New Orleans, Louisiana. There was no use trying to do any sightseeing, and also there was no use getting up and walking around in the dark, so I continued on laying amongst the paper and finally did doze off, but not really asleep.

I wake up in a little while, feeling pretty cold, so I unwrap my bundle and cover myself with it and sort of turn over on my side and find that my pardner had either moved or rolled further away or had got up and was standing somewhere about the car. I dozed off again and I don't know what it was that woke me up but when I did I had a feeling that all was not as it should be in that car. I reached over feeling out lightly with my hand to find out if my pardner had really just moved over or had for some reason or other got up. I reached over as far as I could with my hand but couldn't find him there.

The feeling that something or other was radically wrong still prevailed, so I got up and called out a couple of times, but I received no answer to my calls.

Now, by this time, the feeling increased so I walked as far as the side door and lit another match and researched every corner of that car by its dim light, but he was nowhere around that car.

By this time I was feeling real fearful and sure something really was wrong, so I said half-aloud, "Gee, that is funny. Where could he have gone to?"

I stood by the door, peering into the darkness, trying to figure out how he had managed to get off (if he did), with the freight still keeping its top speed. I was positive it did not stop since we left that side track—I am positive of it—for invariably I always wake up when any vehicle I might be sleeping on comes to a stop.

The only explanation I can offer for his disappearance is he must have been standing in the doorway and the train gave a lurch which caused him to lose his balance and fall out into the darkness and at this moment being somewhere back along the track, seriously hurt or perhaps dead.

"Well," I said to myself with resignation, "He is gone. There is nothing to be done now. I am sorry I wasn't there to save him, if that was how he disappeared."

For awhile I tried to occupy my mind with other thoughts than that he was hurt or dead. The more I tried, the more I thought of it, and then, just as I was dozing off, again his words and remarks about the "Laws of Retribution" came back to me with more significance than ever.

Then perhaps, I thought, he only saw in its quick reaction on those two men for stealing his coffee just what he could or was expecting would happen to him sooner or later for something he himself was guilty. What he really was thinking of at the time he made the remark when he said, "Yep, I guess they are right," was perhaps only a confirmation in his own mind of a similar warning he himself had received at the time he had also committed offenses against some party or parties.

"And then again," I thought to myself, "I may be all wrong, for he may have been as innocent as a babe of any wrong doing all through his life. He was just an innocent victim of an untimely accident of which there are thousands every hour of the day, week, and year on a railroad."

That taught me a lesson, too, for ever since I have never leaned or stood near an open door of a box car when it was standing or in motion. Isn't it queer that some suffer and die for other humans to learn and thereby live longer to enjoy life and all good things in this world?

"Well, it must be about time we were pulling into Mobile," I thought, so I went back to the pile of papers expecting to see from my corner any moment some evidence or sign that one generally sees when you hit the outskirts of a town or city or railroad yard.

We didn't reach there as soon as I thought, for it must have been almost two hours after the time I expected we would. But when we did, we sure pulled in with a bang, for the engineer didn't slacken speed on entering the yards very much. I had to wait until she came to a standstill.

I slid down out of the car and made my way across the tracks seeking a way out of the yard and away from the rest of the men who were riding, by now scattered all over the yards.

I found an outlet and by a quick short run I was clear, but the rest of them kept running hither and thither and didn't seem to be in a hurry whether they ever got out or not.

I started towards the center of Mobile and I had not got more than halfway when three automobiles passed me with about seven passengers in them. At first I didn't pay any particular attention, but when a fourth one came up the road, I saw just what kind of passengers they were and too, I saw by the license plates the cars had stars fastened on just above them.

"Sheriffs, I said to myself. "And what a nice haul they made of those darn fools who would advertise themselves by wandering around the yards."

To say the least, I considered myself lucky by getting out of there before the "Fee Grabbers" got into action.

Well, a miss is as good as being a mile from the mark, so I was as good a shot or a miss as I would have been on a bullseye in that particular instance. Gee, what a narrow escape from the chain gang. What an experience that would be—one that I sure wouldn't want and one that I would never be able to live down.

When anybody mentions a jail or a chain gang I start to shudder, a fear seems to grip me, and I always say to myself, "God, anything but that!"

When I finally arrived into Mobile proper, my first thought was of that feather bed I had slept in when I first visited. I had some difficulty in finding the house and finally, when I did, I am told there were no vacancies.

My next thought was a restaurant and a good meal and after that I would have to hunt up a place to sleep.

I tried a few places but turned them down as not much better than a boxcar, so I kept on walking around Mobile and thinking pretty seriously of returning to the railroad yards and continuing on with my journey.

I had just turned another corner when a man stopped me and asked for a pipe of tobacco. I accommodated him and then asked, thinking he might know of a good place to sleep in.

"Why don't you go over where they take care of the transients? It don't cost you anything. I would if I was you and on the road."

He gave me the directions and, thanking him, I started out for the place hoping it was worth bothering with.

I found the place after walking over an area of about three miles of Mobile. No one would expect the building from its appearance to be anything but one of the many old-time Colonial houses that still are standing and giving some pretty good service yet in the South.

I looked the place over and found on one of the posts the number the man gave me. So up the[1] steps I climbed and then across a wide veranda to the front door. Just as I was about to put my hand on the latch to open it, someone on the inside beat me to it and appeared in the doorway. He looked me over kind of as though to say, "Who are you and what do you want?"

I ignored his searching look and stepped aside to let him pass. When he did, I entered and found myself in a poorly lit room. I stood there for a second or two to get my eyes accustomed to the half-lit room, and as I was about to return outside, someone in another room off to one side of the room I had entered said, "Yes, what is it you want?"

I followed in the direction of the voice and found myself standing in front of a high-top desk. On the other side, seated, was a middle-aged man writing. When he had finished, he simply reached over the top

---

1. Here John draws a series of dashes in the notebook, representing the steps he climbs.

and handed me two slips of paper and said, "Take these and get your dinner in the mess room just next to the room you first entered. Then, after you have had your dinner, return to me."

I did as I was told and I must admit it was not a bad meal considering it was for nothing. After I finished I returned to the man at the desk and he handed me a slip on which there was but one word: "bed."

"Well," I thought to myself, "This isn't so bad at that."

If I had only taken the time to spend a few moments looking around, I certainly wouldn't have hesitated one moment about returning to the yards and picking out a boxcar to get what sleep I could while waiting for the next freight out. But instead I did a little scouting around Mobile and at that I didn't see much more than I did on my first visit.

I wandered around the railroad station and along the bay. I saw there some pretty large tramp steamers, all of which, from the debris around and on the wharfs, must be in the South American trade. Bananas seemed to be the main cargo. Outside of that, I didn't see anything out of the ordinary or anything that one doesn't see in any other city of its size throughout the whole USA.

There was one outstanding fact about Mobile I did notice above everything else and that was most of the menial work was done by the Negro. He seemed to be the only one that really had any life about him. Also, I noticed that the white element didn't look so healthy or as prosperous as they were wont to be. This struck me as being queer, for I thought, if most of the work was done by the colored element, the white element must be on the paying end. But as I mentioned, they sure didn't have the look that goes with being financially independent.

Well, it was getting time for me to be getting back to my supper and bed. So I eased my way there and just made it, for as I was ascending the front steps, someone was ringing a bell and shouting out of the window, "Come and get it!"

I heard a general rushing of feet further back in the building, so I waited until they came and entered and was seated. I then followed the last one in and presented my slip of paper to a man standing inside the door of the dining room. He took it and pointed over to one of the tables and said, "Take any one of those seats and eat."

Supper in any of these places generally is a light repast, with tea as a beverage instead of coffee. I thought it was alright as free meals go. After eating you could sit around and chew the rag with the rest of the men, or if you preferred to do so, you could take a walk uptown and get back safely in time for the required time you are supposed to be in. If you happen to miss this hour you run the risk of losing your bed.

I walked uptown and had a cup of coffee and got back in plenty of time to be on the safe side of any likelihood of losing out in regards to sleeping quarters.

When I finally decided to go to bed, I found the man who assigns you your bed. So I showed him the slip which entitled me to one bed and he got up and said, "Follow me."

I followed him into a very large room, which seemed to extend the whole length of the building. It took up about one third of the width of the entire building. There was no ceiling but the roof. It put one in mind of a mammoth storage room. I looked around for the beds or cots that these places generally use for sleeping accommodations, but I couldn't see any. That didn't worry me much, for I thought they could as well be at the other end of the room. It being as large as it was, it was hard to see anything clearly from where we entered.

As we entered, another man got up from a stool he was sitting on and advanced towards us. He met us in about as businesslike a manner as if he was in one of the largest hotels in the country.

The man who brought me in handed the slip I had given him to the other fellow and said, "Give this man a bed and treat him right."

"Right," said the other fellow. With that over, he said to me, "Follow me," kind of officious like.

I followed on behind him until he stopped about halfway down the room. Here he looked up towards what I made out to be a row of shelves attached to the walls and held up by stanchions about four feet apart. The shelves were about six feet wide. There were about four tiers of them and they extended along about one half of the length of the room. I didn't even number them.

Then he pointed up and said, "Take the second row and the third space from that post."

I turned my head and looked at him and he returned the look and said, as though to read my thoughts, "I know it's awful, but there it is, and if you kick about it, they will tell you to take it or leave it."

"But it reads on that slip 'bed,' doesn't it?" I asked.

"Yes, it sure does, and that is the bed," he answered, hanging back as though to hear me hollering.

"Well, good night. Hope you sleep well," he said, and then disappeared into the dim light of the room and resumed his post, sitting down to wait for the next sleeper.

"Well," I said to myself, "I asked for it and here it is, so take it or leave it."

I had half a mind to leave it, but on second thought I said to myself, "Here is something to write home about, so here it goes."

Up to the second row and the third space from that post I go.

I got up without any trouble, but when I saw that the shelves were slanting out, I just about gave it up. Believe it or not those shelves were at least eight inches lower on the outer end than the inner end. That was the last straw, so I got down and looked around in the dark for some other place where I could lie down. I couldn't find any other so I finally decided I would have to accept the shelf and make the best of it. So up I go again and lay down to get a rest the best way I knew how under the circumstances.

There wasn't even a cover for the boards. There wasn't even a cover to pull up over you. It was just a bare shelf. So I spread my overcoat as smooth as I could and tried to sleep.

I stretched out full length on my back and dozed off, only to awaken shortly after and find I had slipped down the shelf almost half my own length. I pulled myself up on the shelf and tried it again by pulling my knees up. I finally dozed off again, only to be awakened again. This time, instead of my legs being over the edge, I find myself dangerously sleeping full length near the edge—just one foot and I would have fallen a full six feet to the ground. I pulled myself up again to give it another try, and as I did, I happened to swing my arm upwards and hit my knuckles against something on the wall behind me. Whatever it was it was hard and sharp enough to take the skin off one of them, so I lit a match to see where the object was situated in order to know how to miss or keep away from it. In the light of the match, I find that it is an old iron ring riveted into the wall. I didn't think much of it at first, but just a few moments after, someone else did the same thing I had and let out a curse, exclaiming "Damn it to hell, why in hell don't they take those g--damn slave rings and chains out of here?! There ain't no slaves anymore."

"So that's it," I thought, cocking my ear to hear whoever it was that had said that, but they had no doubt turned over and went back to sleep again.

I reached up to investigate the ring and chain with my fingers and found they were as he had said—slave rings, or shackles.

"So that was the explanation of the whole layout," I said to myself.

Undoubtedly, I was in one of those buildings that had been built back in the old slave days and this portion of the building was where they had lived and slept. The shelves were used for sleeping accommodations and the rings were no doubt used to keep them from sliding off by shackling them to the rings. Or perhaps it might be that there were some unruly ones among the slaves and to the rings they shackled them, perhaps to keep them under control or to keep them from wandering around or possibly running away.

I may be wrong in the foregoing deduction of the place, but after setting up for awhile with my knees pulled up and my head resting on them trying to rest until the morning came, I gave thought to some of the stories I had read when I was a boy of the days when slavery existed. In some of them, I recalled some of the descriptions of some of the buildings and ways of handling slaves. This building and its shelves and rings and chains in the wall and the type of living quarters certainly compared well with those descriptions.

I was awakened from my thoughts by someone calling out, "Rise and shine!" Rise and shine—if ever I welcomed a call it was that one. I actually slid off that shelf to the ground. After I got my things together, I started to look for a place to wash. The man in charge saw me searching around and with a sort of sneer on his face asked, "What the hell are you looking for?"

I didn't cotton so well to his attitude, so I said in as sneering a way as I could muster: "What the hell do you think I would be looking for the first thing in the morning?"

He answered me back and advanced a little closer to me by saying, "Getting tough, eh?"

"Yes I am getting tough if you care to call it that. So what?" I came back at him and then advanced until I stood in front of him. He didn't say anything for a minute or two. Then, as if thinking better of the matter he said, "OK, bud, forget it."

"OK, bud, I'll forget you, but there is one thing I'll never forget and that is last night and this place," I said with conviction.

He smiled and then said, "You and me both. I am pulling out myself tonight. How about teaming up with you?"

"Thanks, bud, but I don't team up with the best of them. I am a lone wolf," I said. And with that, I gathered up my duds and walked out of the place and on down the street towards the center of Mobile to get my breakfast. Then I headed for the yards for the next freight out.

Even with last night's experience I still liked Mobile and if I had enough money with me, I am certain I would have taken a chance of stopping for awhile and trying to get something to do, for I am sure I would have been satisfied to stay there indefinitely.

What is it about Mobile that attracts me? I am unable to this day explain, but it does.

I finally managed to get aboard a freight even though the railroad officers were especially active on this day. I saw them chasing others off railroad property, but none of them saw me, for I kept under cover just a little bit outside of the yard. So when the freight was ready, I watched the railroad officers as I eased my way towards the engine. I figured they would be busy keeping the other fifteen or twenty men who were trying to catch her at about halfway up the yard. And if they would only stay there keeping them off at that point, my chances of getting on near the engine could be good when she started out. So far, everything was going along in my favor, for none of the officers even looked my way. I finally get right in front of the engine and then over on the opposite side of the freight and started to walk along it when someone hollered, "Get the hell out of there!"

I didn't pay the least attention to whoever it was, so I continued along for another length of a car, when the freight started up and on I went. I had climbed the ladder that is always on one end of a boxcar about halfway up when I happened to look sideways and then I got scared. For coming down the side of the train on a run was one of the officers with a pistol in his hand and hollering, "Get off that freight or I'll shoot you off."

I stopped for a moment wondering whether I should get off or continue on up the ladder and take a chance on the train speeding up and being too fast for him to catch up with me. I decided to take the chance and continued to climb on up as fast as I could to the top. Just as I reached the top, I heard the crack of a pistol shot and then another and then another and then I heard two of the bullets hit the side of the car not more than a foot on each side of me.

When I heard those bullets hit the car I knew then that boy was good—and out to back up his words with lead. Right now if he could get ahold of me, I no doubt would get the whole works when I got in front of a judge.

The freight was a manifest and of course she just ripped along as fast as the engineer could push her. I had to lay flat on top in order to keep on her, for the wind was so strong I could hardly keep my cap on. I lay there looking up at the sky, thinking to myself about how lucky I was that I didn't get shot.

"Well, a miss is as good as a mile, old timer. Pretty close but not close enough. Better luck next time, but I hope not," I said to myself, sort of jubilant that I had won out.

I tried to sit up again to have a look at the countryside for this was a little different route than I had taken going west. I sat up for a few moments but the force of the wind forced me to lay flat again. Then I tried being on my side and, just as I was enjoying some scenery along the way, the car gave a lurch and I came near rolling off. So I resumed laying flat and kept that position until a trainman came along and sat down alongside me.

The first thing he asked was, "Did he hit you?"

I shook my head sideways and said, "No."

With that he seemed relieved and then said to me, "You no doubt will get a 'hot' reception in Montgomery so be careful," and then added, "I'll tip the engineer that you are OK and he will slow down a little bit just before we get into the yards and if you are wise you will get off then."

I said "OK, pard, thanks! And don't forget I am sending my regards to the engineer with thanks, too."

"Same to you, boy." And with that, he continued on towards the engine. When he came back he said as he went by, "It's all fixed, so it's up to you."

Chapter Thirty-One

On to Montgomery

I continued to keep down and out of the wind. We were making pretty good time and if we kept up the speed we ought to get into Montgomery in record time and if not we will certainly be on time.

Once in awhile, I thought I felt a raindrop, but I watched the sky and couldn't see any signs of wet weather. But down here in the South one never knows when it will change from fair weather to foul, especially in the winter months. So it wouldn't be a surprise to me if it didn't start out of a clear sky, like it did once in Decatur, Alabama, when I stopped there on my way west.

I was feeling kind of disappointed I wasn't riding inside of a car. I did want to get a good look at this part of the country. Well, traveling like I was, you can't expect "Deluxe" services, so I just contented myself with gazing up at the clouds, hoping everything would be OK at the other end of this diversion. It was then I got to thinking of the last few words the trainman said to me on his way back. I repeated to myself his words and started to become kind of in doubt just as to how to take them. He said, "It's all fixed, so it is up to you." The last six words didn't bother me as much as the first three. "It's all fixed." I didn't like them, for they could as well have a double meaning as well as a singular one. Something told me to be on the alert for a double cross, as they say, although I had no reason just then to doubt the sincerity of the trainman.

To be on the safe side I'll just keep my eyes open when we get near our destination.

So with that intention in my mind, I gave it no more thought than to say to myself, "I am glad I thought of that," and then started to watch a nice black cloud forming further south of us. And if I know my clouds, I was due for a soaking and also a possible sojourn in some hospital in Montgomery, Alabama.

The cloud wasn't long catching up with us. It was coming cross country. There was no escape, so I sat up and creeped to the end of the top of the car and descended over and onto a ladder in between the car I was riding and the next one.

I got down just in time. The rain came down in torrents and if I had stayed on top, with the force of the wind against me, I certainly would have been wet through in a second's time. As it was I had some chance of my overcoat protecting me pretty well. After the first spell of rain it slackened up to almost a drizzle. By this time it was getting dark so I was afraid to stay in between as it is dangerous enough riding astraddle in the daytime. One is liable to get tired in one position, and if I was to miss my footing changing about, well, there is no telling: No more riding; no more divisions to make. It is certain death. Or, if you have been born under a lucky star, you might get out of it alive but minus your limbs. But I think I can safely say it would be death—99 out of every 100 accidents of this nature are generally fatal.

The rain has stopped and I am again on top.

I looked ahead and saw some pretty bright lights. I am not sure it is Montgomery, Alabama, although we have been long enough and the speed fast enough to be just about pulling in there.

All of a sudden we slacken. Then I looked back towards the caboose and I see a hand held up, waving me to be ready to hop off. I got down off the top and over and onto the side ladder, then on down to the step and as I did, the engineer put on the brakes as if to test them and that was the signal to let go and I did.

I don't know of any other words to emphasize my avowed intention of never to try again to get off a train going as fast as this one was, but: Never Again! I didn't realize how fast it was really going so I let go of the handle and when I hit the ground I was hitting it at about a speed of 25 miles an hour. That is a little too fast for human feet to travel without getting them tangled up. The roadbed on the side of the track was filled in with some pretty large cracked rock, so when I struck them it was like hitting a lot of jagged roots or stumps. Consequently I didn't even get a proper footing when I landed and as a result I tripped and flew through the air, like a plummet, only to land flat on my stomach. Then it was that I went into a slide that didn't stop until I had gone down a ditch and halfway up the opposite side.

I laid there stunned for a few seconds and then, thinking of the train, I looked after it. There, standing on the rear platform of the caboose, was the whole train crew laughing so hard some of them were doubled up. I gathered myself up and brushed myself off and while doing this was also checking up on any possible injuries, scratches, or cuts. I didn't feel none and as for any marks I didn't have any that I could see. My face felt OK too, so I had one more look on down the track towards the train and said to myself, "Laugh, damn you, and I'll bet none of you would have the nerve to try it nor would you take a chance on dodging bullets either." And with that off my chest, I looked around to see just exactly where I was.

Well, this is getting to be a trip of narrow escapes, for on my arrival in Mobile, I just miss going to jail—but don't—then I run the gauntlet of the railroad officers and one of them tries to shoot me off the train—but he doesn't—then I get darn near killed by dropping off a freight going at a speed of 26 miles an hour—but I didn't. So, I thought to myself, what next?

It started to rain again and that brings me back to the business of either getting under cover or finding some quick route into Montgomery and a good meal and a bed.

After walking a block or so I came to a crossroad. As I stood there undecided as to whether to go up it or not, I saw a street car crossing it about a quarter of a mile away. When I saw it, that of course decided one, so on up the road I hot footed it to catch the next one. I had to wait about 45 minutes to catch the next one and first thing I know I am in Montgomery, Alabama, safe and sound.

Well, after I got through eating I started looking for a moderate priced room and on one of the streets I was hailed by someone calling to me across the street. I looked over and there I saw the train man who had "it" fixed for me to get off before I hit the yards. I crossed over to him and when I stood in front of him, he says to me, "Say, where did you come from? Have they all got as much nerve as you have?"

I told him; but as for nerve, I told him I didn't know about that.

"Well, I am glad you are all right, so good luck and so long," and then he went his way.

"Well," I said to myself, "that is one white man that steered me right."

I continued on looking for a room but after an hour or more I gave it up and then stopped another fellow who looked as though he was on the road himself. I asked just where I could find a place to stay. He looked at me and smiled and then said, "That's funny, that is just what I am looking for myself."

We stood there looking at each other for a few seconds and then he suggested we go back a little bit and ask whoever we might happen to meet. We walked along for about three blocks before we met anybody who we thought might know where we could stop.

We got the information from an old Negro, and from then on it was easy. We finally reached the place just in time to get a bed. From the system the man in charge used checking us in, I was sure I was once more in a Transient Bureau.

I noted the place was very clean and sanitary. The cots and bed clothing were practically new and the sleeping quarters smelled as if they just been freshly painted. So with these observations, I undressed, satisfied at least it was clean. I climbed into bed, for I really was tired. I must have slept right on through the night, for I don't remember even moving or of hearing a sound until early the next morning when I was awakened by the man next to me who had to give me a push to get me up.

I had a very nice breakfast considering it was received for nothing. After breakfast I was told to stop in the office before I left. I went there immediately and the man in charge took my name and pedigree and then asked me in a very pleasant manner if I intended on staying. I told him I was sorry but I had to be moving on, for I wanted to get home before the severe winter set in up North.

"Well, you can stay here as long as you care to. We also could use a man like you around here and it might turn out to be something worth while, for we feel these places are going to be a permanent thing," saying this, hoping perhaps I would be interested.

"No, I am sorry. Thanks just the same," I said as courteously as I could.

From all appearances, this Transient Bureau was a very well kept and managed one. Everything about it smacked of cleanliness and good service. I would have liked to stay a day or so longer, but I wanted to make any time I had to be on a move. Last night was cold, and if it got much colder I would have to confine my riding to daytime.

I made for the railroad yards immediately after I was through and checked out of the Transient Bureau. I didn't get there any too soon, for there she was, all set and waiting for me, it seemed. I walked right up through those yards as though I owned them, and picked out a nice clean boxcar. I had just got nicely seated when the conductor gave the signal and I was off towards Birmingham, Alabama.

Chapter Thirty-Two

Birmingham

The sun came out nice and warm on this particular morning, so from my seat in the boxcar I did get a pretty good idea of this part of the country. Although I couldn't see much difference in this vicinity of the South than any other. There was only one variation I noted and that was that it is a little more thickly populated and there were far more small places along the railroad. Here and there I saw some old farm building that had been vacated and was now rotting into almost total ruin. The farms around them were covered with weeds, which gave evidence they had not been tilled for years. It was just about the same as any other part of the North, I thought.

We were stepping along at a nice speed and I hoped we would get into Birmingham a little early. So I sat there, thinking of some of the incidents of this trip coming east. I was sort of worried I wouldn't make it when I had hoped I would. Well, so far I had been lucky. I still had about fifteen dollars and, if worse came to worse, I had enough to pay my fare. If only I could get as far as Charlotte before I got froze off the road.

To tell the truth, I really was beginning to like this mode of life. It isn't exactly that it is a carefree one, but I liked seeing different places and people. In other words, I liked the change of scenery one sees traveling about. Best of all, I seemed to be happier and more contented than ever before in all my life. It seemed as though I was gratifying a desire I didn't know I ever possessed or a latent one that needed only just such an experience I was going through. My health had improved to a point that as far as any nervousness was concerned, it couldn't have recovered anywheres near the degree it was now at if I had paid a million dollars to the best physicians in the country. That was worth something more than all the wealth in this queer old world.

It is really hard to explain, but I do know it is a fascinating life. It is one that surely will bring out what there is in a man. You can go wrong very quickly if you are so inclined, but if you are not, you will grow kinder in your thoughts towards humanity; especially do you towards the poor unfortunates you see—and I have seen plenty on this short trip from New York City to Oakland and back to where I am at present. I have often given thought that if there are as many unfortunates to every mile in this country as I have run into in the miles I have covered, then they must run into the millions. I have no solution to the problem and I can offer no reasons or cause of this condition, but one thing I do know: It does exist.

But to get back to the subject of the mode of living I was now enjoying, I can further testify it will also make one more self-sufficient and his intuition made far more keener than if he continued on living under more favorable conditions. You just have to use your wits or else you don't make out.

Well, I should be getting near Birmingham, so I got up and stood over to the other side of the car and peered out through the darkness. To be sure there it was, so I prepared to leave the train as soon as an opportunity presents itself.

We rolled along for a short distance and come to a stop with a jerk and a bang. The door almost shut completely. Fearful that something had happened, I hurried to the door and pushed it open and looked out and ahead. I was jerked into action by what I saw. There they were again, and there I was again, caught in between railroad officers. Two were coming in the back end and three from the head end. I slid off and, at the risk of my life, I crawled under the train and out the other side.

I look up and down and I find I am clear of them temporarily.

I gave a quick look ahead up in the darkness and I made out a short, steep hill ahead of me, so I took a chance and started to climb up. Before I got halfway up, I began to slide back down again, for the whole bank appeared to be covered with a slimy covering of some kind. I tried it again, putting more speed to my ascent, and I finally made the top. There I find I am barred from any further advance by a barbed wire fence. Well, thought I, I am not going to be caught, so here goes. I get my foot on one of the wires and down comes both of the posts and that scares me.

I give one leap and I find I am in someone's orchard. I wander around in the darkness, bumping into tree stumps, and finally I come to another fence. This I climb over without any trouble and, lucky me, I am on a country road and out of harm's way. Once more I have managed to keep out of a possible stay in some jail.

How I found my way in the center of Birmingham, I to this day couldn't tell you. I recrossed the tracks in the yard twice before I finally got on the right street. Then, even after I did, I still didn't have the right direction. However, I did finally come out somewheres near the section one generally looks for to obtain moderate priced lodgings.

It was too late to bother the Transient Bureau, so there was only one thing to do. That of course was to start looking for something in the way of a hotel within my means. After going from one place to another, I finally found myself on a street on which about every other door was a hotel entrance. At each door there sat a colored man shouting to those that might be passing, "Hotel! Hotel, Boss! Hotel for the night!"

I had observed this way of getting hotel trade before, pretty well all over the South, especially in the Deep South. But as I always was pinched for money, I never had the opportunity or price to patronize them.

Most of these hotels were six bit houses, and six bits is a lot of money for an itinerate traveler to be spending for a flop. On this particular occasion I felt too doggone tired to be walking around all night looking for something perhaps just two bits cheaper. Besides, I was always somewhat curious about these places that had a doorman selling rooms like he had rooms under his arms and was selling them like so many newspapers on a street corner.

So I thought that considering the cost of my return trip, I could afford a little treat in the way of a decent room for once in a month and a half of travel. So I crossed the street and walked right by the colored man to go on up the stairs. He got up on his feet and followed in the rear. As I got to the landing, he looked through the railing and called out, "Roomer coming up!"

From behind a desk, a woman pops up like a Jack in the Box. She reaches for the register and places it in front of me and says, "Sign here, please. Name and address."

When I had registered and had paid over my six bits, she said sweetly, "Thank you, Sir," and then tapped a desk bell. Hardly had the bell stopped its ting-a-ling than a colored porter and a bevy of women and girls made their appearance so quietly and suddenly that it seemed they had popped from behind the chairs or had come up through the floor as if by magic.

Naturally (What man wouldn't?), I looked them over.

That is what they are there for, and I observe them showing off their personal qualities. Some are quite young and somewhat attractive (but dangerous); others older and painted and powdered in a vain effort to hide the ravages of dissipation—old bats long in the business.

There was one, a voluptuous creature, a blond, who was chewing gum a mile a minute and dressed only (I mean only) in a gaudy kimono of bright scarlet and figured with floral designs of black and green. She was lolling in a Morris Chair with her legs and feet stretched out full length in front of her, as though she owned the place and hadn't a care in the world. The lazy thing. Dressed as she was in scarlet, she reminded me of a huge piece of linen that by some queer quirk of nature a set of shoulders and a head and a pair of legs and feet had attached themselves thereto. Then again she reminded me of an old cow chewing her cud in a clover patch.

She was well aware of my scrutiny but she didn't seem to mind, for she gave me a broad smile and a knowing wink, as if to say, "How about it, kid?"

The Madame (sharp old timer she was) saw the wink and, as we went on down a hall to show me my room, she said to me in an undertone, "She's nice, ain't she?" Then as an added piece of advertising, she gets sort of confidential by telling me, "She's the best in the House." I gave no answer to her complimentary remarks or her hidden hints, but I was thinking that as far as being a good judge of desirable women was concerned, she would have been a better judge of beef or horse flesh. I bid the Madame good night and closed the door and turned the key and flopped into one of the chairs. Without any notice, I and the chair went crashing to the floor. The chair was reduced to a hundred pieces and I sprawled out atop of them, cursing a blue streak. I was voicing my opinion half aloud and damning all the hotel gyps in the country, especially those of the South.

I finally got myself righted and kicked the debris over against the wall and then sat on the bed and prepared to retire for the night.

If collapsible chairs and rickety furniture weren't enough to make me wish I had kept on my way or make me curse the management of cheap hotels, I certainly had ample reason for complaint after I had been in bed for about twenty minutes.

The first evidence of the fact that I was not going to have a very good rest in that bed was the feeling of something crawling along on my neck. I got up and put the light on to investigate. I was amazed at the number of bed bugs I saw scurrying to all points of the compass.

There were thousands of them, there was an army of them. They were so thick it reminded me of a hive of bees that were crawling all over its white surface looking for and wondering what it was that had disturbed them.

While I was standing there gazing at that horde of blood suckers, someone knocked softly on the door and said in an undertone, "Anything wrong Boss? Can I help you?"

I stepped to the door and opened it to find a colored man standing there blinking from the sudden glare of light.

"What's the matter?" says he.

"Matter? Just look at this bed full of bed bugs!" I said, pointing to the bed.

He stepped inside and when he saw that army of bed bugs, he stood there as if he couldn't believe his eyes. Then to emphasize his amazement, he said, "Man, oh man. Hot damn. There's bed bugs and nothing else but. Man!"

I started to get dressed while he was still watching the bed and finally satisfied he saw enough, he turned to me and said, "What are you all going to do about this, Boss?"

"Just this. I am getting my money back or someone is going to get hurt around here."

Then I asked him where the Madame was.

"She's gone to bed," he informed me.

"Well, you go and wake her up right away, and tell her I want my money or else!"

He left and in about five minutes he returned with the money saying, "Here you are Boss. I don't blame you."

I gave him two of the six bits and went on my way down the stairs into the cold air. I hied for the railroad yards and arrived there about a half hour after and found a boxcar. There I finished the night out rolled up in enough paper to keep me out of sight and warm as toast and with no bed bugs or vermin to bother me.

I didn't wake up until the sun was up high in the heavens.

"There will be no freight until four pm and you had better get the hell out of here before the Bull comes on." This the yard man informs and advises me when I made inquiries as to the schedule of freights leaving Birmingham, Alabama.

So I had plenty of time to get a pretty good idea of what Birmingham looks like.

Before I do any wandering around I have two duties that must be attended to—one eat, and the other, get cleaned up.

Three day's growth of a fast growing beard doesn't help your appearance, so before I ate, I looked up the passenger station and used its lavatory as a place to shave.

To the boys on the road, or to any itinerant traveler who really wants to look halfway decent, these railroad stations are a Godsend. One might well wonder why they have to use them when anyone knows there are any number of missions and the like, but it is surprising the absolute lack of accommodations, forlorn social requisites, one finds in them. In some places (outside of perhaps an improvised shower or two), there isn't even a place to wash your face and hands. If you do happen to get into one that has accommodations you are hindered either by the hours or the great number that might be using them. In some the doors are not opened soon enough and closed too soon for a complete readjustment from filthiness to cleanliness. So like hundreds of my fellow travelers, I use the railroad stations and brave the dangers accrued thereto of being yanked out and arrested for vagrancy. But damn them, I do keep clean in spite of the busybodies who seem to like or go out of their way to even deny a poor sucker a basin of water and a piece of soap while thousands of dollars are being squandered on unnecessary and useless things.

"How much does a basin of water and a piece of soap cost?" I ask.

"Nil, in comparison to the benefits," I say.

Birmingham, Alabama is one of those cities that when you think of it, you must name the state as well. Birmingham, Alabama, seems to be more complete than to use just Birmingham, for in this city is reflected the whole state of Alabama. In other words, as far as I can judge of what I have observed of the state as a whole (and I have been from one end of it to the other), you will see something representative or something close to it in Birmingham. I have never been in any other city in the whole country where this fact is so pronounced.

After finishing my morning ablution, I set out to take in the sights of Birmingham, Alabama. I was particularly interested in its far-famed steel mills.

I ask for directions to one of the mills from an old Negro and he gives me the directions that will get me there securest and quickest.

WAITING FOR THE TRAIN

I am not long in reaching a point where I can see one of the largest in Birmingham and as I approach it I notice everything seems to be at a standstill. There is not even a wisp of smoke coming from the tall flue-like smokestacks on the smelters that shoot up from the many acres of buildings like so many barren trees in a fire-swept and burned out forest.

Despite the fact I may not be able to get on the inside to see the inner workings of a steel rolling mill, I kept on towards it, thinking that perhaps I could get a little glimpse of it somehow.

I finally reach the entrance and find the gate wide open and a-swing on rusty hinges, through which in the recent past perhaps thousands passed to enter for their daily labors. But now, at this writing, I don't see a living thing save for the flocks of sparrows and swallows and a few pigeons who are taking advantage of the shelter and its solitude.

It is like a graveyard; no voices, no hissing of steam or roar of forced draft in the smelters. No moving of cranes or the clanging of chains or creaking of beams, groaning under the burden of tons of weight; no heat or glare from molten metal. All is silent. Industry seems to have died and now lies rotting beneath the chaos of the scene before me.

As I go through the gate, it seems like entering a mammoth junkyard. Everything is strewn all over the yard haphazardly, as though everything had been dropped as if too hot to handle or at the sound of the whistle announcing the end of the workday.

Tools, parts of machinery, piles of scrap iron and steel, sand, cinders, and coal are everywhere. Everything is covered with rust and the paint is peeling off the building and the windows have long since been broken or smashed by mischievous boys.

Off to one side I see a little donkey engine that looks as though it had been in a wreck and left standing on a side track; as not being worth the trouble to repair. Its running days seem to be over.

I had no trouble in gaining access to the interior of one of the largest buildings and, as I stepped inside, it felt so cold and drafty and hollow-like, it made me shiver.

As I look around, I am struck with the enormity of the place and give thought to the loss of the productive hours that is lost by such idleness.

I walk a little farther into the interior and I hear more clearly in the hollowness of the building the flapping and banging of the doors in the breeze. As I look up fearful that something might come loose and drop on me, my eye catches the ends of ropes and cables and strands of wire and chains, some of which are frayed from use, others broken off short. Others are longer, dangling from big silent cranes, some from the roof and others from blackened beams like cloudy or mud-colored icicles hanging from the roof of a subterranean cave, deep in the bowels of the earth.

Just looking at silent machinery and cold smelters doesn't give me much of an idea of the actual process of making steel plates or rails or other steel products, but it does give me an inkling of the vast amount of massive machinery and the great number of men it must take to run a mill this size. And that recalls to my mind once more not to the loss of productive hours but to the enormous loss in wages and buying power. And its subsequent misery and want and suffering.

As I wandered through the buildings, I was rather forgetful of the time.

So I consult my Ingersoll and find I still have about two more hours to spare. I quicken my footsteps and go through one or two more buildings and leave by the rear of the mill and hasten on back to Birmingham metropolitan district.

When I had arrived into the business district, I had about one hour and a quarter to spare. Giving myself a forty-five minute margin to get back to the railroad yards, I stopped in one of Birmingham's many department stores and made a few purchases. While I was in there, I was struck with the courtesy of the clerks and that smile that goes so well and is indicative of good management. I experienced the same welcome and service in the restaurant I ate my last meal while here.

It is time now to get going, that is if I don't want to stay another night. Still feeling somewhat disquieted with the previous night's experience, I am not such a glutton for punishment. At least not to such an extent that I would invite any more experience with bed bugs and vermin. I still can picture quite vividly that swarm of blood suckers. I itch all over when I think of it.

Everything about Birmingham is nice but its "Six Bit Cat House Hotels."

Well, there are the yards and it is ten minutes to four o'clock, so I ease my way quickly along the edge of the yards, keeping under cover behind the line of gondolas. I come to about abreast of the middle of the freight and wait in between until she gives the signal that she's all set to go.

Chapter Thirty-Three

An Eventful Ride to Chattanooga

We pulled out of Birmingham at exactly on the hour and I was surprised there was no interference from any railroad officer, for Birmingham had a bad name—or rather, the railroad officers had.

I said, "*We* pulled out."

That is right, for on this freight I believe for every car in it there were at least ten riders, and what a bunch of ragged, dirty, and unkempt bums and freaks they are. There were some pretty clean men among them, but the majority, well, they looked like a swarm of scarecrows just escaped from a cornfield.

It would take days to describe in detail the different conditions and array of their apparel. Suffice to say every shade of the rainbow was represented and about every style of clothing and shoes was being worn, without any thought to size or fit. All in a most ragged condition.

I guess if you mixed them all up and cut them into real small pieces they might make a pretty good pile of confetti, but the colors would be sort of dirty like.

After taking a look in regards to nationality and age, I note most of them are American born, and most of them are in their teens.

Such was the nomadic crowd I was riding with on my way to Chattanooga, Tennessee, on this night.

It is turning very cold and I fear I will see snow before many hours. There is a freshness in the air—it smells like snow.

Those who are in the boxcar with me have found places for themselves and have quieted down. Some are stretched out and some have fallen asleep and we are only twenty minutes out of Birmingham.

I envy them in a way. I wish I could just lie down, stretch out and fall asleep just like that—but then again, I wouldn't like to be that way. It's too much like not giving a damn. Too much like the way pigs do—just plop into their own filth and the mire. But such a virtue does have its merits at times, I'll have to admit.

Over in one corner I see a boy not over thirteen. He looks half scared of everything around him. Then, as I watch him out of the corner of my eye, I detect in his bright little eyes that are not missing anything a certain little sparkle of light that tells me he is enjoying the ride and is getting the thrill of his lifetime. Looking forward to adventure—as all youths naturally do—ships at sea, railroads, tropical islands, our own great country, the Army and Navy, and Hobos. Boy, doesn't that kid take me along back over the years down to my boyhood, when I dreamed and dreamed of such places. But there was no realization of any of them until almost fifty years later.

It is starting to snow. The cold wind is steadily shifting around and every minute the temperature is getting lower. Some of the riders are shivering and walking up and down, trying to overcome the chill. The little boy over in the corner is shivering so bad, his teeth are knocking together. Others don't seem to mind—hardy rascals with no underwear, no hat or cap, no overcoat— they put me to shame. I with a good Ulster[1] on and feeling cold. But I make excuses for myself by saying to myself, "They are still young. I am not, so what can I expect?"

But that only seems to make me all the more colder, so I start to do some walking and I get the circular turn going and feel a little warmer for the exertion.

I look over at the boy once more and now, instead of his teeth chattering, he is actually shivering all over. He can't control his muscles. His legs are playing a rat-tat-tat on the floor of the car. He lost his balance when the train rounded a curve and tumbled over on his side.

Poor kid, I thought. What the hell is the idea of a kid riding around like this on freight cars? I curse the Fates for him in sympathy and then I ask all in general (but silently) to myself, "What kind of people are they to let a kid get away from them to skant around this way?"

I cannot stand to see that kid suffer any longer so once more I am called upon by my sympathies to forsake the warmth of my Ulster to a kid to keep him from freezing.

I am put on the mat for letting the boy take my coat by a rat-faced gimlet-eyed half-starved looking fellow who says, "You're a damn fool. That punk's only putting on, look at him now, he ain't shivering now. You ought to let me wear that coat," in a crackling and squeaking voice.

All the while he was laying me out he had his face stuck into mine as though he was about to bite my nose off. I could smell the odor of cheap booze (and no doubt smoke) on his breath. It stunk like as if he was saturated with ether or some other kind of drug that had

---

1. A type of overcoat, popular from the Victorian era, usually wool.

turned his stomach sour. It reminded me of a swill can gone bad and fermenting in the heat of the sun.

I felt like jamming my fist down his throat, but I saw all the rest of the men had formed in a circle around us like a pack of wolves ready for the kill.

So I let him have his say, for I am not sure whether he is alone, or with a few, or with all of them.

I return to the side of the boy and sit down beside him with my back to the wall, just in case someone should take a notion to trip me over and pounce on me.

It was gradually getting dark and now that the sun had gone down, the wind and cold were keener. And same for the few who were sitting on the floor just taking it. Most of the men were walking up and down the length of the car. Some were just walking, others doing an imitation of a dance, others tapping the toe tips of their shoes against the wall, and some going through a sham form of calisthenics in a vain effort to keep warm.

The man who laid me out passed me three or four times, looking down at the boy and me with a cynical sneer on his face. Something told me he and I weren't exactly through with each other. We were just experiencing one of those few minutes of any armistice in the space of which each other was growing to an increasing dislike to each other. The more we looked at each other it seemed to be turning to a hatred. If that was the way he was feeling, I sure could assure him the feeling was mutual if he should ask or started any funny business.

We sat there, the boy and I, watching that parade of men and boys walking back and forth. I don't know what the boy might be thinking of—perhaps home—but I was thinking of this rat-face, gimlet-eyed guy who seemed by his actions still had it in for me. When I came to think of when he climbed on back in Birmingham, Alabama, the way he looked at me I thought he knew me. Now it comes to me quite clearly that it wasn't a look of recognition, it was one of dislike and I remember too I responded to it quite unconsciously. I remember too how he put his hand deep into his pockets and shuffled to the extreme end of the car. I remember a feeling that I was being watched by boring eyes from the rear, but for the moment or until the incident of his taking exception to my sympathies for a kid that was damn near freezing, did I pay much further attention to him.

The climax of this whole affair came when darkness really had set in and I had dozed off. It was the boy who warned me with a nudge; it was he who said, "Wake up Mister!" in a high-pitched voice. Then he followed up his warning by leaning towards me and sort of whispering in my ear, "Look out for his foot!"

Cornered as I was sitting on the floor against the wall, I couldn't very well retreat from an attack which from the warning I had received I could expect any second, so I pulled up my knees and covered up my face with my arms and waited for whatever might come out of the darkness.

It came in the form of a thud up against the wall beside me, so close I had no trouble in recognizing what it was by the smell of leather, mixed with the odor of dirty socks and feet.

"So that's it," thought I, "A kick in the face."

And then my Scotch blood arose within me to such a degree that I thought for a second I was going to have a paralytic stroke or cerebral hemorrhage; but as suddenly as it arose, it dropped and in my anger I was once more cool. So, instinctively, I let go one of my long, long legs and let whoever it was have the full force of its forward force and thrust right on their shins. I had on a pair of those heavy CCC[2] shoes, the heels of which were strapped with steel plates.

"How," I said, "you SOB, did you like that? You lousy bastard!"

I told the boy to remain where he was at all costs and then I got to my feet and searched around for whoever it was. I found him over by the door, nursing his shins and groaning and gasping for breath between attacks of excruciating pain.

I don't know to this day why I did it, and I write this part of what happened with shame. I will never forgive myself. I must have gone temporarily out of my mind when I let fly my booted foot into his face while he was stooped over. This I did saying over and over again, "Kick me in the face, eh? Kick me in the face, would you?" Then, not quite yet returned to normal thinking, I grabbed him by his coat collar and punched him on the point of his chin. Out of my grasp he went sprawling on the floor of the car with me standing over him, saying once more, "Kick me in the face you would…you…you…" and then a feeling came over me like as if I was coming out of anesthesia.

I seemed to be rising upward, upward, and then I felt faint and weak and I could feel the beads of sweat on my forehead. Suddenly it seemed as if I had walked from a darkened room out into the brilliant sunshine which seemed to blind me and make me dizzy and sick and a sinking feeling in the pit of my stomach.

I turned and went groping around in the darkness back to the boy's side and sank down exhausted on the floor.

From that time on, I didn't hear a sound in the car but the groaning of the man and the squeaking of the wooden car and the screeching and the clack of the wheels over the rails as the freight rumbled on through the night.

---

2. Civilian Conservation Corps.

I slowly recovered and the little fellow by my side asked me in a low tone if I was alright. Then in a still lower tone he says, "We are getting near Chattanooga, Tennessee."

"Yeah," I said and then prepared to be the first off that train—the boy and I.

The freight came to a sudden stop and as the boy and I dropped off, I called back over my shoulder to a couple of the men in the back of us to take care of that "smart guy."

Chapter Thirty-Four

Chattanooga and Knoxville

Instead of following the freight further into the yard, we retreated further back towards the caboose and we soon came to a small bridge under which was a paved road. On this we finally arrived in Chattanooga's metropolitan district and got under cover in a thirty-cent flop house. After an hour or two we slipped out, had our supper, and then returned to the flop house and sat around its ill-furnished and dimly lit, dusy and ill-smelling reading room among Chattanooga's bums and riff-raff that usually panhandles their night's flop, or stays there on relief money and as a rule are generally half-drunk.

I had not as yet learned much from the boy about himself and it was not until he mentioned his mother did I venture to ask him his name or where he was going or where he lived. All I cared to know came from him voluntarily when he told me he lived in Knoxville, Tennessee, and that he was returning home from a visit to his grandmother who lived in Birmingham. He was a mannerly little scamp and quite intelligent and had little to say so I let it go at that.

So we retired, I to my bunk and he to a stall or cubicle in which the proprietor said would be better for him.

Perhaps it would be interesting to know (especially for those who never come in contact with any of that number of those who travel along the railroads or hitch hike or who live in missions and the flop houses) the reason for the proprietor taking the precaution to put the boy in a cubicle by himself. Rest assured it wouldn't be for comfort and quiet or any special liking for a lodging be he a boy or a man one hundred years old. It is a precaution against a certain kind of pervert whose victims are generally young and innocent and guileless boys.

The next morning we ate our breakfasts in silence but I noticed he was worried about something, so I asked him if he was sick.

He said no but he was getting worried about how he was going to get home from Chattanooga. He thought, I supposed, this was as far as I was going.

I asked him then if Knoxville was really his hometown and he said, "Why of course. You don't think I would lie to you about it, do you?"

"Well, son, I haven't any way of knowing if it is or not, but if it is, you have nothing to worry about—I will see you through," I said to encourage him, more than anything else.

He seemed to perk up a little bit but he was still worried about something else but I didn't bother him any more about it.

We finished our breakfast and went out into the street and sauntered on down towards the railroad yards.

I never did cotton to Chattanooga and it is another one of those southern cities I don't like. I never took the time to really figure it out. All I can say is, I don't like it, although I never did give the place a once over. Just the appearance of the place, both approaching it and its interior, didn't impress me as being a place I would like to live in.

WAITING FOR THE TRAIN

The boy and I kept on walking slowly towards the yards, keeping off to one side at a safe distance. When we finally got just abreast of it, I told the boy to sit down until I came back from taking a look around to see just where the best place would be and when to catch a freight out to Knoxville. At first I didn't see a soul around the yards, so I took a chance and eased my way a little over the first few tracks. I hadn't gotten very far before someone blew a police whistle, so I looked in that direction and there I saw a railroad officer who was beckoning me over to a small shack. From a distance he looked OK to me, so I threw all discretion to the winds and walked right over to him and asked as bold as I could, "Yes, what do you want?"

He looked at me and then smiled and said, "You know you shouldn't be running around these yards."

"Yes, I know it, but I got a little kid over on the highway that I want to get home," I said, feeling him out to see what he was made of.

"Well, I got kids at home, so bring him over here and we will take a look at him. Where did he say his home was?" he said this a little bit interested.

I told him where the boy's home was and started over to get him. I told the boy what had happened and he came willingly.

When the railroad officer saw him, he took him into the shack and left me standing on the outside. In a few moments he returned and said, "I know this boy's mother, so OK boy, come on in and I will put you both on the next freight which will be ready in about an hour."

I thanked him and entered along with the boy and in about an hour and a quarter we were on our way to Knoxville, Tennessee.

For some reason or other the countryside between Chattanooga and Knoxville does not seem to be very interesting. I didn't see a single thing along this route or distance between the two cities that is worthy of mention. Everything seems to have crawled into its shell or has hibernated for the winter. There is no life or beauty—all seems so deserted and drab. What buildings we come past are either in ruins and decay from neglect or age. I observed too some farm machinery strewn around or left standing everywhere. In one field I saw a plow with its share[1] digging into the ground right in the middle of the field, as though that was as far as the farmer got and decided farming wasn't for him and then and there he quit. So he "hung up the shovel and the hoe," as it goes in Southern song.

There were acres upon acres that, from the appearance of the soil, had not been turned over these many years. The queerest thing of all is I did not see even a single cow. In truth, it looked as if all the farmers had moved to town, or perhaps there had been an epidemic of foreclosures or a succession of them.

The freight we were riding on was a local, and if we were just out for a ride and wanted to kill time, we sure hit on the right kind of a train. I don't believe there is a telegraph pole between Chattanooga and Knoxville that we didn't stop at. Every switch-back, side-track, platform, hamlet town and crossing was our stopping place. At one road crossing, we stopped on the far side and let an automobile pass first.

"What do you think of that?" said the boy as we stared at such rare courtesy from a railroad crew.

It is real cold and the sky is cloudy, and the sun is trying to come out fully to help warm things up a little bit, but it seems to be baffled in its efforts by the big black clouds that seem to be constantly shifting and re-forming as they sailed across the heavens—the big black hulks of ships sailing on a blue sea.

---

1. Lower part of the plow that causes it to dig into the ground rather than ride above it.

The sun, peeping as it did every once in awhile around a cloud, looked as if it was playing a game of hide and seek or that it had lost something and was trying to find it around a cloud. Yes, even the clouds and the sun and the moon and the wind and rain and snow and the seas are all living things the same as we mortals and couldn't they have their sporting and playful moments as well, I thought.

We have sighted the outskirts of Knoxville and here I leave my little friend. After reaching the business district, we said our "adieus" over a cup of coffee in a hamburger joint that stunk of nothing but fried onions.

John's diary stops here, to be picked up several years later, in California, December 1939.

Obituary for Robert L. MacDonald

Robert L. MacDonald, (Bob or Mac), age 85 yrs, of Rimrock, Arizona, died after a brief illness, on February 27, 2014, surrounded by his loving family.

Born in New York City in 1928, he attended schools in NYC and Connecticut. He received a MA in Education from Leslie College. Bob served as a U.S. Marine during the Korean Conflict from 1951-1954.

Bob had an extensive teaching career starting at the Wooster School in Connecticut. He moved to Manchester, Massachusetts, and taught Science, Math and English at the Brookwood School. He coached several sports, notably baseball. He moved to Shore Country Day School in 1974, where he was Head of Upper English

Bob's love for the sea was a lifelong passion. He had a long career of teaching youngsters the art of sailing and was always happy and at peace when sailing his boat, The Reluctant Dragon, to Maine with his beloved wife, Elizabeth, whom he affectionately called Annie.

After moving to Northern Arizona, Bob and Annie formed the Southwest Expedition Institute, a non-profit providing environmental education to youth, especially Native Americans.

When Bob and his wife Elizabeth moved to Lake Montezuma he immediately began to have an impact on the community. He joined the Beaver Creek Kiwanis and, following the untimely death of George Yarrington, donated Southwest Expedition Institute resources and became the advisor to the Beaver Creek School Builder's Club. He also became president of the Lake Montezuma Property Owners Association and, though a group effort, was responsible for the paving of virtually all the unpaved roads in Lake Montezuma. He wrote an index for the much loved *By the Banks of Beaver Creek*, was one of the four original steering committee members responsible for the creation of The Beaver Creek Regional Council, and was almost single-handedly responsible for the preservation of the Back House at Montezuma Well, which he had hoped would someday house an environmental education center and provide an archive for a local historical society.

Bob was preceded in death by his wife, Elizabeth Elley MacDonald, his sister Joanna, and his brother, Willard. He is survived by his two daughters, Jennifer M Richards of Flagstaff, Arizona, and Brooke M Drew of Mattapoisett, Massachusetts; step-children David Newton, Elizabeth Newton, and Ralph Newton, 9 grandchildren and 7 great-grandchildren.

Bob was known affectionately as Mac and will be remembered for his wry humor, philosophical bent, pipe, stories, VW bus and, of course, his Glengarry bonnet.

Death Notice for Willard MacDonald

The following note was sent to Hannah MacDonald on July 12th, 1945 by an Anglican Chaplain of the Royal Navy, Godfrey Bower. He was writing from H.M. Hospital Ship Tjitjalengka, active in the Pacific Ocean.

July 10th, 1945

Dear Mrs. MacDonald,

I would like to convey to you my very deepest sympathy for the death of your son Willard who died on board this ship last Tuesday, July 3rd. I am the chaplain of this ship and a priest of the Church of England—the Episcopal Church—and I should like to tell you that it was my privilege to be frequently at his bedside during his last illness and to give him the sacraments. As soon as he was admitted as a patient on board this ship he sent for me and asked if he could receive Holy Communion which I brought to him the next morning. On the Saturday before he died I heard his confession and gave him absolution and on the Sunday morning I brought the Blessed Sacrament to him again. I shall never forget the look of joy and peace on his face. Very soon after that he lost consciousness and died on the Tuesday morning. People said that it was sad that he should have to die on board a foreign ship among foreigners. But at least the Church and her sacraments which he had always loved so much was not foreign to him. On the Wednesday morning after his death I said a Requiem Mass for his soul. He expressed a wish that I should write to the priest at the Church which he used to attend in New York—I think he said Father Williams of the Church of St. Mary the Virgin, but I am not quite sure. He gave me a little notebook in which he said I would find the priest's name but unfortunately I couldn't find it. Could you please inform him? The doctor worked night and day trying to save his life but he seemed to know he was going to die long before it seemed probable. He surprised me soon after he as admitted by saying that he had a "presentiment." Although very weak, he was often in high spirits and had many jokes with the nurses and attendants. I had many conversations with him and he spoke a great deal about his home and his plans for after the war. He said he had seriously thought of becoming a priest. He spoke a good deal also of his younger brother for whom he had a very great affection.

Once more I would like to convey to you and all his relations and friends my very deepest sympathy.

Yours Sincerely,

Godfrey Bower

Chaplain, Royal Navy

HMHS Tjitjalengka docked at Liverpool, 1942

www.ingramcontent.com/pod-product-compliance
Lightning Source LLC
Chambersburg PA
CBHW070126080526
44586CB00015B/1580